D0209151

*Direct Democracy or
Representative Government?*

TRANSFORMING AMERICAN POLITICS

Lawrence C. Dodd, Series Editor

Dramatic changes in political institutions and behavior over the past three decades have underscored the dynamic nature of American politics, confronting political scientists with a new and pressing intellectual agenda. The pioneering work of early postwar scholars, while laying a firm empirical foundation for contemporary scholarship, failed to consider how American politics might change or recognize the forces that would make fundamental change inevitable. In reassessing the static interpretations fostered by these classic studies, political scientists are now examining the underlying dynamics that generate transformational change.

Transforming American Politics brings together texts and monographs that address four closely related aspects of change. A first concern is documenting and explaining recent changes in American politics—in institutions, processes, behavior, and policy-making. A second is reinterpreting classic studies and theories to provide a more accurate perspective on postwar politics. The series looks at historical change to identify recurring patterns of political transformation within and across the distinctive eras of American politics. Last and perhaps most important, the series presents new theories and interpretations that explain the dynamic processes at work and thus clarify the direction of contemporary politics. All of the books focus on the central theme of transformation—transformation in both the conduct of American politics and in the way we study and understand its many aspects.

BOOKS IN THIS SERIES

Direct Democracy or Representative Government?

DISPELLING THE POPULIST MYTH

John Haskell

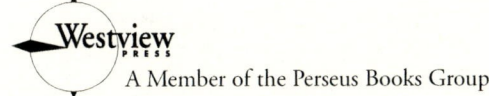

Westview
PRESS

A Member of the Perseus Books Group

Transforming American Politics Series

Copyright © 2001 by Westview Press, A Member of the Perseus Books Group

Published in 2001 in the United States of America by Westview Press, 5500 Central Avenue, Boulder, Colorado 80301-2877, and in the United Kingdom by Westview Press, 12 Hid's Copse Road, Cumnor Hill, Oxford OX2 9JJ

Find us on the World Wide Web at www.westviewpress.com

Library of Congress Cataloging-in-Publication Data
Haskell, John, 1959–
    Direct democracy or representative government? : dispelling the populist myth / John Haskell.
        p. cm. — (Transforming American politics)
    Includes bibliographical references and index.
    ISBN 0-8133-9783-9
    1. Referendum—United States.   2. Democracy—United States.   3. Representative government and representation—United States.   I. Title.   II. Series.
JF494 .H37   2000
323'.042'0973—dc21

                                                                                00-043990

The paper used in this publication meets the requirements of the American National Standard for Permanence of Paper for Printed Library Materials Z39.48-1984.

10   9   8   7   6   5   4   3   2

PERSEUS
POD
ON DEMAND

Contents

Tables and Figures

Preface

Since the double whammy of Vietnam and Watergate thirty years ago, Americans have been disgusted with the functioning of the major institutions of government. Cynicism and apathy are now chronic conditions.

To many, the problems with American politics are so profound as to call for a complete overhaul of the system of representative government developed more than two hundred years ago. How can a policymaking process that was designed to move deliberately and perhaps even inefficiently be appropriate for an era of almost unimaginably rapid technological, economic, and social change? Furthermore, the very ideas that the American system was based on—that officials are elected who in turn make decisions for the people—seem undemocratic and elitist to many observers. This is a populist age; polls indicate that most people oppose the notion that members of Congress and state legislatures should be the ones making important policy decisions on the basis of independent deliberation. For modern-day populists, hope lies in the fact that today, for the first time, it is no longer impracticable for people to rule themselves by voting over the computer or by phone. The prospect of democracy by plebiscite is quite alluring! Why maintain the checks and balances that are meant to protect the people from overbearing public officials when we can rule ourselves?

The *Washington Post* columnist David Broder describes the climate this way in his new book, *Democracy Derailed* (2000):

> I do not think it will be long before the converging forces of technology and public opinion coalesce in a political movement for a national initiative—to allow the public to substitute the simplicity of majority rule by referendum for what must seem to many frustrated Americans the arcane, ineffective, out-of-date model of the Constitution.

In fact, direct democratic institutions such as ballot initiatives and referenda are increasingly popular and are being used with greater frequency in the states to decide some of the most important public issues. Is the movement in the direction of more direct democracy—perhaps even at the national level—inevitable? Is it desirable? Can direct democratic institutions successfully complement representative institutions? Is representative government outdated? This book is an attempt to answer those questions.

I agree with Broder that the movement in the direction of more direct democracy may be unstoppable and that its wider use, as has already been shown in states that have provisions for initiatives and referenda, is ultimately corrosive of representative institutions. It is my belief that more direct democracy promises irresponsible and unaccountable government and constitutes a threat to some of the most basic American ideals. Unfortunately, without a compelling defense of representative institutions, we may not be able to avoid some of the negative consequences of government by plebiscite.

I have tried to provide here a defense of representative government relevant to the new century and a changing society. Building on findings in the social sciences from the last half of the twentieth century that tend to undermine the argument for direct democracy, I have developed a fortified defense of representative government. Perhaps it will in some small way help to dampen the seductive appeal of the populist rhetoric promoting the expanded use of initiatives and referenda.

There are a great many people and organizations I wish to thank, without whose help it would have been impossible to complete this project. First, I am especially grateful to the Smith Richardson Foundation for providing generous financial support that enabled me to take leave to research and write this book. In particular, Smith Richardson's program officer, Mark Steinmeyer, was of tremendous help at all stages. My employer during the writing of this book, Drake University, proved extremely flexible in allowing me to take leave on short notice. I wish to give special thanks to Dean Ronald Troyer, who has always been tremendously supportive of his faculty in ventures such as these; in addition, my colleagues in the Politics Department—David Skidmore, Dennis Goldford, Arthur Sanders, Debra DeLaet, Akitoshi Miyashita, and Eleanor Zeff—were completely supportive and "took up the slack." Lois Santi was helpful on many levels, and I benefited greatly from the research assistance of Donald Rasinen. His thoughts were particularly influential as I developed the material in Chapter 2.

I owe a continuous debt of intellectual gratitude to Professor William Keech of Carnegie Mellon University, who has had more influence than any other person on the way I think about American democracy and representative institutions. Steven Brams spent a great deal of time commenting on and criticizing drafts of chapters, for which I am very grateful. His input was invaluable in the development of the book. At the initial stages, Thomas Mann and Norman Ornstein were kind enough to take the time to provide very helpful commentary on rough drafts and overall themes. In addition, informal conversations with Thomas Husted,

Thomas Summerhill, Alan Ehrenhalt, David Magleby, Caroline Tolbert, Elisabeth Gerber, and Dane Waters sent me in productive directions that I would not have gone on my own. Dave Magleby was especially generous with his time and ideas, sharing his wide range of writings and thoughts on the subject of direct democracy. My editor, David McBride, was more than willing to offer constructive criticism, direction, and support, without which this effort would not have been possible.

Having said all that, of course I take full responsibility for everything in the book.

John Haskell

1

Introduction

In some important respects, American political history has been characterized by a gradual but unmistakable march in the direction of more inclusiveness and more democracy. It took nearly two hundred years, but the franchise was extended beyond propertied males to all white males in the nineteenth century, then to women in the early twentieth century, then to African Americans in the South in the 1960s, and finally to young people aged eighteen to twenty years in 1971. Opportunities for power for the previously disenfranchised and powerless have flowed from that.[1] In addition, the representative institutions of government in the United States, as well as the political parties, have opened up their decision-making processes in ways that distinguish American democracy from every other democracy in the world.

This seemingly inexorable movement in the direction of more democracy has never reached what some regard as its logical conclusion—a political process in which the people *directly* rule themselves—because of the impracticality of direct democracy in a huge sprawling country with many millions of people. Now, however, computers, the Internet, and interactive television can change all that.

Great advances in communications technology have always had profound effects on American politics. In the 1920s, the advent of radio forever changed the relationship between the president and the people. Calvin Coolidge was the first to use the new mode of communication to his personal political advantage, and shortly thereafter Franklin Roosevelt refined the technique with his legendary Depression Era "fireside chats."[2] A few decades later, television further changed how public officials and candidates interacted with the public. The political parties are still reeling from its impact, particularly the ability it has afforded candidates for office to connect directly to voters without the mediation of party leaders.[3]

The twenty-first century promises change of an even more thoroughgoing nature. At the very least, advanced technologies will give citizens more avenues for contacting and petitioning elected officials. In addition, computer technology may be used to make it easier to put more initiatives on the ballot in the states, perhaps one day even in federal elections. It is likely that the Internet and interactive television will affect our politics in other ways—perhaps one day every citizen will be plugged into government at the state, local, and federal level. But will advanced technologies be used in imaginative ways to enhance dialogue and democratic deliberation involving more citizens, or will they be used primarily to promote "instant democracy"—essentially, more frequent plebiscites conducted by computer on the issues of the day? Most political scientists and scholars of American politics think that the trends point in the latter direction.

What are we to make of the potential for dramatic change in the way ordinary citizens interact with, or perhaps replace, elected officials? What effect might these changes have on the American constitutional system? Does the increased reliance on direct and participatory forms of democracy constitute progress? This is the time to take a step back and consider the implications of some of these developments, both those that have already taken place and those that may in the future. In this book we will look at the spread of direct democracy in the United States and the ideas that fuel its spread, speculate as to the direction citizen involvement in policy-making is likely to take, and consider the wisdom of plebiscitary democracy in light of recent scholarship and experience.

This chapter begins with an overview of one of the main issues confronting American democracy at this time: a public that may be more alienated from the political process than it has ever been. Most observers agree that there is something seriously wrong with democracy in America; certainly the public seems to have lost faith in the political system. There is, however, no consensus as to the cause. Informed observers offer sometimes diametrically opposed explanations. Some say we have too much democracy and too much direct access to elected officials who are not given the leeway to make carefully considered and responsible public policy. These critics suggest that politicians are excessively responsive to public opinion when making policy. Others claim that there is too little democracy. Politicians are insulated from real people and out of touch. The United States' political institutions need to be opened up and made more accessible. These observers say that citizens should be able to take policy-making into their own hands; perhaps we should even remove the impediments—including the constitutional checks and balances—that stand in the way of the realization of a purer democracy.

In the second part of the chapter, I present the argument of this book. My aim is to counter and refute the argument made by advocates of more direct democracy, which is this: Representative institutions act to stymie the expression of the popular will and fail accurately to consider the public interest when policy is made. The solution, according to advocates of direct democracy, is simple: allow the direct expression of the popular will by permitting citizens to vote to determine public policy. There are two problems with this solution. The "popular will" cannot be identified with any precision or certainty by taking a vote, a point shown conclusively by a relatively new field of inquiry in the social sciences. In addition, the very idea that the results of a plebiscite should be implemented into public policy is potentially dangerous and illiberal. I argue that in light of our new technological capabilities, constitutional limits on direct democracy actually are now more important than ever before—precisely because of our rough-and-ready populist traditions, precisely because direct democracy is so incredibly seductive in the American cultural context.

The Crisis of Faith in the Political System

Commentators and specialists on American politics from across the ideological spectrum may not agree on much, but they do tend to agree that there is something wrong with the state of democracy in the United States. There is ample evidence that the general public concurs. Polls regularly indicate that large majorities think that the country is "on the wrong track," even now when the economy is going great guns. The public's attitude toward the Congress and the political process in general is one of bitter disdain, an attitude that has proved to be quite stable over the last twenty-five to thirty years.[4] By overwhelming majorities, Americans believe that the country is run by a few big interests and not for the benefit of the people.[5] Even the popular second-term president Bill Clinton is not trusted and was thought not "honest enough" to be president by 52 percent of the public *before* he was impeached for perjury and obstruction of justice, according to a September 1997 *Time* magazine poll.

The most obvious manifestation of Americans' disaffection with politics as usual is that we don't even bother to vote. The trend has been generally downward since 1960. Turnout fell below 50 percent for the 1996 presidential election and was at an abysmal 36 percent in the 1998 off-year congressional elections. This trend is all the more remarkable considering that the population is considerably older, better educated, and richer than it was in 1960—factors that supposedly correlate with a higher likelihood of voting—and many barriers to voting have fallen in the last thirty-five years, such as poll taxes, discriminatory registration tests, and numerous stringent residency requirements.

In a country that is at peace and far wealthier than ever, the government seems hamstrung by the combination of a fiscal deficit (even in surplus we are for the most part living off the revenue from payroll taxes, and the impending retirement of the baby boom generation is likely to lead to a return to large deficits) and a confidence deficit. The vast majority of the people do not trust their government and are unwilling to support a significant national commitment of resources to any of the problems currently plaguing us.[6] Politicians are loath to introduce ambitious legislation of the sort commonplace in the 1960s. An activist Democratic president who idolized John Kennedy and ran the George McGovern for President operation in Texas in 1972 and who proposed a comprehensive overhaul of the entire health-care system in his first term now proudly announces that "the era of big government is over."

Compare that with the robust attitude of the public in 1960, when a much less wealthy country in the midst of an expensive standoff with the Soviet Union all around the globe, and even in outer space, was supremely confident in the government's ability to conquer social problems.[7] Today, Americans of all stripes are better off than their parents and enjoy far more benefits from the government in the form of numerous and sometimes lavish subsidies and tax breaks;[8] at the same time we have no confidence in that government, are more sure that it is corrupt, and are gloomier about the prospects for our children. No wonder that the preeminent political book of the early 1990s, by E. J. Dionne, a columnist at the *Washington Post,* was *Why Americans Hate Politics.*[9]

Commentators and ordinary citizens alike are disturbed by many particular aspects of the political system. Most prominent among these aspects is the influence of special interests in the government, particularly the Congress. In addition, the government is thought to be corrupt, out of touch, spendthrift, and unable to deal with the most pressing issues of the day: crime, environmental degradation, health care, education, the approaching insolvency of Social Security, the increasingly unequal distribution of wealth, chronic poverty, and moral breakdown.

Most important, the public thinks the problem is systemic. Politicians themselves chime in. Retirements from Congress have been occurring at accelerating and sometimes record-breaking rates in recent years, often including the most vital, active, and respected members. Democrats and Republicans alike, such as recently retired Senators Bill Bradley (D-New Jersey), John Danforth (R-Missouri), Tim Wirth (D-Colorado), Sam Nunn (D-Georgia), Alan Simpson (R-Wyoming), and Hank Brown (R-Colorado), describe the stalemate, ineffectiveness, and futility of recent Congresses. The conventional wisdom is that there is something wrong with the system, the way our government goes about its business.

Too Little Democracy? Or Too Much?

Though commentators of different ideological persuasions agree that there is a systemic problem, they disagree, sometimes vehemently, as to the underlying cause of the troubles in our political system. Most prominent observers of American politics tend to fall into one of two camps. One group believes that there is too little democracy in the United States. These "populists" say that politicians are out of touch, are insulated from regular people, and serve only the monied interests that can afford to lobby them. Our constitutional system, populists say, with its checks and balances, separate branches of government, and a tradition of federalism which tends to weaken and decentralize the political parties all feed into the problem of a government too distant from and unresponsive to the concerns of the people.

These critics say that the solution to the problems that confront American democracy is more democracy—programmatic political parties, more direct input, more referenda, more initiatives, more citizen-based action. Observers as various as the venerable scholar of American government James Sundquist and the conservative gadfly and author Kevin Phillips have advocated at least a streamlining, if not a rethinking, of the basic structure and workings of the American constitutional system.[10] The political theorist Benjamin Barber calls for more community-based action and active citizenship to correct the ills of a system hampered in its functioning by a too-distant elitist political establishment.[11] Barber and Phillips, along with a decisive majority of the public,[12] support the use of a national referendum to override or bypass the Congress. Scholars such as James Fishkin and Robert Dahl have proposed statistically representative citizen assemblies to provide policy advice to elected officials.[13] They view this innovation as a corrective to the antidemocratic lack of diversity and the isolation of the political class. Many of these critics view the American system of separated institutions, multilayered checks and balances, and weak decentralized parties as antiquated and fundamentally undemocratic—as roadblocks to the establishment of a more vital and democratic political system.

On the other side are those who claim that the mismanagement of public affairs and the general dissatisfaction with the political system are due to an *excess* of democracy. Twenty-five years ago the political scientist David Mayhew, in his classic essay *Congress: The Electoral Connection*, depicted the Congress as a hyper-responsive body geared to the reelection-seeking goals of the members.[14] According to Mayhew, members of the House and Senate had brilliantly structured the institution both to serve the parochial needs of their constituents and to address larger problems in ways that constituents would find desirable—although in ways that did not necessarily confront these problems in a serious way. The committee system, the party organizations, and the members' offices were all organized to serve the particular interests of the members' constituents to ensure reelection. Congressmen might pontificate endlessly on the

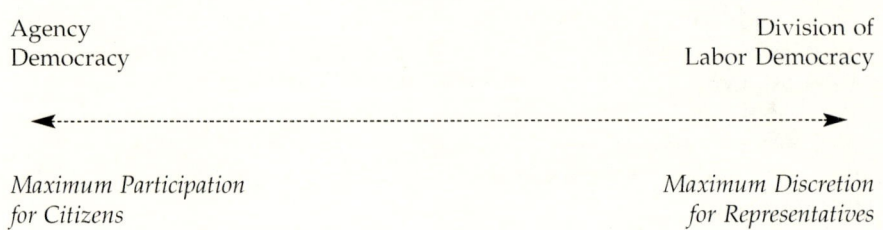

FIGURE 1.1   King's Conception of Representative Government

floor about Vietnam or forced busing or taxes with no apparent effect, said Mayhew, but when it came to serving the immediate needs of their constituents, the Congress as an institution operated with breathtaking efficiency. The journalist Steven Stark found things substantially the same in the 1990s.[15]

Contemporary observers such as the political scientist Anthony King and the journalist Jonathan Rauch find a government both excessively responsive to the people's immediate needs and one lobbied effectively, really hectored, by ordinary people.[16] Rauch stresses that it is "we the people"—yes, the ordinary people—who are the problem. In some respects, Rauch says, the term "special interests" is a misnomer, since many of the special interests lobby for ordinary people by protecting and expanding broad-based entitlement programs. In fact, most Americans are members of some association or interest group that is active in the Washington power game.

It is worthwhile to explore King's thesis as propounded in his recent well-received book, *Running Scared,* more carefully. He begins by developing a slight modification of the old "delegate-trustee" formulation of legislative representation. His conception of democracy is a continuum from "agency" to "division of labor" (see Figure 1.1). In the agency conception, politicians act as agents of the public, carrying out their immediate wishes to the best of their ability to discern them. And the public views its role as an active one, looking over the shoulder of its "agents" as they go about their business. In the division-of-labor conception, politicians are given the space to make decisions without being subjected to constant public scrutiny. In this conception, the public weighs in on Election Day to evaluate the work of the politicians.

According to King, democracy in the United States resembles the agency conception more than in any other country in the world with the exception of Switzerland. As he points out in describing the allure of agency democracy and the drift in the direction of a fully "plugged in" plebiscitary style of democracy:

Representative government of the kind common throughout the democratic world can be only a second-best. The ideal system would be one in which there were no politicians or middlemen of any kind but in which the people governed themselves directly; the political system would take the form of more or less continuous town meetings or referendums, perhaps conducted by means of interactive television.[17]

King goes on to point out that the people in a country with an agency political culture will be constantly frustrated. They will never be satisfied with their politicians in such an environment, he says, since a purely agency form of democracy is impracticable.

This agency political culture is part and parcel of the populist tradition in the United States. Populism connotes a mistrust of the elite along with an abiding faith in the wisdom of ordinary people and their right to govern themselves by majority rule. It has always been a central part of American political culture.[18] The United States is unique as a nation that is founded on democratic ideals as variously expressed in the Declaration of Independence and the Constitution. But there exists a profound tension between the ideals in those two documents. The first document celebrates democracy in its participatory, majoritarian form and is an important source of our populist tradition, whereas the second put in place representative institutions designed to place checks on the direct implementation of majority rule. American political culture has always been torn between populist ideas of direct rule and the republican conception that public opinion is best channeled through representative institutions.

There is no doubt, according to King, which ideas have won the day; the populists have triumphed. Americans believe they should be constantly looking over the shoulder of elected officials, and, whenever possible, they should take matters out of the hands of the politicians and decide public policy for themselves by means of initiatives, referenda, or other forms of direct democracy.

But King contends that politicians can only govern effectively if they are free to lead, free to do unpopular things between elections, and less susceptible to the constant pressures associated with special interest group lobbying and constituent demands. American politicians, he writes, are addicted to public opinion polling, beholden to organized interests, too obsessed with their permanent need to campaign, and deathly afraid of deviating from the path of utmost caution in legislating and roll-call voting. One can only imagine what the outcome might have been had certain momentous decisions—say on the Marshall Plan, the Emancipation Proclamation, or *Brown v. Board*—been made on the basis of a poll, a focus group, or a referendum.[19] Sometimes leadership is required to advance great moral causes or to implement farsighted policies. An excess of democracy, King says, distorts the legislative process and executive branch policy-making, both of which require opportunities for independent deliberation and decision-making in order to function properly.

King encourages Americans to draw on their heritage of heroic leadership, from Washington to Jefferson to Lincoln, to move in the direction of the division-of-labor conception of democracy. He also suggests various reforms meant to achieve that goal, including longer terms for House members, to relieve the pressure of the continuous campaign, and campaign finance reform, both to reduce the burden of fundraising and to strengthen political parties. Parties in America should be more like their counterparts in other democracies, he says, providing some buffer for elected officials from the demands of the citizens. He also suggests a change in the mind-set of Americans, amounting to a greater recognition of the value of leadership and the division of labor.

Were King's reforms to be enacted, they would have at least marginally beneficial results. He is, however, wrong, at least in terms of degree of emphasis, in a few important respects. King rests his case against agency democracy, or its fulfillment in a full-fledged populist-style direct democracy, partly on its impracticability. But, in fact, more forms of direct democracy *are* practicable with advanced technologies, and these technologies will pave the way for the expanded use of existing forms, such as initiatives and referenda.

King also overrates the relative importance of the American "heroic leadership" tradition against the populist tradition. The truth is that two of the country's greatest heroic leaders, Thomas Jefferson and Abraham Lincoln, are in the American pantheon precisely because they dedicated their lives and careers to the cause of more democracy and more power for ordinary and previously disenfranchised citizens. Lincoln is revered because he was instrumental in breaking down what had been improper, illegitimate, and illiberal constitutional and traditional limitations on democracy. It was his radical vision of a national democracy that won the day over states' rights, or at least some states' self-proclaimed right to secede from the Union over slavery. And there was no truer and more influential democrat in American history than Jefferson, whose political career was built in large part on his belief in the common man, the sanctity of majority rule, and his opposition to the Federalists, who were responsible for the restraints on majority rule written into the Constitution.

It is probably true, as King says, that agency democracy leads to the making of poorer legislation by distorting the legislative process, takes up too much valuable time of members of Congress as they obsessively plan and raise funds for their perpetual reelection campaigns, and forces members to be too receptive to the appeals of special interests.[20] It is also true that a fully plugged-in interactive democracy would only make matters worse. But I think it is important to put into proper perspective his arguments. Calling on the American tradition of heroic leadership has almost no value in heading off the movement in the direction of agency democracy. Americans will continue to monitor their elected officials whenever their rights, interests, and values are at stake. Furthermore, claiming that a full-fledged populist democracy is "impracticable" is, for all intents and purposes, no longer true. King's arguments regarding the value of relatively independent deliberation and leadership are good ones, but the siren song of direct democracy will win the day in the United States unless a more convincing counterargument can be made.

Democracy in America: The More the Merrier!

What is unique and relevant in the contemporary setting—and helps fuel the "too much democracy" versus "too little democracy" debate—is the extent to which the barriers to fuller and expanded participation, and even direct democracy, have been and are rapidly disappearing. We can voice our opinions to people in power (and be heard!), gain access to elites, and participate directly in politics in ways never before possible. American culture makes more and more characteristics of direct democracy irresistible temptations as they become technologically feasible.

Never has the American political system been more open than now to the participation and inclusion of more people, and not just by technological advances like the fax machine and e-mail, sophisticated polling techniques, and interactive television. The political parties are more permeable than they ever have been. All kinds of people previously excluded by ethnic variations of the white male good old boys club are influential in our politics today. It no longer astonishes anyone when African Americans, women, Hispanics, and Asian Americans are elected or appointed to prominent positions in public life. Evangelical Christians, who were once generally uninterested in political participation and unwelcome in "respectable" political party organizations, have taken over the organizational structure of the Republican party in more than a dozen states in the last twenty years. And the parties aggressively recruit new voters from among the native- born poor of all races, as well as the newly naturalized.

Even money is no longer an insuperable obstacle to political power in contemporary America. Alan Ehrenhalt, in *The United States of Ambition*, documented the increasing accessibility of the political system to housewives and teachers, some of whom are making very attractive and successful candidates.[21] And those who teach politics in the nation's colleges and universities can chime in with numerous tales of students from very modest backgrounds who dedicated their lives to the political system and now hold positions of responsibility and authority.

But one need not participate as a candidate or an activist to have an impact. For those preferring to stay on the sidelines away from electoral politics, there is the Internet, constant polling, talk radio, referenda, initiatives, sophisticated interest group structures, etc., through which to channel opinions, press a case, and protect or advance interests. In the age of computers, with advanced technology for instant communication, interactive television, and instant polling, we now have the means to rule ourselves directly.

These new possibilities are incredibly seductive. There is no country on earth where the power of the voice of the people holds more sway than in the United States. In view of that fact and of the breakdown of the practical barriers to direct democracy, the relevance and centrality of our constitutional system of checks and balances comes into question. It does not seem illogical to contend that the constitutional limitations on direct democracy are the last great barriers to the achievement of a true democracy. After all, observers going back as far as Alexis de Tocqueville recognized the irresistible allure of direct democracy in a country where the voice of the people is so venerated.[22] As we shall see, numerous prominent scholars and journalists are intrigued by the promise of achieving a "true" democracy; they have responded by advocating modifications in the constitutional arrangements. They ask: Why have representatives making all the decisions for us when we can make them ourselves, particularly when these representatives are corrupted by powerful monied interests? Don't the people have a better sense of what is in the public interest?

The constitutional restraints were put in place in large measure to protect ordinary citizens against ambitious people in positions of power. James Madison wrote in defense of the Constitution in *The Federalist Papers*: make "ambition counteract ambition" by separating the institutions into different branches in order to provide checks to restrain those in positions of power.[23] But if direct rule is possible now, why not modify or do away with the complicated system of separated branches sharing powers that stand in the way of the implementation of the popular will? We don't need to be protected from anyone in power anymore if we can take power in our own hands in a true democracy. Why not restructure the system to take advantage of the new opportunities to rule ourselves?

Defending Representative Democracy: The Traditional Arguments

Defenders of representative democracy—government by legally constituted bodies of elected officials—usually base their case against the arguments made in the previous two paragraphs and against the institution-alization of direct democracy on two main points:

Point 1. Only representative institutions can fill the need for informed deliberation, consensus, and compromise, all of which are necessary for good government in the public interest.

Point 2. Arguments for direct democracy either explicitly state or imply that the opinion of the public has a special character: the majority by right should rule. Such a viewpoint can lead to the violation of minority rights by majority tyranny.

Both of these arguments are intellectually powerful and have had and continue to have adherents of the highest pedigree. By the same token, both are frequently attacked as elitist by those fashioning themselves as true democrats, since they seem to suggest that ordinary people are not fit to rule themselves.

As advocates of the first argument, E. E. Schattschneider and V. O. Key, two of the most prominent scholars of American politics in the middle of this century, were perhaps the most persuasive in warning against putting too much faith in public opinion polls or other plebiscitary forms.[24] Key stressed that the public made responsible and informed choices at the polls in support of or in opposition to the party or official in power. But that is as far as it should go, he said. The public is not in a position to be able to micromanage government.

Similarly, Schattschneider pointed out that politics is most democratic and ordinary people can wield power most meaningfully when the public rules by means of a vote supporting one party or one candidate and rejecting the other on Election Day. This is what the public is equipped to do, and it is the most democratic way to do the business of government. Interest group politics is skewed in favor of the affluent, but Election Day politics is relatively fair. After all, Schattschneider wrote, on Election Day it is one voter, one vote, whereas the chorus of lobbyists "sings with an upper class bias." Moreover, people simply don't have the time to devote to becoming expert on the details of public policy.[25] So a properly functioning democracy is set up so that the people can weigh in on Election Day, rejecting those they dislike and rewarding those they think are doing a good job.

These arguments may sound good in theory, but in the current climate of mistrust coupled with the new opportunities for direct public influence, they have lost most of the appeal they may once have had, and they certainly do not hold much sway on the imagination of the public and activists, not to mention many pundits and scholars. People are profoundly suspicious of representative institutions and the politicians within them, accusing them of serving the special interests instead of the public interest.

As for the threat of tyranny by the majority, it is fair to say that Americans are blasé on that point. It is hard to convince most people living in a country that has functioned democratically for more than two centuries that the threat of tyranny is a real one, although some people, especially African Americans, gays, and some immigrants, may be more sensitive to this possibility than others. It can even plausibly be argued that many Americans, when push comes to shove, are not committed in practice to the basic protections against tyranny by the majority in the Bill of Rights.

In the end, the simplicity of the populist argument is winning the day. Populists and most ordinary citizens believe that representative institutions, particularly as they are arranged in the United States, prevent the people from seeing their will implemented into public policy. At root, they say, this is because elected representatives take into account their own career interests (which usually turn out to be one and the same as those of the special interests that fund their campaigns) instead of the public interest when considering legislation. For populists, if the politicians won't listen to the people, there is a very simple solution: let the people vote, whenever feasible, to determine policy. The people will take into account the common good when casting their votes; the politicians will consider their narrower professional concerns while in office.

Direct Democracy Versus Representative Democracy

The Populist Theory of Voting

The populist argument implies a certain way of thinking about voting; the populist theory of voting is that the outcome of an election or a plebiscite reflects the popular will. Populists believe that the popular will identified by a vote should then be implemented into public policy. Not only that, since the people are more attuned to what is good for the overall community than self-interested elected officials, they contend that the outcome of a vote is the best representation of the public interest. Since voting is the central participatory act in a democracy, this theory of voting is the foundational premise of the populist conception of how a democracy should operate.

Public choice, a relatively obscure field of inquiry in the social sciences, is the study of decision-making processes in politics and economics. Scholars of public choice have tested the populist theory of voting—that the outcome of an election can be interpreted to reflect the popular will—

and discredited it, effectively undermining the premise of the populist conception of democracy. However, their discoveries have for the most part been published only in academic journals and have remained inaccessible to most people, as a result of the highly technical jargon and advanced mathematics that characterize the research. This is unfortunate because many of these findings are relevant to contemporary American politics—I would argue that they need urgently to be brought to bear—and what is more, the concepts are surprisingly simple and straightforward. It is the main aim of this book to explain these findings, to explain why election results cannot be interpreted in the ways that populists wish, and to develop a broader defense of representative institutions that incorporates the findings of public choice scholars.

Refuting the Theory

In the middle of the twentieth century, pioneering scholars of public choice made some inquiries into the processes involved in counting up people's preferences by taking a vote in order to come to a group decision. Their basic discovery was what they called the "paradox of voting"; after this initial finding, public choice scholars made numerous other discoveries that served to refute the populist theory of voting. I have summarized the relevant findings here. Chapter 5 is devoted to explaining these in more detail.

- The paradox of voting concerns the relationship of individual choice to group choice. The paradox is that whereas an individual can make a rational, logical, and coherent ordering of choices, options, or candidates presented to him or her, it is often impossible for a group, even one made up of well-informed and rational individuals, to order its choices coherently.[26]
- Majorities in electoral party politics are really unstable coalitions of minorities that rarely if ever express clear and comprehensive policy instructions.
- Different legitimate and widely used methods of voting often produce different winners.
- Any decision-making process used by a group to decide among three or more options may be manipulated by strategic voters.[27]

We can never be sure that the popular will is reflected in the result of a vote.

In effect, it can be shown that *identifying the popular will by taking a vote is literally impossible to do with any certainty or precision*. Can voting achieve what populists intend for it to achieve? The answer is no. The populist theory of voting is discredited, as is the conception of democracy espoused by populists. Attaching special significance to the results of elections or plebiscites presents other problems, as well, some of which are described below.

A good way to get a handle on what is wrong with populists' ideas about democracy is to compare appeals to the popular will in politics that are so common in the United States to similar appeals to divine will in politics. The comparison makes for some surprising and revealing parallels.[28]

The Voice of the People and the Voice of God in Politics

It is generally acknowledged in the contemporary United States that it does not make sense and may not be appropriate to depend entirely on scriptural support for a political position, if for no other reason than that Americans are so religiously pluralistic and so thoroughly secular in so many ways that such a tactic is not likely to succeed. But by no means is religion regarded as out of bounds in the public discourse. Quite to the contrary. Activists on the left and the right regularly appeal to the religious sensibilities of the public in advancing positions on moral questions. In recent years, the conservative end of the spectrum has gotten most of the attention when it comes to the mixing of religion and politics,[29] particularly on social issues such as abortion; but the left, too, relied on sympathetic denominational organizations in its opposition to President Ronald Reagan's policies in Latin America; and, of course, the core of the civil rights movement in the 1950s and '60s was the evangelical Protestant black church. Liberal denominations remain active today in environmental matters, issues of economic justice, the gay rights movement, and other issues. Religion is, quite simply, the foundation of the morality of the great majority of people in the United States, left, right, and center, and questions of the most profound moral significance are often addressed in politics. As a result, religion will be a part of our politics as long as it remains a source of morality for so many.

The point is that, while religion is an important and integral part of American politics, most people recognize that it is impossible to be sure exactly what God has to say on any particular political question. A person's sense of moral structure derived from religious traditions will inform her politics, but this is something far different from a claim of divine authority. Appeals to divine authority are also generally thought to produce an intolerant attitude to diverse viewpoints—after all, going against the word of God cannot safely be tolerated—and to lead to efforts at repression.

In the United States, the popular will has very nearly literally been apotheosized—elevated to divine status—effectively taking the place of divine authority. This makes sense to a lot of people, because, after all, the people are meant to have ultimate authority in a democracy. And just as going against the "will of God" carries (or carried) great risks in some countries, going against the "will of the people" is regarded by some as antidemocratic at best and subversive at worst.

The relevant thing that scholars of public choice have discovered is that gaining a precise sense of the popular will in politics is a concept just as elusive as divining God's exact position on the issues of the day. Not only that, the populist idea that election results (or poll results, or the results of plebiscites, etc.) have some special significance, and should be translated into public policy in something like their unadulterated form, is about as dangerous and potentially oppressive to vulnerable minorities as the notion that someone or some church should translate the word of God into public policy.

Essentially what we now know is that the populist theory of voting—self-government by plebiscite—is both unachievable, because elections and plebiscites cannot be interpreted in the way populists intend, and undesirable, because the apotheosis of the popular will can lead to tyranny by the majority. In this book, exposing the faulty premise of populism is the first step in making the case for a practical, meaningful, and achievable role for voting and developing a broader defense of representative institutions. I summarize that argument below.

Defending Representative Democracy for the New Century

Discrediting the populist theory of voting may do serious damage to the case for institutions of direct democracy such as initiatives and referenda, but that in and of itself does not make a positive case for representative institutions. But we can build on the findings of public choice scholars about the nature of voting and elections to construct a case for representative institutions relevant to a future in which populist ideas more generally are likely to be ever more popular. Not only that, these arguments hold the promise of breathing new life into the traditional arguments for representative democracy described earlier.

Often those who challenge the wisdom of having people rule themselves directly are labeled "elitist" or "antidemocratic." They are said to believe that the people are too stupid to rule themselves. If you say that the people should not rule themselves, the argument goes, then you must be saying that there are better sorts of people who should be ruling—and what could be more antidemocratic than that? In fact, representative democracy is neither antidemocratic nor elitist.[30] Representative institutions are actually more democratic than direct democratic ones, because they are based on a theory of voting that gives people more control over agenda setting and policy-making than the populist theory of voting does.

In the first place, populists' ideas about people's views on issues tend to oversimplify those views. People frequently have a rather nuanced take on policy matters, and sometimes people's positions on one issue are contingent on the resolution of other matters. Institutions of direct democracy rarely can capture the complexity of public opinion, particularly on those issues that people have considered with any care, nor do they often capture the complexity and interrelatedness of controversial public policy questions. Representative institutions are arranged, in large measure, to take into account exactly those relationships.

Populists also contend that the public interest is better served by direct democratic institutions. After all, isn't it a truism that career-obsessed politicians serve their own interests while deciding legislation, as compared to the more civic-minded voter? In fact, the idea that something resembling the public interest can come from a plebiscitary process is ludicrous. The registered opinions of millions of people, many probably arrived at the last minute, as expressed by a yes or no vote in a voting booth or in response to a pollster, cannot possibly approximate something as elusive as the "public interest." The people's interests are much too various and intertwined to be represented effectively by an act as simple as casting a vote. Properly constructed representative institutions can and do a much better job of representing the diversity of interests in a complex society.

But more important than anything else, the public interest in a liberal democracy should not be subject to the dictates of anyone or anything, not even an electoral majority; it must be thought of in process terms. The public interest is served by fair procedures and agreed-upon rules that permit a fair hearing for all interests. If we can accept the reality that no decision-making process, whether direct or representative, is perfect and that unjust outcomes will occur, we can place the appropriate value on fair deliberative procedures that are designed to provide opportunities for redressing and repairing those outcomes. Simply put, the public interest is much better served by fair procedures that permit contentious matters to be hashed out face-to-face than by the imposition of the results of a plebiscite.

Even if we were to assume that the outcome of an election could identify the popular will, is it really desirable to have an institution that imposes the majority view on the basis of a one-shot once-and-for-all decision-making process? Populists, in effect, apotheosize the popular will. They believe that the majority should rule by right. It is this apotheosis of majority opinion implicit in populism that puts no break on tyranny of the majority and no limits on what a government of the people can legitimately do. Representative institutions designed on the U.S. model offer no guarantees, but they do place numerous obstacles in the way of tyranny of the majority, principally in the form of legislative procedures minorities may legitimately use to protect their rights.

Most important, unlike direct democratic institutions, representative institutions are based on an achievable, coherent, and meaningful theory of voting. In the *Federalist Papers*, James Madison, John Jay, and Alexander Hamilton made the case for representative democracy. In such a system, the objective of popular participation in elections is simple—the only purpose for voting is for the people to decide who should hold positions of authority in government. The people govern themselves, thereby exercising their sovereignty, by controlling who is in office and prescribing boundaries for those officials by the threat of the veto on the next Election Day. The people's reasons for keeping incumbents in office or replacing them are entirely up to their free choice. Voters may be deciding simply to get rid of one evil in favor of a lesser evil; they may be voting prospectively to have their representatives attempt to implement this program or that platform or to advance this set of values or that set of interests; they may simply trust one candidate to serve the nation or carry out duties prescribed in the Constitution more than another. They may have no reason other than some free-floating desire to "throw the bums out." And the people are utterly free to try to contact, cajole, and otherwise attempt to influence elected officials.

By contrast, populists depend on the vote to express the will of the people on policy—something election results cannot do in any meaningful way.[31] In addition, the proposals that are placed before voters for them to decide are frequently devised by people who are inexperienced in writing legislation and unaccountable to the people. Agenda setting and legislative drafting are, in effect, taken out of the control of the people. A properly functioning representative democracy gives people control over the policy-makers at the ballot box.

In sum, representative democracy does not depend on the idea that the results of an election or the results of a poll or plebiscite should *rule by right*, which is the theory of the populists. Instead, carefully constructed representative institutions—institutions accountable to the electorate—are designed in such a way as to tame the passions of the moment and to consider legislation from a variety of perspectives.[32] Furthermore, there is an understanding that the public interest is better served by providing a forum for deliberation than it would be by automatically and mechanically implementing the results of a referendum or election. In the process, representative institutions are meant to secure the liberties of the citizens, which may in some circumstances mean serving as a bulwark against the imposition of majority opinion.

This endorsement of representative democracy should not be construed as advocacy for the elimination of participatory forms of democracy or the stifling of "excessive" participation in politics by citizens. There is no reason to discourage participatory democracy and participation in politics by citizens. In any event, this could not be achieved in this country. The United States has a vigorous and sometimes raucous populist tradition, as well as an abiding mistrust of those in power, and it always will. A free-wheeling participatory environment featuring citizens' direct access to policy-makers is as integral a part of our political culture as the separation of powers and the system of checks and balances. The American constitutional system of separate branches of government and checks and balances is so valuable *because* of our populist, anti-elitist traditions—characterized by Americans' centuries-long suspicion of those in power and the special interests that influence them. It is *because* we are an open and participatory society with few barriers between the governed and those who govern that these restraints are so important. It is because direct democracy will become ever more feasible that it is so important to develop a defense of representative institutions relevant to the twenty-first century.

Plan of the Book

In this chapter, I have laid out the contours of my argument. We have seen some of the reasons why Americans' profound disaffection with politics has led them to be seduced by the populist notion that it is better for people to rule themselves directly. We have seen why people have rejected the best traditional arguments in defense of representative democracy. Finally, I summarized my main contention: that the populist notion of democracy is in fact unachievable and potentially dangerous, and that representative democracy is based on sounder principles that better serve the public interest.

The remainder of the book is divided into two sections. The first, Chapters 2–4, provides background and context for the contemporary debate over institutions of direct democracy. The topics are the development of populist political culture in the United States (Chapter 2), the spread of direct and participatory forms of democracy in the country (Chapter 3), and the major issues dividing proponents of direct democratic institutions and representative institutions (Chapter 4).

In Chapter 2, I explore how powerful the populist ideal has been since the Founding period. At that time, populism was espoused by the losing side, the anti-Federalists, in the debate on the adoption of the Constitution. In the end, the Constitution reflected the views of the Federalists, who instituted numerous checks on popular rule. But even though the anti-Federalists lost the battle over the Constitution, they seem to be winning the contemporary war of popular opinion. From case studies of controversial issues during the last decade, we shall see how nowadays, populist ideas about the fundamental meaning of the Founding are held more widely than those of the Federalists.

In Chapter 3, we look at the rise of direct democracy in the twentieth century and the directions it is likely to go in the future. About thirty years ago American democracy became dramatically more open to citizen involvement and activism—some scholars describe this as the era of participatory democracy. Citizens and interest groups aggressively pursue new ways of exerting influence on policy-makers, some of which involve high-tech innovations. One of the upshots of this change has been the increased interest in and use of ballot initiatives and referenda. In this chapter we see why Americans are inclined more toward these plebiscitary forms of participation than toward forms that would entail direct involvement in the nitty-gritty details of agenda setting and policy formulation.

In Chapter 4, I consider the state of the debate in elite circles on the merits of direct democratic institutions versus those of representative institutions. First, I look at the case for direct democracy made by populists across the ideological spectrum. We shall see why some scholars and activists believe we have too little democracy and shall look in some detail at the corrective measures they prescribe, including national referenda, alterations in the Constitution, and new high-tech forms of interactive democracy. Then we shall look at the major issues dividing advocates and opponents of direct democracy. The debate among academics, activists, and journalists revolves around some of the following issues: Are initiative campaigns just as susceptible to undue influence by special interests as legislatures are? How prepared are the people to participate in plebiscites? Are the rights of vulnerable minorities really at risk with direct democracy? Does direct democracy contribute to or detract from responsible government? The simple populist argument seems to be winning the day, even though some evidence from states that allow forms of direct democracy such as ballot initiatives and referenda casts doubt on the wisdom of using direct democratic institutions. Despite such evidence—which is not well known—many people do think that the popular will is reflected in plebiscite outcomes; they do think that the public interest is best served by these institutions.

In the last section of the book, Chapters 5 and 6, I develop my defense of representative institutions. In Chapter 5, we see why the populist theory of voting doesn't hold up to close scrutiny. Recent findings in the field of public choice show conclusively that elections and plebiscites cannot serve the purposes that populists are convinced they do serve. In short, the results of elections, or polls, or referenda cannot be interpreted in the way populists would like, and populists' conception of public opinion is wildly oversimplified.

We see in the final chapter that representative institutions operate under a different set of assumptions about public opinion, assumptions that square better with the complexities of both public opinion and contentious political issues. Furthermore, representative institutions have been furnished with checks and balances specifically to provide some protection against overzealous majorities, among other things. Representative democracy is not "elitist" as its critics contend. Instead, it is based on a theory of voting that makes sense and that actually gives citizens *more* control over policy-making than direct democratic institutions.

This is not to say that the criticisms of our system of government summarized in this chapter are baseless. In some respects our representative institutions are indeed failing to live up to their promise. I end with some recommendations for enhancing the representativeness and accountability of these vital institutions.

2

The Heritage of Populism in the United States

The populist impulse in American politics is as old as the nation itself. Early populists played an important role in the debates at the Founding about what form democracy should take in the new nation, and populism has always colored our politics, providing a language for reform, and sometimes reaction. Though populism has had ugly nativist tendencies, it has also inspired and laid the groundwork for some of the most far-reaching reform movements in American history. In addition, it has been an organizing principle in American politics, especially for influential third party movements. Perhaps the best testament to its lasting appeal is that the rhetoric of populism has been indispensable to the left and right, Democrats and Republicans alike, for at least a century.

The historian Michael Kazin, in his recent book *The Populist Persuasion*, defines populism as "a language whose speakers conceive of ordinary people as a noble assemblage not bounded narrowly by class, [who] view their elite opponents as self-serving and undemocratic, and [who] seek to mobilize the former against the latter."[1] Populism, Kazin suggests, gives voice to the people's opposition to the "establishment" or, more generally, the elite in business, politics, and the culture. In important ways, it is the language in the United States for what the Founders called "pure" democracy—or direct rule by the people.[2]

As a result, the populist impulse has been harnessed in support of a particular conception of the meaning of democracy in America. Populism is really, then, more than just an impulse in American political culture; it is a full-fledged theory of democracy that can be summarized as the belief that a legitimate democratic political system should be arranged to ascertain the popular will (usually by the majority-rule principle) and then to implement that will as public policy.

The initial focus of the chapter is the controversy during the Founding period over competing visions of democracy in America. The debate pitted *constitutionalism*, which sought to constrain majorities, against *pop-*

ulism, which sought to erect political institutions that would obey them. Throughout American history these ideas have coexisted, sometimes in an uneasy alliance—Thomas Jefferson is credited with reconciling the ideas within the American federal system—and sometimes in contradiction, as expressed by Theodore Roosevelt. We will see how populism became deeply entrenched in and an essential part of American political culture during the nineteenth century, eventually influencing the most important reform movements in the twentieth century.

Today, Americans continue to distrust their elected representatives and other elites—perhaps more than ever—and they support efforts to change the political system to make it easier for the citizenry to bypass the politicians. Political controversies in the 1990s provide numerous examples of how the populist impulse remains a potent and increasingly influential force that politicians ignore only at their peril. In fact, the very same debate that characterized the Founding period—that between constitutionalism and populism—continues to define the debate over the future of democracy in America. If anything, the tension between the two ideas is greater than ever. Americans regard their representative institutions with growing disdain at the same time as direct democracy is more popular than ever, as referenda and initiatives are used with increasing frequency in some states, and technological innovations offer new ways to bypass politicians.

Constitutionalism Versus Populism

The new nation that was established in 1776 was founded on the radical notion that the people must consent to the form and structure of their government, instead of upon the Old World ideas of nationhood usually linked to ethnicity, territory, or religion. The legitimacy of the American regime rested, as the phrase goes, upon the "consent of the governed." But there was hardly a consensus as to precisely what it meant to have a government that derived its powers and legitimacy from the people. How do you put into place a government of, by, and for the people? What institutional arrangements are required? Exactly what role do the people play?

The debates over the adoption of the Constitution in 1787 and the extent to which it should reflect constitutionalism or populism pitted the Federalists against the anti-Federalists. The Federalists' views concerning the source of the people's sovereignty in a democratic state were very different from the anti-Federalists'. Instead of sovereignty deriving from popular majorities, the Federalists believed sovereignty was expressed by the principles and ideas in the Constitution. The people were wise enough to know, according to the Federalists, that majority rule did not constitute the most meaningful expression of their sovereignty. Rather, the true will of the people was expressed through their support of the republican principles outlined in the Constitution.

This constitutionalism sought to check the potential dangers associated with the passions of the moment and provide for deliberation and reflection on policy matters by elected representatives. In the view of the Federalists, direct popular rule would constitute a threat to individual liberty.[3] And just as ordinary people wisely defer to doctors on medical questions, these constitutionalists believed, so should ordinary people defer to statesmen on matters of state. This idea didn't detract from the democratic nature of the system, according to the Federalists—the people reserved for themselves the ultimate power by holding their elected representatives accountable on Election Day. Thus the government did exist by consent of the governed—the people were truly sovereign. Regular and frequent elections were the key to establishing the legitimacy of the regime.[4] The threat of the next election would keep those in power from abusing the liberties of the people, while giving elected officials room for the independent deliberation that is crucial to making public policy for the good of the community.

The anti-Federalists advocated a strongly democratic view of the concept "consent of the governed"—a *populist* view, if you will.[5] They distrusted distant and unaccountable power, and they believed the people should, to the extent possible, govern themselves directly. The very essence of their idea was that the people's sovereignty resided in popular majorities. This represented to them the only legitimate expression of the idea that people must consent to be governed.

At the very least, the anti-Federalists believed, popularly elected representatives should wield the most power, and they should be closely watched, with annual elections to hold them accountable. The president should also be directly elected, the anti-Federalists contended, and he should not be eligible for reelection, lest one man accumulate too much power in one branch of government, constituting a threat to liberty. The anti-Federalists were particularly suspicious of institutions some sought to establish whose office-holders were not directly elected by the people, including the presidency and also the Senate (the proposal was not to require direct election of senators), as well as the federal courts. Any institution not directly controlled by the people by means of elections held within it great potential for abuse of power. The most vehement debates centered on just these issues—precisely what role people should have in governing themselves and what institutions, if any, should be free of direct popular control.

But the anti-Federalists lost out at the Constitutional Convention in 1787 and the subsequent ratification debates in the states. Though the

Constitution was a document forged from a series of compromises, on most of the big issues the populist anti-Federalists lost.[6] The president was not to be directly elected; instead, the Electoral College would choose the chief executive. The indirectly elected Senate was established as a part of the legislative branch co-equal with the popularly elected House of Representatives. The House would be the only body in the constitutional framework that the people would control directly. And members of the federal judiciary, headed by the Supreme Court, would serve lifetime appointments and would be removable only by a cumbersome impeachment process. In essence, the institutions of government outlined in the document were designed to check the passions of the moment that might be felt or expressed by popular majorities. This fashioning of these institutions was viewed as a series of crushing defeats by most anti-Federalists.

The winners, the Federalists, eventually formed a political party by that name.

When the Federalists assumed power after the first elections under the new Constitution in 1788, President George Washington made a point of including the brilliant anti-Federalist Thomas Jefferson in his cabinet, appointing him secretary of State, in order to promote national unity after the contentious constitutional debates. Jefferson had been in Paris as minister to France during those debates, so he had not made the enemies many of the more vociferous and active anti-Federalists had. Some of these other anti-Federalists were perhaps even more ardent democrats than Jefferson. Thomas Paine and Patrick Henry, for example, suggested that representatives be bound to support the views of the majority of their constituents in the Congress. (Such a provision was seriously considered for the Bill of Rights and was a part of some states' constitutions in the early days of the country.[7]) Jefferson was a more palatable choice to build national unity, even though he was in the populist camp. He was, of course, a widely respected figure—truly a member of the "natural aristocracy" the Federalists championed—with considerable talents and political skills Washington knew would be useful.

Jefferson played a crucial role in another aspect of the philosophical debates between the populists and the constitutionalists. The two camps had distinctly different visions of the future of the nation, as well as distinctly different ideas about the role the central government should play in realizing their respective visions. Jefferson envisioned a great and expanding country (which he brought about with the Louisiana Purchase and other policies after assuming the presidency in 1801) reflecting the virtues of educated and hardworking small farmers and tradesmen who would govern themselves. He saw the future United States as a great country stretching from the Atlantic to the Pacific taking advantage of the bounty of the continent, especially land, which would be populated by people close to that land.

Leading Federalists such as Alexander Hamilton, on the other hand, saw a great nation emerging on the basis of a mercantilist and increasingly modern economy directed by influential bankers and statesmen in the east who had the best long-term interests of the country in mind.[8] The realization of this vision would be facilitated by the strong, energetic executive provided for in the Constitution, who would not be directly elected, thus less prone than the Congress to shortsighted and parochial policies that might be dictated by the passions of the moment. While Congress as the lawmaking body would have the most power, the members of Congress, Hamilton reasoned, would be essentially local politicians who would not see the big picture on economic policy, and certainly not on foreign policy. The executive must be free to see the big long-range picture; as a result he must be able to pursue some policies (particular in the realm of foreign affairs and trade) without too many impediments from the Congress.

Though the two conflicting visions, as we shall see, were crucial in framing subsequent debates about the meaning of democracy in America, the essential philosophical tension was between the two ideas about what "consent of the governed" meant. It is a tension that has stayed with us throughout our entire history. For the populists, majorities were always sovereign. It was better to trust the goodness and wisdom of ordinary people than rely on the judgment of an American version of an aristocracy. For the constitutionalists, the sovereign expression of the people's will was reflected in the wisdom of the checks and balances built into the Constitution that could work to thwart majority rule.

How could Thomas Jefferson be said to be a true patriot when his views about American democracy seemed directly at odds with those expressed in the Constitution of the United States? Jefferson, as well as some others sympathetic to the anti-Federalist viewpoint, took an ingenious position that reconciled the seemingly irreconcilable differences between populism and constitutionalism. To Jefferson, sovereignty resided with the people *in the states*. Constitutional checks and balances were meant to restrain the potentially powerful and distant government in the nation's capital so that the good and virtuous citizenry of small farmers and craftsmen could rule themselves by democratic principles at the state and local levels. Thus, Jefferson established a populist position that could coexist with and even complement, however uneasily, the constitutionalist position.

These early populists believed that the central government was a threat in two ways. First, a distant, strong central government can too easily encroach on the sovereignty and liberties of the people. Second, the people who propose to place more power in the hands of the central government (the Federalists, such as Hamilton) advocate moving the country in a direction, the direction of mercantilism and industrialism, which would take from the small farmer and craftsman the control over his livelihood that makes self-government possible. How can a man be truly free unless he has control over his government *and* his livelihood? Both were necessary conditions for democracy, Jefferson believed.

Jefferson is credited with founding the longest-lasting political party in the world—the Democratic-Republicans, which evolved into the Democratic party—to reflect these principles. The party's philosophy was simple: people must be allowed to rule themselves at the state level as they see fit, without intrusion from the central government or the domineering eastern elite.

The roots of American populism could be said to have derived from the Jeffersonian interpretation of the Founding (what I have called the "populist" interpretation). Populism would undergo many changes. One example: The federal government would not always be viewed as a threat by future populists. But the essential points—that the majority should rule by right, and the people needed constantly to be on guard against an overreaching elite—remain constant.

Andrew Jackson and Anti-elitist Populism

American democracy in the age of Jefferson does not appear very democratic from the contemporary perspective. Between the enslavement of the African American population and the lack of woman suffrage, the majority of the adult population was excluded from the political arena. Even among white males, only a minority qualified to vote in many states, owing to property requirements. This had an impact on the political style of even ardent democrats. They did not have to appeal to a broad range of voters, which made the aristocratic bearing of someone like Jefferson less of a political handicap than it might have been in a more democratic polity.

By the late 1820s, however, the nation had gradually become more democratic. The second generation of political leaders didn't have the automatic standing enjoyed by Founding Fathers such as Washington, Jefferson, and others, and far more Americans were voting, for property requirements had been widely relaxed. In addition, the divisions between factions of the political elite were more noticeable.

The political scientist James Young has written that the politics of the 1820s was characterized by severe deadlock; among other things, there was an incredibly contentious presidential election in 1824, which ended up in the House of Representatives and which called into question the very legitimacy of the republic.[9] The too-distant political elite was falling out of favor in this gradually more democratic polity, and the Federalist party was coming apart at the seams. In fact, it is an indication of the eclipse of the Federalists' ideas and political style by more populist-oriented politicians that for all intents and purposes the party breathed its last in that decade.

At about the same time, other political parties—both the Democrats and the emerging Whigs—were gradually becoming more organized and were reaching out around the country to the new voters.[10] In 1828 the Democratic party settled on a war hero presidential candidate, Andrew Jackson, a man whose campaign and presidency set a tone for politics in a democratic age that continues with us today.[11]

Despite being quite wealthy himself, Jackson campaigned as one of the ordinary working people. As a military man, he was the first political outsider prominent in national politics; up to that time major figures had had lengthy records of national political service. Stressing his humble origins, presenting himself as the tribune of the hardworking small farmer and craftsman, he projected a manly can-do image, as compared to the effete intellectuality of Jefferson. Jackson proved to be an extremely successful politician and a highly popular president.

Jackson's veto of the rechartering of the second Bank of the United States was the seminal event of his presidency, and it presaged the anti-elitist tone of populist rhetoric for generations to come.[12] Jackson saw the national bank as being run by a well-placed group of eastern financiers who made decisions about investing and loans that exerted a tremendous amount of influence over the entire economy, potentially making or breaking whole industries. The ordinary hardworking American people who elected Jackson did not have the same priorities as this unaccountable group of financiers, he said, some of whom he portrayed as being under foreign influence.

Already, thanks to Jackson, by the 1830s the voice of populism was clearly defined. The agrarian roots of the country—the "grassroots"—inspired the myth of the hardworking small farmer who had the dignity and the moral courage to run his own life (if given the chance) in a democratic polity. These were the true democrats, the ones who produced goods and didn't live dishonestly off the hard work of another man. The great majority of citizens needed to fight off the power of a distant, unaccountable group of powerful men in the East (some of whom might be more sympathetic to foreign interests than to the interests of the small farmer) who adhered to the mercantile tradition of orchestrating a modern economy by controlling large sums of money and political power. Such power would make it impossible for the average productive man to run his own life. Jefferson's vision of the American future, where hardworking men could run their own lives on the wholesome rural frontier, was at stake.

It was already becoming clear which interpretation of the Founding had captured the imagination of Americans. The party of the Federalists, who had constructed and rammed through a constitution that protected the new nation from the kind of popular government advocated by anti-Federalists (and which provided for energy in an indirectly elected executive branch to fulfill their vision of the American future), was gone from the picture. The Jefferson-Jackson party of local control and states' rights (the Democrats) and the party of legislative supremacy (the Whigs) were ascendant.[13] These two parties adapted themselves organizationally and structurally to a more democratic age, while the Federalists fell by the wayside.[14]

Populism Gets a Party

Populism grew stronger as a political force in the late nineteenth century as a reaction to the dramatic changes brought about by the Industrial Revolution. While a loosely defined populist movement at that time was in large measure a bitter reaction against fast and overwhelming economic change, it also served as an effective call to serious and sometimes drastic reform in a society where the inequities brought about by corporate industrial capitalism were increasingly apparent and distressing. Small farmers were finding it more and more difficult to maintain their dignity in the face of what seemed now to be the overwhelming power of eastern industrial and financial interests.

Not surprisingly, late-nineteenth-century populism found its most potent voice in the rural areas in the South and the Middle West. The Populist party formed at that time served as a fusion vehicle for a wide range of largely rural protest movements and parties. The centerpiece of its appeal was in the form of a partly mythical nostalgia for a bygone era in which the small farmer was in control of his life and a deep suspicion of those people and forces responsible for change. In most of the country, including the nonslaveholding parts of the South, farming was equated with independence, democracy, and self-government, not with a feudal tradition as in some other countries. Agrarian life was the source of the American democratic tradition, and Populists' belief in democracy derived from those roots as well as the belief in the essential goodness and wisdom of the common man, particularly as compared to the wickedness of those among the elite in the East who looked down on them and cared nothing for their way of life.

But the Populist party was based on far more than just wistful nostalgia. Contemporary historians stress the insistently radical nature of the

Populist platform, which called on the federal government to redistribute wealth and take responsibility for the common good and smooth out some of the rough edges of corporate capitalism.[15] Populists proposed an increase in the money supply and strict regulation of the railroads so that farmers who depended on the rails for distribution of their products would no longer be gouged by the industrialists. They called for the right of labor to negotiate with management, an end to brutal strike-breaking practices, shorter workdays, as well as numerous changes in the political system to move in the direction of more direct democracy in order to bypass the corrupt politicians and political parties that were bought off by big corporations. The party promised that these reforms would bring back the days when the individual had a chance to compete before true free enterprise was destroyed by rapacious and predatory industrial monopolists. The party had its successes, but was hampered in its attempts to widen its following among the poor in the cities by the fact that many of the city dwellers were foreign born and didn't cotton to the rhetoric and style, which were anchored in the party's agrarian heritage.

In 1896, the Populists ended up endorsing the Democratic presidential candidate William Jennings Bryan, who promised to fulfill the Populist platform and bring the financial establishment to heel.[16] The party withered quickly after that, but its spirit lived on. The Populists' rhetoric and sometimes their programs were quickly hijacked by the major parties and other movements. Most important, the Populists' message was part of the inspiration for the Progressive movement, which proved to be so influential in twentieth-century American politics and culture. Their spirit spoke to something so profoundly in keeping with American democracy that it was impossible to ignore—the deepest democratic yearning to have control over one's destiny, to not feel helpless in the face of distant forces perceived to be undemocratic and parasitic.

The Progressives:
Putting a Middle-Class Face on Populism

The Populists' agitation for democracy and social and economic reform came to its political maturity, in some senses, with the Progressive movement. Where the agrarian populists often expressed a gut-level, sometimes antimodern, reaction to the rapid social and economic changes in the last decades of the nineteenth century, Progressives put a more measured, middle-class face on reform. They were more comfortable with modernity, thus were not reflexively distrustful of change. Where the Populist reformers were anti-elite, frequently lumping together economic, social, and political elites in their rhetorical attacks, some of the Progressives themselves came from the elite class and saved their most virulent disdain for corrupt politicians and the new class of industrial-ists.[17] Where some Populists were reactionaries resistant to modernity and change, the Progressives sought to channel change in ways that would improve the community. Their program was less radical than the Populists', yet many Progressives still advocated far-reaching social and economic reforms and a continuation of the call for institutions of direct democracy. As such, Progressives were populist in the generic sense—they believed in the wisdom and community-spiritedness of the common man, and they sought above all to make the political system more re-sponsive to the will of the majority.

In truth, Progressivism consisted of a variety of strains, including but not limited to the temperance movement, efforts to clean up corruption in politics and the political parties at the state and local levels, and na-tional efforts to break up monopolies and use the federal government as a competing force against powerful economic interests.[18] The historian Richard Hofstadter described Progressivism as "that broader impulse to-ward criticism and change that was everywhere so conspicuous after 1900, when the already forceful stream of agrarian discontent was en-larged and redirected by the growing enthusiasm of middle-class people for social and economic reform."[19] The first major history of the Progressive movement, written by Benjamin Parke DeWitt in 1915, de-scribed it this way:

> The first [tendency of Progressivism] is found in the insistence by the best men in all political parties that special, minority, and corrupt influence in government—national, state, and city—be removed; the second tendency is found in the demand that the structure or machinery of government, which has hitherto been admirably adapted to control by the few, be so changed and modified that it will be more difficult for the few, and easier for the many, to control; and, finally, the third tendency is found in the rapidly growing conviction that the functions of government at present are too re-stricted and they must be increased and extended to relieve social and eco-nomic distress.[20]

DeWitt felt that the political system in the United States was in dire need of restructuring so that it was not so easily captured by groups with interests inimical to those of the whole population. In this way, the Progressives rejuvenated the debate—essentially dormant since the days of slavery—about what kind of document the Constitution was and how the idea of "consent of the governed" should be interpreted. The more committed Populists and Progressives believed that the document stood in the way of democracy, that it represented government by the few. To some, the Declaration of Independence better represented the true mean-ing and spirit of the Founding than the Constitution, which many believed was written by men with property in order to protect their privileged status.[21]

In coming to grips with the Progressives' perspective and impact on American democracy, one must understand their paradoxical view of human nature and their position on the proper connection between people and the government. Progressives were typically Protestant moralists who believed in the essential dignity of the individual and his or her right to liberty, but also believed him to be innately sinful. This latter belief did not, however, lead them to resignation when faced with the failings of individuals and society. While a conservative might conclude that every step forward by mankind would be nullified by one step back (or maybe two or three steps back), Progressives believed it was possible to remove temptations (by making alcohol illegal, for example) and rein in some of people's darker impulses with progressive legislation and reform.[22] Certainly the government can and should be used as an instrument of the people to improve society by controlling the abuses of corporate capitalism.

Progressives had an abiding faith in the capacity of people to act in the interest of the community. Despite people's failings as individuals, in the political sphere they could be communitarian, rising above their innate sinfulness. The ordinary man can make good decisions in public policy—he had the *right* to. The average person is not influenced and controlled by the special interests; he or she takes the view of the whole community into account, unlike the typical corrupt politician. Adding up the opinions of interested citizens resulted in a kind of ultimate wisdom. As a consequence, Progressives seemed to have an almost dogmatic faith in the validity of corporate judgment. (It could be said that they seemed blind to the possibility that that very corporate judgment could infringe on individual liberty.) The crucial idea was that community action can make the society better, creating the "city on a hill" envisioned by the Puritans.[23]

As a practical matter, in the Progressives' view, it was absolutely necessary to rid the political system of corruption, open up government processes, and make them accessible to the people, and it was desirable whenever possible for ordinary citizens to govern themselves. (Certainly direct democracy was preferable to government by self-interested politicians who might be on the take.) The essence of this idea can be found in the words of one of the state Populist platforms co-opted by Progressives: "The majority of people cannot be corruptly influenced."[24] In order to realize the goal of true self-government in the public interest, the political system must be cleansed of venal and corrupt politicians in representative institutions and in the political parties who have a vested interest in the workings of the political system and have lost sight of the common good.

The Progressives ran with many of the ideas for political reform and direct democracy that had been advocated by the Populists in the late nineteenth century. These included the direct election of U.S. senators; the institution of referenda, provisions to recall elected officials, and initiatives in many of the states; the use of primaries to select candidates for office at the state and local levels, and of presidential primaries to select convention delegates; and numerous municipal- and state-level reforms.

Their biggest and most important targets were the political party machines, which were seen as being in league with corrupt special interests in stymieing the will of the people by choosing party insiders and flacks as candidates for elected office. The Progressives viewed the parties as constituted at that time not as helpful intermediaries between the people and the government, as some theories would have it, but rather as roadblocks to the true expression of the popular will in public policy. Political parties were the lynchpin, since they controlled the politicians who represented the people in the legislatures but were beholden to their party bosses.

The institution of the direct primary to nominate candidates was the vital reform in weakening the hold of the political parties on politics and government. It enabled voters to choose their party's candidates, even sometimes against the wishes of the machines. The machines were also hurt by other reforms, particularly good government reforms that put the provision of basic services, including everything from trash collection to welfare payments to the down-and-out to government contracting under the control of professional bureaucrats. Thus were bypassed party officials and ward heelers, who had become accustomed to controlling the distribution of various services and contracts for their political benefit— sometimes improving their own financial situation in the process.

Progressives were represented in both parties in those days, but it was the ideas of the Progressive Republican president, Theodore Roosevelt, who entered office in 1901, that had the most impact in the new century. In an important sense, he *nationalized* populism. Jefferson's master stroke had been to reconcile a federal-level constitutionalism with populism at the state and local level; now Roosevelt proposed using the constitutional arrangements as a vehicle for carrying out the popular will at the national level. Roosevelt reasoned that the energetic executive created by the constitutionalists to be strong but insulated from public opinion could be used by the people and for the people.[25]

Roosevelt's thinking went this way: In the early nineteenth century it may have been the case that people could run their own lives at the state and local level and needed to be protected from an overbearing central government, but in the early twentieth century the situation was entirely different. The states and regions of the country were so interdependent in the modern age that it was often necessary for that central government to step in and act in the interest of the people. The federal government was needed by the people as a protection against the economic power of the railroads and other industries that crisscrossed the country. Where else could the people logically turn other than their only nationally elected office, the presidency? Who could speak for the people better than their president?

Roosevelt's balancing act between populism and constitutionalism was far more problematic than Jefferson's. Why have the checks and balances at all if the purpose of government is to fulfill the people's wishes as expressed at the polls? At the very least—as Woodrow Wilson argued—the system needed to be streamlined along the model of parliamentary government.[26]

Roosevelt's ideas took firmer hold as the century progressed. The federal government would no longer be thought of as merely an arrangement of institutions meant to provide a few crucial services, such as defending the country when threatened by hostile forces, but strictly limited so as not to pose a threat to the people's liberties. The federal government, and particularly the presidency, could express the aspirations and will of the people.[27] The Progressives' populism was not one of resentment and retrenchment and reaction, as some forms of populism could be. Instead, Progressives had a positive and expansive vision that encompassed using the federal government for the good of the whole community.

The Progressive movement is sometimes depicted as petering out by the late 1910s, but actually the Progressive spirit animated the New Deal as well as the political reforms of the 1960s and early 1970s.[28] For example, before the 1970s, presidential nominations remained largely under the control of party leaders, unlike nominations for most other offices. One of the most important reforms in the seventies was the spread of presidential primaries, inspired by latter-day progressives, which injected the populist expectation of direct rule into the inner sanctums of presidential party politics as an effort to fulfill Roosevelt's wish that the president truly be able to speak for the people.[29] But perhaps the most important legacy of the Progressives was the spread of certain notions—that the only cure for the corruption inherent in representative government is more democracy, and that the populist theory of democracy applies at the federal level, not just at the state and local levels.

The Populist Message in Contemporary Politics

Populist political language in some ways remains unchanged from the days of Andrew Jackson 170 years ago. The people know better; the distant elite establishment controls government illegitimately against the wishes of the majority of average men and women, today; ordinary people are stymied in their efforts to gain access to the political system.

The historian Michael Kazin points out, however, that many of the targets of populist dissatisfaction in recent years are new—often the liberal cultural and political elite and liberal interest groups, instead of robber barons, Wall Street, and bankers. The left is perceived as the defender of a corrupt status quo by many, and some on the right and an angry nebulous center have successfully generated popular resentment against a supposed left-wing elite establishment. In fact, the welfare state, originally instituted as a buffer for ordinary people against the vicissitudes of the marketplace, was characterized by conservative populists such as Alabama's Governor George Wallace in the 1960s as serving minority (usually African Americans') and elite (often social workers' and bureaucrats') interests against the wishes of the majority.[30]

The Democrats' New Deal coalition was torn asunder in the sixties and seventies by the likes of Wallace, who railed against the "pointy-headed bureaucrats" who were conducting "social experiments," such as busing to achieve racial integration, on ordinary folks; Richard Nixon, whose vice president, Spiro Agnew, vilified the "effete intellectual snobs" who were thwarting the "silent majority;" and Ronald Reagan, who rode the tax revolt to the White House as a protest against confiscatory taxation used by "gov'ment" to support welfare and other unpopular programs.[31] The white northern blue-collar and southern components of the Democratic coalition—at one time the mainstays of the party—were deeply offended by liberal racial policies and the perception that Democratic politicians were soft on crime. (Many Democrats' reflexively liberal stand on crime issues was particularly problematic politically in the sixties, as the nation suffered through one of its worst ever crime waves.) These white southerners and northern workers left the Democratic party in droves, at least in presidential elections, making it nearly impossible for a Democrat to be elected president for nearly a quarter century.[32]

One of the best ways to understand populist resentment in late-twentieth-century America, or perhaps throughout our history, is to look at one of its perennially favorite targets, the Supreme Court. The liberal Warren and Burger courts of the 1960s and '70s instituted new, more lenient, and very unpopular, rules in criminal proceedings and forced busing to achieve integration, policies involving highly controversial constitutional interpretations that stoked the fires of popular rage. How could an unelected, elitist institution rule on such sensitive areas with virtually no accountability? Populists viewed them as high priests in black gowns who should have no special place in a democratic polity. Jefferson himself had seen no particular reason why these justices' interpretation of the Constitution should take precedence over that of the other branches.[33]

Of course the justification for this exalted role was the constitutionalist view that the Constitution should trump public opinion when the two came into conflict. Tellingly, this argument did nothing to quell the firestorm of protest. Majorities were incensed. Majorities were also incensed in the 1930s when a conservative court regularly nullified New Deal legislation, which stoked the fires of reformist populism.[34] Again, the justification was the constitutional one—and this justification is a weak reed against populist outrage! An institution like the Supreme Court by its very nature incites the populist resentment that is always so close to the surface in American politics.

Today, populism sometimes takes less ideological forms than at certain times in the past. In 1992, Ross Perot, perhaps the wealthiest man ever to mount a serious presidential campaign (he founded the Reform party in order to do so), became the voice of populist outrage, railing against the political establishment, organized interests, and foreigners who were influencing American politics against the wishes of the majority of Americans. He got on the bandwagon of a populist movement to institute term limits (an approach Andrew Jackson hinted at more than a century and a half before), and advocated the implementation of national town-hall meetings and national referenda. Politics needed to be wrested from the career politicians and the special interests; a businessman from Texas, who had the public good in mind, could better run a government mucked up by corruption and could "get under the hood" and fix the economy. His remarkable performance—at one time he led the major party candidates in the polls and ultimately received about one fifth of the vote despite wildly erratic behavior during the campaign—told a great deal about the strength of his message.

More recently, the former professional wrestler and Navy SEAL Jesse Ventura stunned the political world by defeating strong major party candidates—one was the son of Hubert Humphrey, a legend in Minnesota and national Democratic party politics—to win the 1998 race for governor of Minnesota as a populist reformer. (Ventura ran as the Reform party candidate.) Ventura's appeal was essentially nonideological; he railed against the thoroughly corrupt political parties and out-of-touch career politicians, rallying new voters with an updated version of an old-fashioned theatrical style of politics. He warned that the vast majority of Americans are thoroughly fed up with unresponsive politicians in the major parties and more ordinary citizens like him will run and win if the parties don't wise up.[35]

Given the redistributive bent of populist politics in the past, oddly enough the left has had relatively few populist politicians who have made a noticeable mark in recent years. The most notable exception is Jesse Jackson, who preached an old-time economic populism updated by racial inclusiveness in his quests for the presidency in 1984 and 1988. Jackson broke through in 1984 with a few victories in Democratic primaries and caucuses, and in 1988 he won many more. Only Michael Dukakis stood between him and the nomination that year. But Jackson's successes had more to do with his powerful appeal to the influential African American constituency than it had to do with the positions he took on economic issues.

Bill Clinton and his consultants created a soft kind of economic populism to generate support for his presidential candidacy in 1992, represented best by his "putting people first" slogan and folksy manner. But he turned out, by his own admission, to be a green-eyeshade "Eisenhower Republican" on economic policy.[36] More commonly the left has been pressed into retrenchment to maintain programs that polls show to be unpopular with a majority, such as affirmative action and arts funding, and to address the concerns of unpopular and vocal constituent groups like gays and lesbians. Clinton's wide popularity during his second term in office was due to his part in welfare reform and tough anti-crime legislation[37]—both right-wing populist issues—far more than for his advocacy of the liberal cultural agenda.

Public Opinion

Today populism is manifested most noticeably in Americans' disdain for the political process. Though the center and right have captured the language of populism, there is a growing widespread distrust of elites in government, the political parties, and the media. Americans believe as firmly as ever, by margins of more than two to one in most polls, that the "interests" are controlling the politicians and that politicians are fundamentally corrupt and out of touch—government must be cleaned up and run efficiently, as though it were a business.[38] Most people do not like Congress, and they distrust incumbent politicians. Neither party is trusted by most people to handle what they perceive to be the most important problem facing the country. By a large majority most people would not like to see their son or daughter go into politics.[39]

Americans believe that widely popular movements to change the system have come up short for the same reasons as always: government is fundamentally corrupt and the views of the people are shut out. One of the best examples of this is the failure at the federal level of the term-limits movement, the movement to limit the number of consecutive terms of office members of Congress can serve. The term-limits movement captures perfectly the bitterness toward politicians and the alienation toward the political process that so many people feel. If only ordinary citizens with no ax to grind could get their chance to break into the political process, advocates of term limits say, government would work better and the grip of the special interests could be broken. But the movement, while successful in many states, was stymied in the courts and by the super-majority rule (requiring a two-thirds vote) on constitutional amendments in the Congress.[40]

Americans are so suspicious that they don't even trust the Congress with the arcane business of budgeting. A highly popular constitutional amendment to require a balanced budget received the necessary super-majority in the House to send it to the states for ratification, but missed passing in the Senate by a single vote.

Perhaps most important, Americans believe that politicians routinely ignore their desires when they cast their votes in Congress. In a recent poll, 63 percent of Americans wanted members of Congress to "stick closely to American public opinion . . . including results of polls" when making legislative decisions, whereas only 34 percent said members should "do what they think is best."[41] Such a result should come as no surprise in a country where the voice of the people is so venerated.

Certainly, some of the public cynicism is well founded, but much of it probably represents nothing more than an intense dislike of the inevitable messiness of democratic politics, and the anger just seems to get worse the more public and open the process becomes. In fact, Congress is surely *less* corrupt in most respects than at almost any time in U.S. history. But its activities are more open to scrutiny than ever before, with constant coverage by C-SPAN, numerous all-news cable channels, and commentary aired on a dozen or more political talk shows. This fosters the climate for dramatic, but really symbolic, statements like the term-limits movement and the Balanced Budget Amendment, both of which are apparent quick fixes but don't really address the root causes of special interest influence or chronic deficit spending and might, if implemented, have very little effect on them at all.

The irony is that politicians do listen to the people; they are almost obsessive consumers of polling data and other sources of information about what their constituents think, including letters, phone calls, e-mails, and faxes. As a result, there is less and less space for independent deliberation by elected officials. The political scientist John Geer argues that rational politicians would be crazy not to pay close attention to the best sources of information available to them about what people think.[42] And most politicians are neither crazy nor irrational. Geer and many others have documented the attraction polls have for politicians. A former presidential speechwriter, Peggy Noonan, has written: "Polls are the obsession of . . . every political professional, Republican or Democratic. . . . In every political meeting I have ever been to, if there was a pollster there his own words carried the most weight because he is the only one with hard data, with actual numbers on actual paper."[43]

Geer asserts that great leaders of the past—even Lincoln and Churchill—would have consulted polls had they had that resource. In fact, successful democratic politicians have always used whatever gauge they could to determine what people were thinking. To a great extent, doing this well has been what determines success in politics. Today the means are just a bit more systematic and scientific than they used to be, if not always terribly precise. The question is: What do politicians do with that information? Do they search out ways to convince people of their positions and develop better arguments tailored to the way people are thinking about an issue? Do they take leadership positions on issues that people are ambivalent about or ones on which they haven't focused? Or do they simply pander to what the majority seems to think?

The ubiquity of public opinion polls and the ability of the citizens to communicate their views puts the politicians in a bind: When do you attempt to lead? When do you follow? When the costs in terms of votes are high and are made plain, politicians tend to bend to the will of the majority on almost any issues that catch the people's attention, no matter how ill thought out or reflexive the public's views. The anti-elitist tone is as strong as ever, too, as evidenced among members of both parties. A few examples from the recent past illustrate these points well.

Congress Plans to Raise Its Pay—Without a Vote

Populist outrage was most vociferously expressed when, in early 1989, the House of Representatives planned to give its members a 51 percent pay raise without actually voting on it. The raise would put at $135,000 salaries that had been at $89,500. In return, members of Congress would forego most of their honoraria and speaking fees. A salary review board had suggested the hike on the grounds that higher salaries would be more apt to attract the best and brightest to public service, and that paying members better would make them less susceptible to special interest influence. Members, as expected, were supportive; many complained of the cost of maintaining two homes and the relatively lucrative opportunities people with their skills could have outside of public service. Speaker Jim Wright arranged that the pay raise would go into effect if the House did *not* vote *not* to have the increase.

But the "specter of radio populism"[44] reared its head, as talk-show hosts around the country stirred up what *Newsweek* described as the "tea bag revolution"—a kind of modern-day Boston Tea Party protest.[45]

Capitol Hill offices were flooded with tea bags from constituents, many coming with pointed and even violent messages. A varied crew of populist agitators spanning the spectrum from the conservative talk-show host Rush Limbaugh to the liberal consumer advocate Ralph Nader decried the large raise, whose arcane details regarding speaking fees and the like had no deterrent effect on the outrage.

Quite rapidly the pressure became too great, and Wright was forced to hold a vote. The pay raise went down by a 380–48 margin. In this case it appeared that the pols in Washington were utterly out of touch with how people might respond to what appeared to be a kind of subterfuge, how this maneuver could feed the populist belief that politicians were out of touch more generally. Not only were members giving themselves a large pay increase, they were going to institute it without taking responsibility for it. The public was incensed, as reflected in polls and, more tellingly, in constituents' direct contacts with their representatives' offices, many of which were inspired by talk-radio hosts. Once the feelings were made known, the House responded with amazing speed and notable decisiveness.

The Mexican "Bailout"

But not all populist outrage is caused by simple issues such as the pay raise. There was an interesting case in 1995 involving the Clinton administration's plan to provide $40 billion in loan guarantees to help stabilize Mexico's failing economy. The President had lined up an impressive array of bipartisan support, including that of prominent Republicans such as House Speaker Newt Gingrich, Majority Leader Bob Dole, and Former President George Bush. In fact, it was apparent from the start that Clinton would get much more support for his plan from Republicans than from Democrats. He also had the enthusiastic support of the widely respected Federal Reserve Board chairman, Alan Greenspan, who believed that it was crucial for U.S. interests to stop the possible ripple effect throughout Latin America of an economic collapse in Mexico.

In some sense the bailout case was a replay of the debate over instituting a North American free trade zone (NAFTA) in 1993. Labor-oriented Democrats and some populist Republicans resented what they regarded as a "bailout" for Mexico. Senator Hank Brown (R-Colorado) said, "There's no reason U.S. taxpayers have to bail out people who make large unsecured loans to Mexico. I think it's crazy."[46] Representative Zack Wamp (R-Texas), after listening to the defense of the plan from Greenspan, said, "Sitting and listening to Mr. Greenspan last night, I couldn't help but realize that he's a whole lot smarter than the

people of east Tennessee who I was elected to represent. But I am going
to vote with them this time and not with Mr. Greenspan . . . even if one
out of ten times the people are wrong, then so be it. We've got to listen
to them."[47]

And the radio talk-show hosts were not quiet. Limbaugh stated that
"President Clinton is very decisive in giving away our money and taking
away our sovereignty."[48] Congresswoman Marcy Kaptur (D-Ohio)
chimed in by criticizing the bailout of a country that has mismanaged its
economy for "as long as I've been an adult."[49]

With polls showing nearly 80 percent of Americans opposing the plan,
even the support of the President, Greenspan, and the Republican leadership could not carry the day. All claimed that the plan was in the national security interest; the majority in the Congress didn't care. As
Congressional Quarterly put it: "In the wake of the [1994 election results],
lawmakers have become more sensitive to the concerns of their constituents than to the demands of their leaders."[50] In the end, the President
circumvented the Congress with a scaled-back alternative rescue plan for
Mexico that did not require congressional action.

The political scientist and television commentator William Schneider
announced the triumph of populism in 1995. "The Establishment of this
country has lost so much legitimacy that it now has to govern by decree.
That was the larger meaning of President Clinton's recent decision to
issue an executive order bailing out the Mexican economy," he wrote in
a political journal. "The Mexican loan guarantee was not a left-right issue
or a Democrat-Republican issue. It was a populist issue that divided the
Establishment and the people. Washington and Wall Street supported it.
They knew it had to be done. The people were against it by better than
4–1."[51] The people saw no reason to "co-sign a note for Mexico" when we
have so many pressing problems at home.[52]

Not much had changed since Alexander Hamilton and the anti-
Federalists debated constitutional powers in the 1780s. In the Mexican
loan case, Hamilton's energetic executive exerted constitutional powers
directly against the will of the people to implement an establishment-
backed foreign policy initiative. Foreign policy was being implemented
undemocratically, as Hamilton thought was sometimes necessary for the
good for the country.

Interestingly, polls indicated that people who knew something about
the subject tended to support the loan guarantee, but this didn't matter
to hyper-responsive politicians who were adept at stoking the populist
fires. An increasing number of Republicans in the Congress were strongly
"anti-establishment." And the majority of Democrats were solidly against
almost any international trade accord or bailout. This case and others
vividly show that populism in America isn't a liberal thing or a conserv-

ative thing. Democratic House Minority Leader Dick Gephardt of Missouri, the Reverend Jesse Jackson, and Ralph Nader on the left, Pat Buchanan, and Congressman (now Senator) Jim Bunning (R-Kentucky) on the right, as well as centrists like Ross Perot and Jesse Ventura all qualify as populists. All, with the exception of Ventura, were vocal opponents of NAFTA and the Mexico plan.

In the aftermath of the Mexican loan guarantee debate, Thomas Friedman, a *New York Times* columnist, described the Congress as being loaded with "nativist, anti–foreign policy types who think that representative democracy is accurate poll-taking, not judgment. . . . Thank goodness nobody did a focus group before President Truman announced the Marshall Plan."[53]

The Nomination of Zoe Baird for Attorney General

In the first month of the Clinton Administration, a major stumble occurred with the nomination of Zoe Baird for the post of attorney general. She would be the nation's first woman attorney general, which appealed to liberals, and her highly successful career as a corporate attorney appealed to conservatives. Members of both parties sang the praises of this impressive, highly qualified nominee. Initially expected to be a slam-dunk in the Senate, her nomination quickly became problematic.

Soon it came to light that Ms. Baird had employed two undocumented Peruvians to provide childcare and perform household chores. The law states that employers must verify the status of their employees and can be fined for hiring undocumented aliens. To the establishment this was no big deal. A typical response was the *Los Angeles Times* editorial which said that, although this scandal was a minor embarrassment, it should have no effect on her qualifications to be attorney general.[54] The conservative *Wall Street Journal* was enthusiastic about her candidacy. The leaders of the Senate Judiciary Committee, Orrin Hatch (R-Utah) on the Republican side and Joe Biden (D-Delaware) on the Democratic side, were not particularly concerned, either. The establishment view was nearly universal: *everyone* does this.

According to the scholars Benjamin Page and Joseph Tannenbaum, who wrote a trenchant analysis of the scandal, among the prominent members of the national media only Cokie Roberts and Russell Baker expressed much concern. Roberts, on her Sunday morning television show, said: "I'd like to know what she was paying them, frankly, because she made enough money to hire Mary Poppins. . . . The idea that the only people that you could get under these circumstances are people that you have to hire illegally is just not the case with somebody who makes that much money."[55]

The radio talk-shows quickly reflected the majority sentiment. They were like "town meetings," according to Susan Estrich, a talk-show host who was Michael Dukakis's campaign manager.[56] All across the country the people were expressing outrage that a wealthy lawyer avoided making Social Security payments by hiring an illegal immigrant. Apparently some people could avoid the rules that everyone else has to play by, and get away with it. And she was going to be attorney general? Nominated by a president who at the 1992 Democratic convention invoked the forgotten Americans who "play by the rules and pay their taxes"?

Capitol Hill was flooded with phone calls. Senator Dennis DeConcini (R-Arizona) had 305 calls against her nomination and 4 in favor. Senator Paul Simon (D-Illinois) had 1,987 against and 217 for. Senator Patrick Leahy (D-Vermont) said, "I had never seen so many telephone calls, spontaneously, in such a short period."[57] This was the important point: both on the Hill and on talk shows around the country the response apparently was unorchestrated. And the polls went against Baird's nomination as well. By about 60 percent to 30 percent the country opposed her nomination, and many people in the majority seemed to feel intensely about the issue.

Page and Tannenbaum write that three preconditions have to be met to generate this sort of populist outrage, all of which were met in the Baird nomination case. First, on a high-profile matter, elites act on values and beliefs that are quite different than those of most ordinary citizens. Second, a large number of people become aware that they are acting in this way. Third, the public finds a way to express its outrage.

Page and Tannenbaum suggest that it may be fairly common for the first condition to be met, but in most cases the public is never made aware of the elite's actions, or the issue may not catch the public's attention, or the matter may be highly technical with no interested activists able to figure out a way to attract the public's interest. They find that populist outrage that does get expressed usually does not lead to useful discussions of the topic at hand. "Yet," they write, "it is important that such an instrument exists for 'enlarging the scope of conflict' and for bringing about more democratic outcomes, at least under certain limited circumstances."[58]

What is not in doubt is that the Congress will respond swiftly if the public can find a way to convey its sense of outrage. And it is reasonable to assume, given the increasing sophistication of interest group networks and the greater opportunities afforded by advanced technology for contacting members of Congress, that politicians are more sensitive than ever to and are more likely to respond to the potential for expressions of public outrage such as those described here.

Constitutionalism Versus Populism: The Clinton Impeachment

In December 1998 the House of Representatives impeached President William Jefferson Clinton for obstruction of justice and perjury in the Lewinsky sex scandal, the second time in American history a president had been impeached. Also for the second time, a trial in the Senate ensued. Perhaps never before in the lifetime of any living American had the interpretation and the wording of the Constitution received the level of public scrutiny they did during the trial. Senators, law professors, journalists, and ordinary Americans weighed in an ongoing debate about the meaning of "high crimes and misdemeanors," the criterion by which a president may be impeached and removed from office. The clash between populism and constitutionalism in our political culture was highlighted in vivid relief during this great spectacle. As it turned out, for even the most avid defenders of the Constitution, the choice was difficult.

The Constitution acquired the status of Holy Writ during the impeachment debate and the trial. Time and again senators and congressmen of both parties committed themselves publicly to the constitutional process that must be followed in an impeachment. The movement to avoid a trial in the Senate was waylaid by references to "constitutional duty." The efforts to short-circuit impeachment by censuring the president for his transgressions also foundered on the argument put forth by opponents of censure that such a move was not explicitly permitted in the Constitution.

But public opinion was certainly not ignored. Though Americans may at some points in the scandal have wanted the President to resign, by about a two-to-one margin they did not support his conviction and removal from office. In this era of constant public opinion polling, senators were fully cognizant of the political risks they ran in going up against these strong sentiments on such a salient issue.

The most interesting case involved Senator Robert Byrd, a Democrat from West Virginia, the second longest serving member of the body, a former Senate majority leader, and a recognized expert on the Constitution and Senate history, procedure, and precedent. There is probably no senator who reveres the Constitution and the Senate's place in the system of separated powers and checks and balances more than the senior senator from West Virginia. In an amazing interview on ABC several days before the Senate was to vote on the articles of impeachment, Byrd told the reporter Cokie Roberts that he believed that the President had committed high crimes and misdemeanors. There was no doubt in his mind about that, he said, but he intended to vote against conviction on both counts, the perjury charge and the obstruction of justice charge. (He followed through on those intentions.)

Roberts was taken aback. How can you say that the President committed high crimes and misdemeanors and yet not vote for conviction? she asked. The renowned expert on the Constitution wavered for a moment. He claimed first that the country could not risk the instability that would follow from the ouster of the President at this time. (This argument was disingenuous in view of the fact that the country was about as stable as it had been in at least seventy years at that moment. The United States was not at war. The Cold War was over. The Dow Jones Average was nearing 10,000, and the economy was growing and had been for about six years.) Perhaps more significant, Byrd also cited the support the President had among the people. These were reasons enough not to convict the President, he said, even though Article II, Section 4 of the Constitution states: "The President . . . shall be removed from office on impeachment for, and conviction of, treason, bribery, and other high crimes and misdemeanors."

Byrd's was a truly remarkable statement. Though not explicitly going against the direct letter of the Constitution (it doesn't say that the Senate *has to* kick the President out for high crimes and misdemeanors), it did constitute a great deal of wiggling for the one senator who more adamantly than any other declared his allegiance to and respect for the document. For him, public opinion won the day over the rhetorical obeisance to the specific words in the Constitution. He was not the only senator on either side of the question whose vote did not reflect his interpretation of "high crimes and misdemeanors." There were other senators and representatives, including members of the President's party, who early in 1998 warned that the President was through if he had perjured himself, but later backed away from such pronouncements in the face of public opinion.

Conclusion

Where does this leave us today with this "antidemocratic" Constitution of ours? Of course Americans still revere it, at least in the abstract. That was made abundantly clear in the media and in the Congress during the debate on impeachment. The very words "separation of powers" and "checks and balances" hold special significance for most people. We are left with the same two conflicting ideas: Americans' reverence for popular rule and public opinion and their reverence for a document that was written to rein in majority rule in some circumstances. Though Americans are ambivalent, conflicted, and downright contradictory in their feelings, their views about the meaning of democracy seem to be reflected better by the populist position than by the constitutionalism of Hamilton, Washington, and John Adams.

Jefferson's brilliant reconciliation of his populist beliefs with the checks and balances and the separation of powers in the Constitution—the restraints that in his view were meant to protect the people from a potentially overbearing federal government while they governed themselves at the state and local level—is no longer a reasonable accommodation. The neat distinction Jefferson drew between the roles of the different levels of government simply does not apply anymore. Teddy Roosevelt recognized this in the first decade of the twentieth century. And beginning with the New Deal in the 1930s, the federal government became much more involved in nearly every aspect of people's lives. The New Deal sounded the death knell of what was known as "dual federalism"—a doctrine that laid out a fairly clear delineation between what were state and federal government responsibilities, with most responsibilities remaining at the state level.[59] Today there are no meaningful barriers to the direct rule of the people by the Congress and the president. Yet checks and balances continue to thwart citizens' ability to rule themselves at the national level.

Americans may have the good sense to see value in both constitutionalism and populism. But the acute tension in American political culture between these ideas is increasingly difficult to paper over, if it can be done at all. First of all, Americans are used to looking to the federal government to address their needs and fulfill their desires. At the state and local levels many Americans have recourse to initiatives and referenda to overcome the obstacles of separated powers. In addition, many governors have the kind of power and authority in their states to carry out their perceived mandate that presidents can only dream of. In most states the legislatures are part-time assemblies without the visibility or resources to challenge the governor as effectively as Congress can challenge the president. At the national level, the Congress and the president are like two evenly matched heavyweights going toe-to-toe in a championship fight, and there are myriad ways to stop legislation from passing.[60] In spite of Teddy Roosevelt's formulation, which essentially sought to give the president special status as spokesman for the people, national electoral mandates usually vanish overnight[61] in the struggle for power in Washington, leaving the people increasingly frustrated with their national governmental institutions.

Furthermore, as the government in Washington becomes more and more discredited in people's eyes, populist notions gain ever more support. Respect for representative institutions and their way of doing business is almost nonexistent. Already members of Congress only cross the public (as happened with the pay raise, Mexican loan guarantee, and Baird nomination cases) because of gross miscalculations.

Eventually the public will demand the opportunity to get involved more directly in the legislative process. This is already happening with increasing regularity at the state and local levels. There may be a day when the pressure for national referenda and maybe even electronic plebiscites will be too strong to resist.

Constitutionalism might one day be seen as about as anachronistic as the Electoral College is today. While presidents are still technically chosen by the electors and not by the people, presidential elections are now universally regarded as candidate-centered plebiscites. The Electoral College is only tolerated because it hasn't obstructed the people's choice in more than a century. It might be that legislative processes are moving in the same direction—tolerated only so long as they do not stand in the way of the popular will. Increasingly, that is exactly what is happening in states that allow ballot initiatives and referenda.

In the next chapter we look more carefully at both the sorts of direct democracy current in American politics and some experimental innovations. Though advances in technology open up almost unlimited possibilities for direct citizen participation and access, we will see why only some forms are likely to take root here.

3

Direct Democracy:
Past, Present, and Future

Although the authors of *The Federalist Papers* specifically dismissed "pure democracy"—their term for direct democracy—as impractical and undesirable, the notion of direct rule has always been an attractive one to Americans. In the last thirty years or so, the development of a highly participatory policy-making environment has inspired greater interest still in initiatives and referenda as a means to make and influence policy.

After a brief glossary of relevant terms, this chapter begins with a look at the spread of direct democratic institutions during the twentieth century. Although populist ideas have been an important part of American political culture from the beginning, institutions of direct democracy were not put into place in any state until 1898. In the two subsequent decades, about half of the states instituted measures that facilitated direct control of government by ordinary citizens, including the referendum, initiative, and recall.

In more recent years, the populist impulse in American political culture not only has led to a remarkable quintupling of the use of referenda and initiatives, but also has penetrated the once-hallowed inner sanctum of presidential nomination politics. In the second part of this chapter, we see how and why American democracy has become dramatically more open and participatory in recent years, a development spurred by the growth of government in the 1960s and '70s. In this new environment, more groups than ever try to have an impact on public policy, and there is ever-growing interest in new ways to influence (or bypass) policy-makers. We look in detail at the growth of new forms of participatory democracy and experiments in direct democracy.

Finally, I speculate on the likely future directions that direct citizen participation in American politics will take. I conclude that direct democracy of the plebiscitary type—where citizens decide policy at the ballot box, perhaps enhanced by advances in technology that have, for example, made voting at home by computer feasible—is the most likely to flourish in the American political cultural context. Also, it is a sure bet that interest groups and active citizens will continue to take advantage of new forms of technology in their attempts to influence policy-makers. Institutions of direct democracy that require the involvement of citizens in agenda setting and policy formation, which some propose, will have a tougher time taking root here, despite their manifest appeal to many activists and scholars.

Defining the Terms

Many important terms in the discourse on direct democracy are used rather loosely and sometimes interchangeably in common parlance. What follows is a glossary that differentiates between them and indicates how they will be used in this book. First are the various forms of direct democracy, followed by terms commonly used to describe polities characterized by a great deal of citizen participation in politics and/or direct involvement in lawmaking.

The term *referendum* is often used generically to refer to any direct legislating by popular vote. In my use of the term I will maintain the important distinction between referenda and initiatives. In general, all referenda, with the partial exception of the popular or petition referendum, involve legislative action. In other words, referenda are ordinarily put on the ballot by legislators. *Initiatives,* on the other hand, are put on the ballot by citizens.

The term *ballot proposition* is also often used generically to refer to both referenda or initiative—any item that is placed before citizens for a vote. I will limit its use to refer to initiatives. The general terms *plebiscite* and *measure* will be used to refer to all kinds of legislating or advising by popular vote and thus cover all forms of direct lawmaking by citizens.

- *Constitutional referendum:* All states except Delaware put constitutional amendments that have passed the legislature before the people. Most states require a supermajority (commonly two-thirds) vote in both houses of their legislature and a simple majority vote of the people to ratify an amendment.
- *Petition referendum* (sometimes known as a *popular, protest,* or *direct referendum*): A petition referendum is a statute enacted by the legislature that is placed on the ballot for a vote as a result of a petition by citizens. Twenty-five states permit citizens to petition to place some types of statutes on the ballot. As is the case with all forms of direct democracy, there is considerable variation among the states as to the number of signatures required. The requirements involve either an absolute number of signatures of

registered voters or some percentage of either registered voters or participants in the last election. The petition referendum is distinctive from other types of referenda because *it is the only kind of referendum placed on the ballot by citizens.*

- *Mandatory referendum:* This is a referendum that is required before certain types of legislation can become law; a majority of the states have this. For example, in twenty-five states an act pledging the "full faith and credit" of the state as backing for a bond issue requires a referendum.
- *Advisory referendum:* The purpose of an advisory referendum is to find out how the voters feel about some issue. Some states have provisions that allow the legislature to put a question on the ballot for a vote. A second kind of advisory referendum permits citizens to petition to put a matter on the ballot. The results are only advisory and are not binding on the legislative body.
- *Direct initiative:* A direct initiative procedure permits voters to put either constitutional amendments or ordinary statutes up for a vote after a sufficient number of signatures are gathered by petition. As with all plebiscites, the required number of signatures is either a fixed number or a percentage of the voting population. When the term "initiative" is used alone, it usually means a direct initiative.
- *Indirect initiative:* An indirect initiative is one submitted to the legislature by voters. In some states if voters secure enough signatures, they may submit a statutory or constitutional initiative to the legislature for approval. If the legislature either does not act within a specified time or changes the proposed statute in a way unsatisfactory to the original proponents, then the proponents may attempt to gather the additional required signatures to have the initiative put up for a vote. In some states, the legislature may put a substitute proposal up for a vote as well.
- *Recall:* In some states voters may petition for the recall of elected officials before the expiration of their term of office. Recall, unlike all the measures listed above, does not involve legislation or the consideration of constitutional changes. Usually the signature requirements for recall are pretty steep, a considerably higher number than for initiatives. Once the proper number of signatures is attained, a special election is held to determine whether the officeholder keeps his or her position.

Of the various terms used to describe citizen involvement in political processes, the broadest is *participatory democracy*. Participatory democracy is essentially another way of saying *agency democracy*, the term coined by

Anthony King and introduced in Chapter 1. Alan Rosenthal, in his seminal work on state legislatures, *The Decline of Representative Democracy*, describes participatory democracy as a system in which citizens have considerable access to and influence over the actions of their elected representatives. This involves open processes in which representatives are highly responsive to citizen demands. Polls carry a great deal of influence in a participatory polity. A highly participatory citizenry often forces representatives to accede to their wishes and behave more as agents of the constituents than as trustees following the dictates of their conscience.

The term *direct democracy* carries the specific connotation of citizen involvement in lawmaking. This can take the form of either active involvement in agenda setting and policy-making, along the lines of the traditional town hall meeting, or simply participating in deciding legislation or constitutional changes by means of initiatives and referenda. In short, direct democracy is when citizens are directly involved in deciding policy and/or formulating it, by voting or by deliberation and discussion, face-to-face or electronically.

Plebiscitary democracy has a narrower meaning. It refers only to the involvement of citizens in lawmaking at the end stage—when they vote to determine whether a measure is to become law or a part of the state's constitution. In other words, plebiscitary democracy is a subset of direct democracy. Making policy by plebiscite connotes only citizen involvement in the final decision, not participation in the formulation of and deliberation on policy. Sometimes the term *instant democracy* is used as a synonym for plebiscitary democracy.

Discussion democracy means the direct involvement of citizens in the formulation of and deliberation on policy options as a prelude to deciding the outcome by vote. Discussion and plebiscitary democracy are the two basic kinds of direct democracy, differing importantly in the nature of citizen involvement required. Sometimes the term *deliberative democracy* is used in the direct democratic context as a synonym for discussion democracy.

The Past: The Spread of Direct Democracy in the Twentieth Century

The idea that ordinary citizens should take an active role in lawmaking, including in the formation of policy, can be traced back to the ancient Greeks. In the American tradition, the town meeting, dating back to colonial times, has given some citizens the opportunity for direct involvement in policy-making. In the 1800s the Swiss pioneered the use of initiatives and referenda. Influential American journalists such as J. W. Sullivan, having observed their use there, generated interest in direct legislation in the United States in the late nineteenth century.[1]

Various groups rapidly took an active interest in promoting the institutionalization of both referenda and initiatives in the states. Populists are largely credited with being the ones to take the lead, with Socialists and Progressives hopping on the bandwagon in the 1890s.[2] These reformers had many motives for their interest in direct democracy. It is probably fair to generalize that populists and Socialists intended to use institutions of direct democracy to pressure politicians to pay heed to their agenda of economic redistribution and the regulation of corporations, while Progressives tended to stress the importance of ending corruption in politics and the value of direct democracy as a tool in civic education.

All advocates of direct democracy in America had at least one common motivation: the desire to see the influence of special interests reduced in politics. The state legislatures and the political parties that controlled those institutions were the main scapegoats. The legislatures bore the brunt of the dramatic economic and social changes that were so rampant at the turn of the century. The professional politicians who held seats in these bodies, widely believed to be corrupt and unresponsive, were in a position where it would have been impossible to please everyone even if they had wanted to. In an increasingly complex and interdependent economy and society, legislators were called upon to determine policies that affected major industries and the livelihood of groups of citizens in profound ways. There was much more than ever for them to do, more people to offend, greater complexities and less of a margin for error—and, of course, there were more opportunities for corruption.

Critics claimed that the elected representatives were making decisions to further their careers and to pay off their benefactors, not to advance the common good. The whole political system, it seemed to many, had become the playground of the special interests. The people's faith in their political institutions was eroding. Yet another problem: The cesspool of deal-making and bribery in legislative politics was dissuading good people from entering public service.

Reformers felt that it was crucial to bring the legislative institutions to heel. Citizens needed a means to make policy themselves, as well as a procedure by which to recall incompetent or corrupt officials. If citizens could bypass legislators with direct democracy and the recall, the parties and the legislators would have to become more responsive, the argument went. The institution of initiatives and referenda as the centerpiece of a reform agenda would go a long way to restoring the faith of the people in the political system. In fact, for many Progressives, the advocacy of direct democracy became almost an obsession.

It was not the case, however, that the reformers were actually aiming to replace legislatures with direct democratic institutions. The principle of representative democracy was not really being questioned; it was the bastardization of the process by rampant corruption and the professionalization of the political class that caused legislatures to fall out of favor. The potential of citizen-initiated legislation together with other reforms like the primary election would, it was hoped, entice better sorts of public-spirited people to run for the state legislature.[3] Reformers saw the need for a restoration of sorts to a time when good men came to public service with the interest of the larger community in mind, not that of the special interests and the corporations.

The Progressives were particularly effective at putting in place initiatives and referenda in the states. They also achieved some of the most significant direct democratic successes, including the institution of the direct election of U.S. senators and woman suffrage in some states. As it turned out, in a relatively short period of time, from 1898 to 1918, twenty-three states adopted provisions for petition referenda or initiatives or both (see Table 3.1). Though in recent times there has been a groundswell of interest in bringing initiatives and referenda to more states, only one new initiative state has been added in the last twenty-five years. Over the course of the twentieth century, some states have added provisions for more types of initiatives, but most of the implementation of these institutions occurred during the Progressive Era. Table 3.2 provides a comprehensive list of all the initiative and petition referendum provisions permitted in the states today.

The Present

The Populist Expectation and Nominating Presidential Candidates

As we have seen, one of the main aims of the Progressives in the early part of the twentieth century was to purify the political parties so that they could be vehicles for citizen participation rather than brokers for powerful interests. The Progressives' central goal was to have a government that better reflected the will of the people in its policy-making. Progressive writers, including Woodrow Wilson in his days as an academic prior to his ascension to the White House, saw political parties, properly constituted, as the instrument for achieving that goal.[4]

Wilson believed that the parliamentary, or responsible, party model, where the top-down lines of authority are clear (something like Great Britain's system), was a far more democratic arrangement than the federalized party system in the United States. The Democratic and Republican parties in the United States have a decentralized organizational

TABLE 3.1 Adoption of Direct Democracy in the States

State	Year Adopted
South Dakota	1898
Utah	1900
Oregon	1902
Montana	1904
Nevada	1904
Missouri	1906
Oklahoma	1907
Maine	1908
Michigan	1908
Arkansas	1909
Kentucky	1910
New Mexico	1910
California	1911
Washington	1912
Ohio	1912
Nebraska	1912
Idaho	1912
Colorado	1912
Arizona	1912
North Dakota	1914
Maryland	1915
Massachusetts	1918
Alaska	1959
Wyoming	1968
Illinois	1970
Florida	1972
Mississippi	1992

Reprinted with permission from David Magleby, "Let the Voters Decide? An Assessment of the Initiative and Referendum Process," *University of Colorado Law Review* 66 (1995): 27.

structure in which the state units are largely independent. The national party organizations have relatively little power in the United States compared to their power in countries using the responsible party model.

Historically, in the United States, the state Democratic parties in particular were tremendously various. In Chapter 2 we saw that the Democratic party was founded on the notion of states' rights. This resulted in Democratic parties in states with different political cultures having markedly different ideological orientations, from ultraconservative in most of the southern states to progressive redistributionist in some northern states. It was said in the 1930s that the most conservative and the most liberal members of Congress were all Democrats. This was still the case all the way through the 1960s. The Republican party had a more co-

TABLE 3.2　Provisions for Initiatives and Petition Referenda in the States

	Initiatives	Petition Referendum
Alaska	DI (S)	Yes
Arizona	DI (S,CA)	Yes
Arkansas	DI (S,CA)	Yes
California	DI (S,CA)	Yes
Colorado	DI (S,CA)	Yes
Florida	DI (CA)	No
Idaho	DI (S)	Yes
Illinois	DI (CA)	No
Kentucky		Yes
Maine	II (S)	Yes
Maryland		Yes
Massachusetts	II (S,CA)	Yes
Michigan	DI (CA) II (S)	Yes
Mississippi	II (CA)	No
Missouri	DI (S,CA)	Yes
Montana	DI (S,CA)	Yes
Nebraska	DI (S,CA)	Yes
Nevada	DI (CA) II (S)	Yes
New Mexico		Yes
North Dakota	DI (S,CA)	Yes
Ohio	DI (CA) II (S)	Yes
Oklahoma	DI (S,CA)	Yes
Oregon	DI (S,CA)	Yes
South Dakota	DI (S,CA)	Yes
Utah	DI, II (S)	Yes
Washington	DI, II (S)	Yes
Wyoming	DI (S)	Yes

Explanation of initiatives
DI: Provision for direct initiatives
II: Provision for indirect initiatives
S: Initiatives for proposing statutes
CA: Initiatives for proposing constitutional amendments

herent nationally focused philosophical foundation: it was founded as a vehicle for the opposition to slavery, or at least its extension to the territories, and in support of government policies promoting a good business environment. Yet even in the Republican party there was a great deal of variety among its state units, with a much more conservative orientation in some midwestern states and a liberal bent in New England. These differences remain, albeit to a lesser degree, although today many of the most conservative Republicans are from the South.[5]

Wilson reasoned that if important political decisions were to be made on a democratic majoritarian basis at the national level, the parties needed to be reformed, unified, and disciplined under the principles of the responsible party model. He also believed that the internal workings of the parties needed to be democratized so that ordinary people could express their views in party politics. Parochial, professional politician-controlled state party units could never hope to express the true will of the people in national politics.

Of course, one way for people to have a real say would be to institute initiatives or referenda on the national level. Certainly Progressives were pushing successfully for citizen lawmaking at the state and local level, but most didn't go so far as to advocate national-level citizen lawmaking. To many this seemed too radical a break with the federal traditions outlined in the Constitution. Furthermore, many felt that political parties could potentially be a more appropriate institutional vehicle than national referenda for the expression of the popular will at the national level, provided the parties could be reinvented.

But how to do this? In the view of many Progressives, including Wilson and Theodore Roosevelt, it would take great leadership from the executive to break the hold of state and local parochialism on the parties and on the Congress. In fact, executive leadership was, in their view, essential to realizing a true expression of the popular will in politics; the presidency was the logical place to look for national leadership, not the Congress. After all, the Congress, unlike the presidency, was designed to look after state and local interests.

A plebiscitary presidential nomination process might do the trick, they suggested. If the president had to develop and articulate a national policy platform in a national primary campaign, then he would emerge as the spokesman of his party with a mandate from the public. A national primary was envisioned as a replacement for the process of haggling among state and local party leaders that resulted in brokered party conventions and candidates for president being beholden to those state and local party leaders. Many of these leaders were also in control of members of Congress, because they were the ones who determined nominations for House seats and often were influential in selecting senators.

To break the back of the decentralized party system, then, would require a radical change in the way presidents were nominated; they needed to get a mandate directly from the people through a national primary that would be instituted either by constitutional amendment or an act of Congress. In the meantime, Progressives pushed for state primaries to choose delegates to the national convention who would be tied to candidates instead of to party leaders. Progressives had success in instituting primaries in the 1910s; many states held primaries in 1912, 1916, and

1920 to help select delegates to the conventions. But the state and local party machines were still too deeply entrenched at that time, despite Progressive Era reforms that had weakened them, for primaries to make a dent in their control of presidential nomination politics.

By the reform period of the 1960s and 1970s, the earth had shifted in significant ways. Party organizations, while still able to exert a great deal of control over presidential nomination politics, did not have the iron grip they had earlier in the century.[6] Progressive reforms of all sorts, including primaries for other offices, civil service reform, and professional administration and management of government, had weakened the parties considerably. Finally, in 1968 in Chicago, where, ironically, the last of the truly old-fashioned party machines still thrived, reformers began once and for all to break the hold of tightly controlled, smoke-filled room politics in presidential nominations.

That year the Democrats did nominate the machine candidate, Vice President Hubert Humphrey, as the presidential candidate, despite the fact that he had run in no primaries and held views about the Vietnam War that were extremely unpopular with the most articulate and vocal faction of the Democratic party. This well-educated antiwar faction was not in the majority in the party, but it comprised a significant and crucial segment of the most active Democrats, so it was impossible for the party leaders to ignore them completely. Instead, they let these reformers in under the tent after the 1968 convention.[7] In short order these reformers changed the rules of presidential nomination politics in order to implement something like the Wilsonian vision of a plebiscitary nomination process designed to ascertain the will of the people and to reform the party in the direction of more citizen involvement.

Beginning in 1969, reformist Democrats such as Minnesota's Donald Fraser, Iowa's Senator Harold Hughes, and South Dakota's Senator George McGovern reconfigured the way the party would nominate presidential candidates by instituting new rules for delegate selection for the state parties. Delegates could only be selected in open processes (the most open were primaries, which became the method of choice in most states by 1976),[8] and delegate selection had to reflect the expression of the popular will in the primary or party caucus meetings. Essentially, these reformers put into the national party's rules stipulations requiring intraparty democracy in the state party units in presidential nomination politics. The Supreme Court ratified this radical departure from longstanding practice when Illinois Democratic party officials contested these infringements on what they regarded as their autonomy.[9] The Court said that the national parties had the right to dictate rules to their state units—a great victory for the reformers.

This was, and remains, the most significant implementation of the populist-plebiscitary democratic ideal at the national level in American history. Rather rapidly, as early as 1976, both parties accepted the notion that their presidential nominees would be selected directly by the people in primaries and open caucus meetings. The presidential candidates had party-based mandates directly from the rank and file that they had never had before. It is indicative of the deeply entrenched support of the plebiscitary ideal today that the concept of a brokered party convention in which party leaders ultimately determine the nominees (the way it used to be done here and is still done in most other democracies) seems horribly antiquated and downright undemocratic to most Americans.

Some of these reformers were truly utopians in that they believed that an open, plebiscitary presidential nomination process would increase interest in politics and generate a true national expression of the people's will. In reality, today's presidential primaries in most states have extremely low turnout, and those who do vote tend to be the better-educated and more attuned segments of the population, not the previously disenfranchised. Some of the reformers who were not so naïve were aware that this new reformed party politics worked to their advantage; in fact, because of these reforms upper-middle-class Democrats took over much of the organizational apparatus of the party from the manufacturing union-labor groups that had dominated the party for decades.[10]

Ultimately, while plebiscitary intraparty democracy may have its merits when compared to the smoke-filled rooms of old, the idea that such an arrangement could produce the true expression of the people's will is based on a false premise. Why would the majority view of even the majority party as expressed in presidential primaries necessarily reflect the majority view of the nation, especially in the low-turnout, low-interest environment of presidential primaries?[11] Primaries at all levels have always been characterized by attack politics more than serious discussions of public policy. After all, candidates in the same party tend to have similar views on policy, so they often resort to personal attacks in order to distinguish themselves from their rivals in the quest for power. Such campaigns seem to depend more on sophisticated public relations techniques and advertising blitzes than on anything more issue-oriented or substantial.

In the end, the party reforms of this period were tremendously important. The greatest accomplishments were the structural changes that opened up the parties to all sorts of people who previously had been excluded. But the central goals of the reformers have gone unrealized. Primaries and open party meetings have not increased interest in participating in party politics, and they have not led to clear mandates for the winners of presidential primaries. If anything, parties are viewed with

even more suspicion than ever, and fewer Americans than ever identify
with the two major parties.[12]

The Age of Participatory Democracy

The changes in presidential politics were part of a more thoroughgoing
trend toward participatory democracy in American politics that culmi-
nated in the early 1970s. Though these changes ordinarily didn't involve
the explicitly plebiscitary element that developed in presidential nomination politics, at all levels of government American democracy became
dramatically more participatory. In fact, it would not be going too far to
call the period starting around 1970 the beginning of the Age of
Participatory Democracy in the United States. This new environment presaged a renewed interest in direct democracy.

One of the most important consequences of this change in American
politics was that by the 1970s the once-tight hold of the political elite over
access to the system was broken for good. Ordinary Americans of both
genders and all races and ethnicities were winning elections with increasing frequency. Politicians were forced to be more responsive to citizens and groups. Increasingly, Americans were a part of the bargaining
and policy-making process in Washington and in state capitals around
the country. Where there had once been a fairly stark division of labor between citizens and politicians, now the lines were blurred. An unprecedented opening of the political process had been achieved, in both electoral and legislative politics, unlike anything in any other democracy in
the world. It was an American *glasnost*, but like its counterpart in the
Soviet Union in the 1980s, it didn't resolve the discontent in the political
system—not by a long shot.

In the legislative arena, the chief targets of reformers were the same as
always—corrupt political parties and politicians and representative institutions too susceptible to the influence of special interests. Legislative institutions in the United States at the state and federal levels had traditionally been characterized by a norm of deference to seniority, and
agenda setting was usually engineered by a relatively small cadre of elite
leadership. These agenda setters were typically committee chairs or party
leaders. But by the 1970s, almost everywhere in the country, and certainly
at the federal level, the structured legislative environment was quickly re-
ceding in favor of a far more free-wheeling atmosphere in which agenda
setting and policy-making were up for grabs.

The single most important factor in the opening up of American electoral and legislative politics was the revolution in the American party system that had begun in the Progressive Era. In the 1960s and '70s the parties completed their seventy-year transformation from organizations that

controlled politicians (principally through their control over the nomination process), that were an integral part of the community through their influence or control over public-sector jobs and services, and that set agendas for legislative bodies into organizations that existed largely to provide services to independent-minded candidates who received party nominations by virtue of winning primary elections. The new party system in the United States was, as the political scientists John Aldrich and Richard Niemi have described it, "candidate-centered." Parties and their leaders served the candidates, instead of the other way around. A whole range of people who before had been able only to dream of a career in elected office could now run and win by dint of their hard work and perseverance.[13] While in office, politicians no longer obeyed the traditional norms that required a long apprenticeship while one learned the ropes. Rules changes in the legislatures made people in leadership positions accountable to the backbenchers, and the policy-making process was opened up to public and press scrutiny in ways heretofore unknown in modern democratic politics anywhere in the world. Most proceedings were held in public and votes on even minor amendments would now be recorded in the public record for all interested parties to see. Independent, career-minded, entrepreneurial politicians—even during their very first terms in office—aggressively pressed for their pet agendas, rejecting norms of deference and unwritten rules requiring informal apprenticeships.

Though politicians enjoyed the newfound freedom they had from the parties, there was a downside: although they were no longer fettered by the parties, they weren't protected by the parties either. In a way never before seen in American politics, politicians controlled their own destiny—they were truly independent entrepreneurs whose affiliation with a political party was more a welcome convenience than a hindrance—party membership hardly inhibited their flexibility for position taking on policy matters.[14]

There was another factor that increased the exposure of elected officials. Beginning in the 1960s there was a rapid expansion in the breadth and scope of government activity, starting in the Great Society years of Lyndon Johnson and the liberal Democrat–dominated Congress (especially 1965–66) and continuing during the activist administration of Richard Nixon (1969–74).[15] The provision of services by the federal government, many of which were administered at the state level, reached unprecedented levels, and businesses were subject to a much wider range of regulations than ever before. These developments, coupled with the much more ideologically divisive politics that had grown up in the sixties and revolved primarily around cultural and racial issues, led to a tremendous increase in citizen activism and involvement. Much of this increase was manifested in the startling growth of interest group activity of all kinds—on behalf of business and on behalf of consumers and the environment, on behalf of progressive racial policies and against these policies, for abortion and against abortion; the list seems endless. The number of lobby groups in Washington doubled between 1970 and 1990, and today the total number is approximately 25,000.[16] A similar explosion of activity by organized interests has occurred in the state capitals.[17] Elected officials were confronted by a much more energized citizenry madly organizing, hiring lobbyists, and contacting elected officials directly. Consequently, these new-era politicians were much more responsive to the public, particularly with the more widespread use of public opinion polling.[18]

What resulted in Washington (the situation was similar in an increasing number of state capitals) was an entirely new policy-making environment. National policy was to be made out in the open by legislators who were much less deferential to party leaders and committee chairs. Citizens and interest groups leapt at the chance to get involved by meeting with members, providing useful information to overworked staff in order to gain access, monitoring committee meetings all over the Capitol to protect their interests, recording the votes of all of the members, participating in administrative branch regulatory hearings, and getting involved in financing campaigns with the new rules that encouraged the formation of corporate and other political action committees (PACs).[19]

The policy-making process in a participatory democracy resembles an open, unregulated marketplace with constant bargaining and negotiations among a multitude of actors, on appropriations, authorizing bills, and regulatory decisions. Thousands of decisions are made (many out in the open) on all the intricacies of policy, both regulatory and statutory, in a kind of vast democratic bazaar of members' offices, committee and subcommittee meetings, party caucuses, and hundreds of executive agency hearings, all accessible to the well-heeled and the well-organized. There is no identifiable central planning mechanism, in the form of party leaders in Congress or an executive, that can dictate policy or even an agenda without its being upset by events, persistent and effective lobbying by any of thousands of groups, and the whims of the entrepreneurial rank-and-file members. Compare that to systems with stronger, disciplined parties where the parameters of public policy are much more predictable, because they are usually determined by a cabinet made up of majority party officials.

In this market there are certain resources that contribute to success, and most involve gaining access to the policy-makers. Inside knowledge of Washington's ways is critical, as is money to contribute to campaigns.[20] The ability to mobilize letter-writing campaigns and arrange meetings between members and their constituents can help an interest group get a fair hearing or generate support for or opposition to a bill. The well-heeled, the well-organized, and those with active constituencies do well in this environment. The poorly organized do not.

At the national level, the result is public policy that rewards established and well-connected groups like the gun lobby or farmers. Contributing to citizen cynicism is the continued ability of very narrow, well-heeled interests to get what they want in tax laws, appropriations, and the legislative process in general.[21] But broad-based middle-class interests do well, too, provided they are well organized. Groups representing the elderly and other constituencies have successfully expanded and increased spending for what are by far the three biggest government programs, Social Security, Medicare, and Medicaid.[22]

The end result? Huge government programs that provide substantial subsidies for the vast middle class and everyone else in the form of three programs (Social Security, Medicare, and Medicaid), and thousands of smaller decisions, some of which reward more narrowly focused and intensely felt interests. And make no mistake about it, the grand scope of government activity is widely popular. Even conservative Republicans who were swept into office in 1994 on what they thought was a wave of resentment against big government learned the hard way that, though Americans may dislike big government in theory, they like it in practice. The congressional Republican leadership pushed the issue by eagerly forcing a showdown with the Clinton Administration that led to the government shutdown in 1995. The result was a profound embarrassment for them, as the public expressed in no uncertain terms its dislike of what they regarded as reckless and irresponsible behavior by the Republicans.[23] By 1999, conservative Republicans, still in control in the Congress, were trying to figure out ways to break the spending caps put in place in 1997 as part of the effort to balance the budget and limit the growth of government, in order to fund the thousands of programs and projects their constituents want.

It is important to note that there are some surprising winners in the policy-making bazaar. For example, the far-flung home-schooling movement, speaking for less than one percent of all Americans and hardly comprising the wealthy and connected, stopped Congress in its tracks in 1994 when the House was poised to pass a bill that included the requirement of subject-area certification for home-school teachers. A wave of faxes and phone calls generated through highly sophisticated computerized lists organized on the basis of congressional district turned the vote around to the point where only a single member of the House voted for the certification provision.[24]

The home-schoolers are a good example of how accessible the policy-making arena has become as a result of advances in communications technology. Contact over the Internet and through computerized phone banks was crucial to organizing the disparate group of home-schoolers. Today, in some parts of the country more than half of the population is tied into the Internet, and nearly all of the many thousands of groups with an interest in what goes on in Washington use some form of advanced technology to augment their face-to-face lobbying efforts. As Fred Wertheimer of Common Cause (a liberal public-interest group) has pointed out, every group, it seems, from the Campaign to Ban Landmines to those spewing out the most hateful racist messages, has a Web site and attempts to influence other citizens and public officials.[25]

Almost anyone can find out the status of legislation through the Thomas system, on the official Web pages of the Congress. In congressional offices, on a regular basis a controversial issue will be raised that gets the machinery of the lobby groups generating letters, faxes, and requests for meetings with members and their staff. Sometimes talk radio hosts identify an issue that resonates, and almost instantly the affected groups are able to mobilize ordinary citizens for effective grassroots communication with the White House, Congress, and the bureaucracy by energizing computerized networks of supporters.

Participatory democracy is here to stay at all levels of government, enhanced on the one hand by the increasing sophistication of the groups that know how to mobilize ordinary people and on the other by the populist ethic that is so powerful in the political culture. Some populists still insist that the policy-making environment is "elitist," but in truth this is something of a stretch. Though interest group politics surely still "sings with an upper class bias," as E. E. Schattschneider wrote forty years ago, the vast middle class is not helpless. In this participatory age one of the most important resources is the ability to impress policy-makers with a show of public support for a position—it isn't necessarily just the fat cats who can do this. Most Americans are members of one or more groups active in Washington and/or their state capitals.

It is most important to emphasize that the tremendous growth of activity is, for the most part, anything but a form of protest against what government is doing. The people are most decidedly *not* shut out of the process, in part because of their increased capacity to keep tabs on what is going on. People organize and join because doing so can be effective in defending or advancing their interests—they like much of what the government is doing and want more of it. Many of the new technologies even work to level the playing field, particularly as more people have access to and become adept with personal computers and the Internet. Government affects everyone directly in important ways, and we now have much more access to the policy-making process. The end result is that citizens and groups are continually searching for new and more effective ways to influence policy.

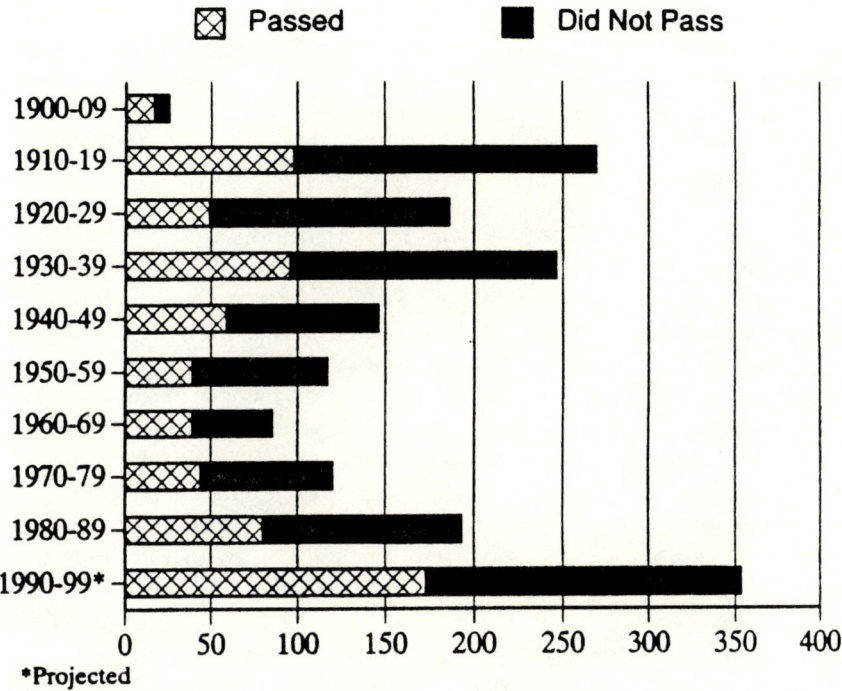

FIGURE 3.1 Use of Initiatives and Petition Referenda in the Twentieth Century
Source: David Magleby, "Let the Voters Decide? An Assessment of the Initiative
and Referendum Process," *University of Colorado Law Review* 66 (1995): 27.

Initiatives and Referenda in the Nineties

One of the ways to make or influence policy at the state level in this new
environment is by the use of initiatives and referenda. Despite the addition of only one new direct democracy state since the Progressive Era, the
last thirty years has seen a fivefold increase in the total number of
plebiscites (see Figure 3.1).

As the stakes in policy-making by government have become higher for
all sorts of interests and segments of the population (witness the dramatic
expansion of government services and regulatory power and the more
highly charged atmosphere surrounding various social issues), the search
for ways to influence policy has intensified. At the state level, some
groups have come to the conclusion that the legislative process might not
be the best, and surely is not the only, venue. The opportunity to put a
constitutional amendment on the ballot could yield a real jackpot. Mere
statutory initiatives can be changed by the legislature, but an amendment
can alter the rules of the political game in more profound ways.

Legislatures are simply not in a position easily to do something about a change in a state's constitution. The initiative process often has been the way to go for people who felt that their views were not being heard in the state legislature. Both organized interests and sometimes grassroots citizens organizations have made use of direct democratic institutions in some states more often than ever before.

Today initiatives are used for a wide variety of policy purposes. David Magleby of Brigham Young University, a scholar of direct democracy and perhaps the nation's foremost authority on referenda and initiatives, has analyzed initiative use since the late 1970s. He writes that "three-fifths of all initiatives have concerned government spending, public morality, or political reform. Initiatives that seek to regulate business or labor or that deal with the environment often generate the most campaign spending but constitute only about one-quarter of all initiatives. Initiatives on civil rights, civil liberties, health, welfare, or education are relatively rare."[26] In the first half of the nineties the greatest increase in initiative use was in the category of government reform, in particular, the term-limits efforts in many states. Other frequent topics for initiative campaigns have been tax limitations, gambling, and abortion.[27] Magleby contends that initiatives not only can achieve the direct purpose of enacting a law or a constitutional amendment, but also are often interpreted by incumbent politicians as indicators of citizen discontent and thus spur legislative activity on hot issues. The tax revolt of the late seventies is a good example of how successful initiative campaigns in some states inspired legislatures in other states to move legislation. In fact, this effect may sometimes have short-circuited direct citizen action in those states.

The term-limits movement of the 1990s and the new century exemplifies well the motivations of many contemporary advocates of direct democracy. Like the Progressives of old, these activists believe that the professionalization of the political class has corrupted policy-making, as career legislators pay back their campaign contributors by making policy that aids the contributors' agendas and thus the politicians' political careers instead of serving the public interest. The solution: End careerism in politics by placing strict limits on how long a person can serve.[28]

Term-limits advocates say that people should get into politics, serve their country or state, and get out. They argue that this would address one of the greatest sources of corruption in contemporary politics: the power of lifetime legislators to exercise control over public money and through the seniority system to exercise authority by chairing committees in Congress and the state legislatures. Lifetime politicians not only wield power undemocratically, term-limits proponents claim, but also are corrupted by the links they developed over the years with bureaucrats and special interests. These three—the legislators, bureaucrats, and lobbyists—work together to further their own ends and not those of the larger community. Term limits is billed by modern reformers as the magic bullet designed to clean up representative processes, as referenda and initiatives were by the Progressives. A broad implementation of term limits, it is believed, would lead to a restoration of sorts to that time when citizen-legislators were motivated by an abiding concern for the public interest.[29] The initiative process is absolutely essential in achieving this end; after all, the political class is not about to term-limit itself.

But these activists of the 1990s who advocate and use direct democratic institutions are not usually "progressive" in the traditional sense of the term. Most Progressives and populists at the turn of the century were on the left side of the political spectrum, sometimes the far left. As we have seen, many were pursuing a policy agenda that included stiff regulations on business, redistributive economic policies, and a pro-labor agenda.[30] Direct democracy was needed, in their view, to bypass or threaten legislatures that were protecting the interests of big business. At the national level, Progressives such as Presidents Theodore Roosevelt and Woodrow Wilson aimed to use the national government as a counterweight to the great power of corporations.

Today the use of direct democratic institutions spans a wide range of causes left to right, from animal rights to ending racial preferences, but most of the energy is on the right. These modern-day populists, exemplified best by the term-limits advocates and the tax rebels,[31] tend to be motivated by a desire not just to restore the citizen-legislator but also to restore what they perceive as the proper, more limited role of government. The people need to step in to rein in a government that is taking too much tax money and is too cozy with organized interests that have a stake in big government. In the view of these activists, government is antidemocratic in the direction of too much regulation and too much taxation and too much social engineering by unelected and unaccountable bureaucrats and judges. Tax limitations are needed to rein in spending; term limits are needed to break the ties between powerful politicians and the special interests that belly up to the public trough and have too much influence on lawmaking and regulatory policy.

The Future

Ambivalent America

In spite of the recent opening of political processes, Americans in general, and not just the committed populists, are unsatisfied with participatory democracy in its present state. The free-for-all environment of policy-making has done nothing to lessen the rampant cynicism among citizens.

If anything, the more participatory and open to scrutiny and influence the political process is, the more people are turned off. The vast majority of Americans simply do not like the normal democratic processes of compromise, negotiation, spirited discussion, and open disagreement.

As government has become a more pervasive part of our lives at all levels and more people mobilize in an attempt to influence policy, we often do not like what we see. The increased activity by lobbies is not always very attractive, as more groups come to the process looking out for their own interest, usually to the exclusion of other interests or the larger public interest. The bitterness of the rhetoric is ratcheted up as a result. The fact that narrow interests can get their way by effective lobbying clearly turns some people off. Politicians, too, look worse in the era of participatory democracy. They are in the fray much more than they were in the past, when the parties protected them from the constant direct contact with voters and active groups that is a part of their everyday existence now. Politicians are on their own and frequently engage in activities that don't reflect well on them in their efforts to attract attention and placate their constituents and contributors. Despite all of this, Americans seem dead-set on continuing to remove barriers to their access to the political system. Why the urge to open things up further when cynicism seems to increase in direct proportion to the opportunities for access to the policy-making process?

There are many factors that account for this. For the committed populist, any hold by the elite on policy-making, however attenuated it has become in recent years, is too much. If we have come this far in opening up the system, why not go further still? There is a strong sentiment in the country that the answer to the ills of democracy is always more openness and more democracy. We could even take the ultimate step: perhaps a truly direct democratic system officially sanctioned by referenda and initiatives at all levels would be the answer instead of this unregulated free market that, no matter how open, is still tilted in favor of those with more resources.

In addition, as the process has opened up our expectations have increased. In the elite-controlled policy environment of the past, people were in effect sheltered from the nuts and bolts of policy-making and accepted things as they were to a significant degree. Now they see that the process at work, even though it is certainly more open, is not always fair. It has become apparent that others may be influencing the policy-makers at your expense. Also, and perhaps most important, it stands to reason that the openness feeds on itself. Interest groups are entrepreneurial. If they lose on one issue today, they will look for new arguments, new methods, and new venues to carry the day tomorrow. And if your competitor gets an advantage on you by lobbying, you have no choice but to organize and enter the arena.

In any event, the floodgates are open, and modern technology promises far more than just an enhanced version of a participatory style of democracy. People and groups may feel that they can do even more with direct, unobstructed access to the policy-making process. What does the future hold in terms of the expansion of citizen access?

Although we are at the early stages of the use of the Internet, technology promises changes of a profound nature. For a country imbued with a populist heritage, the possibilities for cheap and easy participation in policy-making by ordinary citizens are enticing. Many people already have access to nearly unlimited sources of information at their fingertips, and millions of Americans can communicate instantly with each other and potentially with public officials. Could ordinary citizens, in a kind of modern version of Athenian democracy, get directly involved in the deliberation on, even the formation of, policy, regardless of their geographical location? May we be verging on a time when voters determine policy through frequent plebiscites, some or all conducted by computer? What kinds of direct citizen participation will we have—what kinds *should* we have—as interest grows and technology offers more options?

In this section I will discuss some of these issues. As we have seen, the American system has become dramatically more participatory in recent decades. Polling has become an increasingly important, influential, and ubiquitous part of the political landscape. Citizens have more opportunities to engage in political discussion, become informed about politics and policy, and contact and interact with elected officials in a wide range of informal structures. New forms of participatory democracy are emerging all the time. In the future we may experiment with new types of both plebiscitary and discussion democracy. What follows is a systematic look at the forms of participatory, plebiscitary, and discussion democracy already in existence and some of the forms that have been proposed for future consideration. In so doing, we will assess their respective advantages and disadvantages. Following this, I speculate on what forms of direct and participatory democracy are likely to flourish in American politics.

Citizen Involvement in the United States' Future

Participatory Democracy. Perhaps the most conspicuous form of participatory democracy in American politics is the standard random-sample public opinion poll. There are dozens of organizations that do polling for public consumption, and many more that do polling primarily as campaign consultants for candidates for office or as advisers to politicians in office. Television and radio news departments and newspapers use the results of polls as hard news on a regular basis, almost every day on almost every broadcast, it sometimes seems. The belief in the importance of polls is so pervasive that sometimes polls even seem to be conducted in an attempt to get answers to empirical questions (the question "Do you think that the President had a relationship with Monica Lewinsky?" was asked by pollsters when the truth of the allegations was still in doubt) as opposed to just matters of opinion. The scientific measurement of public opinion has become an integral part of every aspect of our politics, from the running of campaigns to the creation of party platforms to the actual making of public policy.[32]

Public opinion polling is widely believed to be flawed for one central reason: the public is quite often asked to weigh in on matters that they have thought very little about. Exhaustive research by political scientists has found a tendency among some people to respond definitively regardless of whether they have even heard of the issue raised by the question. It has even been shown that voters' responses to certain questions can at times be random.[33] Polling organizations are also bedeviled by the difficulties in achieving a reasonably good sample, in part because they can only rely on getting barely half of a randomly selected group of people to respond to questions—even when the sample is screened for likely voters. An additional problem: Some organizations intentionally skew their questions to achieve the desired results and then publicize their results as "scientific." In fact, question wording is a serious problem even for the most reputable of firms; even minor adjustments in the wording of a question can yield almost diametrically opposed results.[34] As important as polls are in our politics, citizens are woefully ignorant about how they are conducted. Even many journalists who report polls are not sufficiently knowledgeable about many of the problems that confront pollsters in trying to measure public opinion with some accuracy.

But public opinion polls are here to stay and are likely to be used more in the future than they already are. Politicians and journalists are addicted to polling, and there is an abiding faith felt by almost everyone, including if not especially the politicians, that the results of polls are meaningful regardless of the methodological and interpretive problems inherent in them. For the politicians, polls constitute something of an improvement in gauging public opinion over the unsystematic guesswork of operatives in the field that was relied upon in the past.

There have been numerous promising efforts to improve public opinion polling with what could be called "informed opinion polls"—essentially, attempts to provide more opportunities for citizens to be informed before they register their opinions. In Washington, New York, Des Moines, and other cities, television stations have organized opportunities for citizens to learn about specific issues on television and then cast a presumably more informed vote by newspaper ballot.[35] In Hawaii, a group of academics identified a random sample of citizens, inviting them to participate in informational sessions on important issues, and then gave them the opportunity to cast a vote by mail or phone.[36]

However, these informed opinion structures have an important drawback: they do not allow for the continuous and instantaneous measurement of public opinion—they take too much time and planning and cost too much for that. And yet, the craving for a quick read on public opinion is nearly insatiable on the part of politicians, the public, and the media. Is there any way to get a quick read on public opinion from an informed sample?

One interesting approach might be inspired by an observation made by the former NBC executive Lawrence Grossman about the stock market. People involved in trading are numerous, diverse (if not representative), and attuned to certain political issues out of self-interest. In the process of buying and selling equities, investors from all over the country signal their pleasure or displeasure with policy made by the Federal Reserve Board, the Congress, and the administration almost instantaneously, using the latest in communications and computer technology. (Sometimes all it takes is a simple statement by a member of one of those institutions to elicit a reaction.) The market's response to the financial implications of government decisions is taken very seriously; everyone knows how supersensitive politicians are to its vicissitudes. As Grossman has observed, the stock market might be the most organized and even systematic example of an informed sampling of opinion going.

One can envision a network modeled on the stock market, made up of a wide range of politically engaged citizens who could be wired to record their preferences on public matters. Perhaps a news organization could plug in thousands of state and local party officials down to the precinct captains. These people would instantly register their opinions on pressing issues before the Congress. This gauge of the opinions of grassroots people with a strong interest in the political landscape might carry a great deal of weight with policy-makers. Essentially what could develop would be a systematizing of the age-old practice of consulting party people at the grassroots. The views of this wide range of politically attentive people at the grassroots would reflect both their role as opinion leaders at certain times and their ability to respond to the strongly felt sentiments of their constituencies. A quick tabulation of their opinions would yield in some ways a more interesting snapshot of opinion than the results of polls of frequently uninformed citizens.

There are no significant technological barriers to this kind of thing anymore. Already, a Web site that tallies the responses of citizens almost instantaneously on a wide range of issues is rapidly gaining national prominence and public attention.[37] Television shows have been taking similarly unsystematic polls on a variety of topics for years over the phone. Of course these efforts do not achieve a representative sample. But if the aim is to get a quick read of a particular segment of the citizenry, the technology is there.

For standard random-sample opinion polling, the most important incremental improvement would be for media entities to be more systematic in the reporting and conduct of polls. Consumers need to be made more aware of polls' inherent weaknesses, and pollsters should be more sensitive to long-term trends in opinion. Polls are only rough estimates of opinion; questions need to be repeated over time and issues have to be addressed in different ways in order to ascertain whether opinions expressed are stable and real or mere artifacts of the wording of the questions.

Much of the new wave of high-tech participatory democracy has a more deliberative character than polling. Every day, through Internet bulletin boards and chatrooms, literally thousands of political discussions and conversations are going on continuously, covering issues of all kinds. Oftentimes these take the form of lengthy interactions that go on for days or even weeks. Social scientists are just beginning to explore the kinds of people and discussions that are taking place, but it is already clear that participants span the political spectrum, although early indications are that conservatives are a bit more active in these formats than those of other ideological persuasions.[38]

The Internet provides many hopeful prospects for expanding and improving political discourse among citizens. One of the more interesting developments is the expansion of low-cost opportunities for third party and other political movements to reach more people. People can easily gather information on the Green party, the Libertarian party, the Christian Coalition, and other groups from the ever-growing number of Web sites these and other organizations have set up. Such sites provide information on petition drives, the status of legislation and court cases, ratings of members of Congress, policy platforms, and many other topics. This sort of communication could potentially be the embryonic stage of a much greater range of political choice, as voters in the future become more easily acquainted with and able to contribute to groups that do not receive coverage from the mainstream media.

In addition, the Internet makes it easy for citizens to gather neutral information on policy and politics. Today, public interest groups, news organizations, and the U.S. Congress make material readily available at the click of a mouse to millions that was extremely difficult or even virtually impossible to attain just a few years ago. There is no question that it is easier today than ever in history to be an informed citizen and voter.

The most innovative developments along these lines involve attempts by nonprofit organizations to promote interactive discussion with elected officials over the Internet. The Center for Governmental Studies has designed something called the Democracy Network, which is being implemented in Orlando, Florida.[39] The system is a comprehensive network that gives subscribers the ability to gain access to position papers from independent sources and from candidates' campaigns, read newspaper articles, watch speeches, review government materials relevant to election campaigns, and communicate directly with some elected officials. Electronic bulletin boards on some issues are also part of the Democracy Network. Many local candidates have participated in debates on the network that have spanned several weeks, often responding to citizens' questions. There have been thousands of hits on the network's Web site, and many observers have been pleased how the discussion between candidates has evolved beyond sound bites and attack politics.

This sort of network has vast potential. Many organizations already provide information on candidates for office, but they are not interactive.[40] The Democracy Network model could enable citizens to question their legislators and congressmen, and even to participate in on-line hearings on major issues.

Political parties and politicians have also worked on outreach through advanced technology. Congressman Edward Markey of Massachusetts was one of the pioneers, making use of a computer conference in 1983 to publicize some of his issue positions on the nuclear arms race. He encouraged subsequent interactions and discussions with those who read his material and wished to comment.[41]

Scores of congressmen today participate in interactive television programs and radio call-in shows to discuss issues with the public. President Clinton has done the same from time to time at the local and national level, and 1999 he initiated the first live interactive presidential discussion format over the Internet. These formats give the public the chance to interact with politicians without having to take the time, trouble, or expense to attend meetings in person. Often focused on a particular issue, such as Social Security, the sessions have proved a good way for politicians to gauge the intensity of the views of people other than those with direct access to their offices. In addition, newspapers and television stations have sponsored interactive issue forums involving policy-makers on a wide range of topics.

The Republican party sponsored an innovative discussion-oriented format called the Republican Neighborhood Meeting in the early-to-mid–1990s, often moderated by the presidential aspirant Lamar Alexander. Alexander spread the gospel of local control, term limits, and shortened congressional sessions to a receptive audience via cable television call-in shows. These shows advanced that issue agenda, advanced Alexander's visibility as a presidential contender in 1996, and perhaps helped energize the party's base as a prelude to its surprising takeover of the Congress in 1994. In fact, Alexander came closer than any of the other GOP dark-horse candidates to toppling the frontrunner, Bob Dole, that year, perhaps owing in part to the visibility that the Republican Neighborhood Meetings gave him among Republican activists.

In many communities and states citizens have had the opportunity to interact with policy-makers in more structured formats.[42] In North Carolina, for example, a three-hour program called OPEN/Net that covers controversial legislative and bureaucratic issues runs on some cable systems. Usually there is a hearing and discussion among policy-makers in the first half, followed by a telephone call-in period for viewers to offer feedback. Berks Community Television in Reading, Pennsylvania, has provided "electronic office hours" with county officials. During these periods, officials discuss their recent actions, taking direct input by telephone from citizens. Sometimes citizens have the opportunity to participate by asking questions in hearings.

These free-for-all deliberative formats give interested citizens more outlets, some quite productive, for expressing their views and in some cases for contacting and interacting with representatives. In addition, the ability of groups of all kinds to provide information on such a wide range of policy issues to so many people can contribute to the development of a better- informed electorate.

Free-for-all formats do have shortcomings, however. Internet discussions often degenerate into flaming sessions and sometimes are characterized more by pontification than genuine discussion.[43] Also, it may be very difficult to discern which information made available through the proliferating political Web sites is reliable. Some also warn of the accessibility of the Web to fringe groups spouting violent and racist messages. It is also often the case that events organized by politicians and political parties, such as Alexander's Neighborhood Meetings or call-in shows with members of Congress, are easily manipulated to the politicians' advantage, despite their apparently open and interactive formats.

But in the end, the existence of more outlets for discussion is generally a healthy development for a democratic political system, even if only certain kinds of people avail themselves of the opportunities. And even though plenty of people and groups put out questionable and even dangerous information over the Internet, there are many highly reputable sources of information of all kinds, including many, as I have mentioned, that are made available by official government entities. Today, citizens have easy access to information on politics and policy in a way that was nearly unimaginable just a few years ago.

Probably the most systematic attempt to address the shortcomings of polling and the more interactive discussion-oriented formats is the brainchild of the political scientist James Fishkin. His innovation, which was underwritten by foundation funding and appeared on PBS stations, was to conduct what he called a "deliberative public opinion poll."[44] Mindful of the shortcomings of ordinary public opinion polls, Fishkin arranged to have a random sample of citizens meet to discuss issues and interact with candidates for president. The idea was to select about one thousand people randomly, so as to have a good chance at achieving a representative sample.[45] They were provided position papers on a wide range of issues as a prelude to question-and-answer sessions with the candidates. In the end, the participants were polled as to their presidential preference. In theory, this sort of poll would approximate what the *whole country* would think about the presidential aspirants if everyone were given the opportunity to study the issues and interact with the actual candidates.[46]

About 72 percent of the original sample responded to an initial phone survey. Only about 36 percent participated in the end—not much different from the response rate of some public opinion polls—but the sample was fairly representative. (The participants' expenses were paid and they received a modest three-hundred-dollar honorarium.) To be sure, the experiment had no noticeable impact on presidential selection, but Fishkin envisions such an event taking the place of the first primary in the presidential nomination process. Instead of having Iowa or New Hampshire start the process, with their unrepresentative electorates and all the advantages that the better-funded candidates enjoy, the deliberative public opinion poll would serve as the first major test. This representative and uniquely well-informed sample of citizens would cast their votes before any of the states, potentially helping to winnow the field of weaker candidates.

The eminent political theorist Robert Dahl also has proposed a discussion format that aims to address the weaknesses of ordinary polling and also to bring a wider range of people into the policy-making process.[47] He suggested the creation of "minipopuluses" of a thousand randomly selected citizens to research and debate a given policy issue over the course of a year. They would produce recommendations at the end of this time, perhaps submitting them to congressional or state legislative committees dealing with the topics under discussion. Dahl's minipopuluses would not necessarily meet face-to-face; instead he would take advantage of advanced technology to permit people the freedom to stay home and participate by computer and interactive television. This format might be more feasible than Fishkin's model, which involves travel, hotel costs, and other expenses.

The Jefferson Center in Minneapolis is already doing something along the lines of Dahl's proposal. Theirs is a grassroots effort to make public recommendations on major policy issues confronting Minnesotans.[48] The center creates so-called "policy juries" chosen from a local community to

examine the views of experts on contentious issues. Local juries then select representatives to meet others from around the state to hear more discussion and consider the issues in more depth. Ultimately, the aim is to
publicize to lawmakers and other policy-makers the conclusions of these
grassroots juries. The results might not be technically representative in
the same way as Fishkin's experiments or Dahl's minipopuluses; twelve-
person juries cannot meet the standard of statistical representativeness
that larger groups can. Furthermore, the selection of people from each
jury to participate in statewide meetings would weaken the representativeness of the sample still more. But promoting the idea that citizen participation in policy debates is a duty analogous to jury duty is an in-
triguing prospect to some.

Plebiscitary Democracy.   In about half of the American states, plebiscitary
democracy takes the form of initiatives and referenda. These methods
give citizens a way to review legislation made by politicians in the legislatures as well as to bring up matters that the legislatures do not address.
In some states the burdens on citizens on Election Day may be considerable: numerous measures may appear on the ballot, and some of them
may be complex and confusing to some voters. Generally, however, initiatives and referenda require relatively little of the average citizen, as the
actual formulation of the proposals will either have been made in the legislature or by interested groups.

Access to direct lawmaking via initiative is, however, hampered by the
burdensome requirements in the states for putting initiatives and popular referenda on the ballot. The process of petitioning is costly and time-
consuming, requiring the collection of many thousands of signatures.
Today it is typical for groups to hire firms, at great expense, that specialize in gathering signatures to qualify measures for the ballot. Another
complaint, in California and some other states, is the amount of time required at the ballot box for voters to read and consider some of the measures they may not have studied in preparation for voting.

New technology does promise the potential for a partial solution to
these problems. A citizens group, the Campaign for a Digital Democracy,
is active in an effort to allow citizens to petition over the Internet. The
technology to validate electronic "signatures" is already available. In fact,
the Democratic party of Arizona is pioneering the use of the home computer in an official capacity by permitting voting from home in its 2000
primary. Other states are also considering that innovation. The use of the
Internet for gathering signatures for initiative petitions has the potential
to cut costs dramatically, making ballot access realistic for citizen groups
that don't have the resources to hire the firms that currently take care of

the logistics and do the legwork. If such a practice were to be sanctioned, home computer users could be alerted through a public interest hotline of campaigns to put initiatives on the ballot. Allowing people to vote at home by computer or in a designated public Internet access site such as a library would give people the luxury of considering complex measures at their leisure.[49]

An even more direct model for a plebiscitary style of citizen participation in lawmaking was tried in a Columbus, Ohio, suburb. In the early 1980s, citizens in Upper Arlington had the opportunity to watch the proceedings of the planning commission and then vote on the proposals through their television sets. There was no interaction with the legislators and the citizens' votes were not binding on the outcome, but this procedure generated considerable interest and is often cited as a model to build on for plebiscitary citizen decision-making.

In the future, the potential for expanding plebiscitary forms of democracy at the local level is nearly limitless. Voting by computer from home opens up all sorts of possibilities. Computer technology could be employed in imaginative ways to group voters into different geographical zones, perhaps even some local neighborhood zones, for the purpose of deciding a relevant issue. A tax for a specific project or road or school, for example, could be considered by a precisely determined local grouping of citizens at much less expense—and without necessarily involving elected representatives. An additional advantage for pressing matters is that decisions could be made by citizens at any time, without having to wait for an officially designated Election Day.

Though initiatives and referenda are very popular and are frequently used at the state and local levels, there is still no provision for national-level referenda. As propositions proliferate on state ballots, is it only a matter of time before popular pressure for a national referendum procedure or even initiatives becomes irresistible? In some states, the issue isn't whether to have direct democracy; it has become one of debating limits on the number and type of ballot measures that are appropriate for citizens to decide. If Internet access becomes or can be made universal (perhaps through public access points) and voting by computer becomes a reality, even these sorts of debates may fade away as the practical obstacles to having voters decide more public matters would be overcome.

But the advent of national referenda would be a big step. The Reform party and many mainstream politicians have proposed the limited use of national referenda for specific issues—maybe just for a citizen veto of certain types of legislation, such as tax increases. Such an idea is widely popular, and, although there is tremendous institutional resistance to it, its advent is far from out of the question. If that barrier were to be crossed, it is hard to imagine that active citizens and groups would be satisfied with restricting the use of the process to a few issues.

For some perspective, it is important to note that countries all over the globe put policy matters and constitutional questions to a vote. Most democracies have provisions for referenda. Far fewer have something resembling the initiative procedure in use in the American states. Only five democracies, including the United States, have never had a national-level referendum. In Canada, some innovative experiments have been tried to bring plebiscitary democracy to party proceedings and legislative voting. The Nova Scotia Liberal party has experimented with having citizens watch party conventions and vote to choose the party leader by phone.[50] Also, the Canadian Reform party recently held a televised debate on euthanasia and permitted a randomly selected sample of its rank and file to cast a vote that was binding on five members of the Canadian parliament.

Curiously, even the most ardent populists are critical of plebiscitary forms of direct democracy. Other than their concerns about ballot access, populists decry the lack of opportunity for discussion, deliberation, and input by ordinary citizens. Almost everyone agrees that plebiscitary forms of democracy run the risk of depending on snap judgments, sometimes ill-informed, by voters.[51] Despite these reservations, direct democracy supporters usually defend plebiscites on the grounds that voters are as fit to make a policy decision as they are to choose representatives (and perhaps about as fit to decide policy as representatives); they also argue that it is crucial, regardless of the voters' fitness for making policy choices, for the people to have a means to bypass an unresponsive legislative body.

There are many other equally contentious issues regarding sanctioned plebiscitary forms of direct democracy. Some of the thorniest revolve around these controversies; the courts are frequently required to pass judgment on ballot propositions after they have passed, and sometimes even before citizens vote on them. By what criteria or justification is it appropriate for the courts to overrule the majority opinion of the people? Do plebiscites threaten the rights of minorities? Should the courts give more or less deference to laws made by legislatures as compared to laws made by the people when those laws could potentially be interpreted as violating constitutional rights? Precisely what standing does citizen lawmaking have in a republic? Advocates claim that if the people are truly sovereign more deference should be given to citizen-made law than to that made by representatives. Courts tend to come to the opposite conclusion. I will deal in more detail with these issues, all central to the debate about the expansion of direct democracy in the United States, as well as other related ones, in the next chapter.

Discussion Democracy. Plebiscitary citizen lawmaking has become commonplace in many states as increasing use is made of initiatives and referenda. But bringing ordinary citizens directly into the policy-making process—actually having them participate in the discussion and drafting of legislation—is rarely done. Nevertheless, the dream of some populists is to do just that, to carve out a role for citizens far greater than just deciding on matters brought to their attention by the legislature or interested parties.

Alaskans have experimented at a rudimentary level with just this sort of thing. Alaska's immense size makes the obstacles to communicating directly with public officials worse for many Alaskans than for citizens in any other state. The Alaska Legislative Teleconferencing Network and Legislative Information Network is an ambitious plan to give Alaskans opportunities to communicate with their legislators.[52] Under it, hearings are conducted and testimony taken from television studios around the state. Citizens have the opportunity to discuss issues directly with legislators and other officials no matter where they live, and officially sanctioned "public opinion messages" can be sent by audience members and participants.

The Alaska experiment has, on the whole, proved to be popular. Substantial numbers of citizens have availed themselves of the opportunity the network provides. Of course being free to participate in hearings is not quite the same as actually writing the legislation. But this is an important innovation, because hearings serve as an early stage in the creation of legislation. Clearly, it is a useful and potentially productive outlet for those who do choose to use it, and it is perhaps more satisfying than arrangements like electronic office hours or call-in shows that are not a part of the formal lawmaking process.

The most ambitious form of officially sanctioned discussion democracy might resemble the "electronic town meetings" that Ross Perot proposed in his presidential campaigns in 1992 and 1996. Perot suggested grassroots meetings at the local level on pending topics such as Medicare reform or taxes or gun control that would be attended by members of the House of Representatives. The citizens attending these meetings, perhaps selected randomly, could deliberate, make policy recommendations, and elect representatives to meet at statewide electronic meetings, chaired by senators, culminating in a national town hall with elected representatives from the fifty states convening to convey their views and present proposals to the president and leaders of Congress. This electronic town meeting concept is not about to happen, but there are certainly no technological barriers to its implementation if the will is there. And if such an arrangement were officially constituted, it would be extremely difficult for politicians to ignore the policy recommendations that would come from them.

The Shape of Things to Come

Peering into the crystal ball to predict the direction of any social trend is always a perilous undertaking, but one can draw some reasonable conclusions about the kinds of direct and participatory democracy that are likely to be popular in the new century.

One thing is certain. In this day and age, with government a part of everyone's life in so many different ways in a uniquely open and accessible political system, interested parties are going to keep trying new and innovative ways to influence public policy. The main reason is that interested parties *can* have influence. It is not a waste of resources for groups to lobby; it is inevitable that groups will try new and innovative methods in order better to press their case. Some of these methods are likely to be among the types covered in this chapter. In a political system like this one, it is the persistent, creative, and resourceful petitioner who is successful.

All sorts of participatory democracy will flourish in the new century. The new technologies that offer opportunities to contact and cajole public officials, mold public opinion, and rally support will be popular with the thousands of groups with a stake in government affairs. Individual citizens, as well, will take advantage of whatever means are available to contact, cajole, and pester their elected representatives, sometimes at the behest of interests they are affiliated with, sometimes of their own volition.

In addition, the public officials themselves have a stake in at least appearing responsive to the public, and there is every reason to believe that they really wish to be. All elected officials must win a campaign by dint of their own efforts; opportunities to appear publicly and address constituents' concerns over the Internet, on television, and in other ways will be useful to them. Entrepreneurial media entities are sure to continue experimenting with innovative new kinds of informed opinion structures that will serve to connect voters and their representatives.

In addition, we can rest assured that traditional random sample polling will continue to be popular, for better or for worse. Polling is crucial to candidates for office, and news organizations, politicians, and ordinary citizens will continue to be fascinated with polls of all kinds. There is a simple reason for this: despite disappointments and cynicism, Americans believe that what the people think matters. Polls are the simplest and most reliable and efficient way to get a measurement of that. Of course polls have myriad problems, as we have seen; we can hope that polling organizations will continue to improve the conduct and reporting of polls and make some effort to inform the public about polling's inherent shortcomings.

Plebiscitary democracy will also remain attractive. Most Americans believe that the popular will can be discerned from a plebiscite. That together with the rampant distrust of representative institutions combine to make initiatives and referenda very popular. Just as important, interest groups and active citizens have found in these methods an effective means to change the law and otherwise influence policy-making.

Many scholars are of the view that the healthiest development would be an increase in discussion democracy, preferably sanctioned formally— or at least sanctioned informally—by government. The typical view, as expressed by Robert Dahl and many others, is that policy-makers are not representative and it is important to incorporate more kinds of people in the policy-making process. Almost everyone agrees that deliberative forms are superior to plebiscitary forms, because it is believed that discussion formats yield better results and more careful consideration of the issues than the snap judgments that play an important role in polling and voting on referenda and initiatives. The virtues of discussion and deliberation, which according to proponents of these plans would include the enhancement of citizenship and a decrease in apathy, argue for the use of advanced technology to facilitate citizen involvement in policy formation and agenda setting instead of simply for the purpose of registering a yes-or-no vote in a plebiscite.

The problem may be in motivating citizens enough so they get involved in these tasks. Obviously it is much easier just to vote on alternatives placed in front of you than to do the wearying work of setting an agenda and legislating. In addition, if citizen involvement in the policy-making stage is deemed desirable, there is the added challenge of ensuring fair and representative participation.

Are Americans inclined toward active participation in the nitty-gritty of policy-making? All indications point in the negative direction. In fact, despite whatever mythology Americans may have internalized about the nature of citizen participation in the early days of the republic, American political culture does not have the participatory tradition to build on that it is commonly believed to have. The sociologist Michael Schudson argues that it would be a radical break with American notions of citizenship to expect regular participation in a deliberative style of democracy in which citizens set the agenda and make policy.[53] The New England town halls and other similar forms meant to approximate the Athenian model of citizen self-government often were not well attended, and the agenda setting was usually controlled by an elite or a group of political insiders. Simply put, Americans have never gotten involved in governing themselves in a sustained fashion in this country. Schudson claims that American traditions are more "monitorial" than participatory. People are used to semipassively monitoring elected officials and becoming involved only intermittently, when their rights and interests are being challenged or violated.

Studies of recent experiments in deliberative styles of direct democracy come to a similar conclusion.[54] Most of the informed structure formats, including many of those described earlier in the chapter, and other innovations that involve direct citizen involvement in policy formation, have not attracted many participants, despite considerable efforts in some cases to advertise them. Even Fishkin's deliberative public opinion poll, which included remuneration for participants, had a disappointingly low participation rate.

These conclusions jibe well with a commonsense view of the level of political interest among ordinary citizens. It has been demonstrated that a majority of people don't vote on a regular basis.[55] Pollsters sometimes cannot get half of the people they call to answer questions. (Fishkin's deliberative poll managed only a 36 percent participation rate.) In addition, we have many more recreation and entertainment distractions than ever before. From magazines and television programming tailored to every taste to the endless supply of movie rentals on practically every corner to more and better options for dining out on a much wider range of foods to the potentially endless possibilities for amusement of all sorts on the Internet—the list of claims on our attention is long.

American society is growing and changing at a rapid rate, and Americans seem to have an unlimited appetite for entertainment. What reasonable person could conclude that people will willingly choose involvement in the mundane details of public policy-making over more enjoyable pastimes? This raises another question: How democratic can discussion-oriented formats be, particularly those designed to incorporate ordinary people directly in the policy-making process, if only a small number of people—likely the more motivated, educated, and attentive ones—are willing to participate? Invariably, the ignorant and poorly educated would participate less and likely be less influential in such arrangements.

Yet another obstacle is that Americans do not like the disputes and inevitable give and take of the rough-and-tumble world of legislating on contentious issues. As I have argued before, the more Americans see of the political process, with its bargaining, negotiations, and inevitably disputatious quality, the less they like it. Americans hate the Congress more in recent years in part because they can see on television what goes into legislating. What on earth would make anyone think that citizens want to participate in an activity that they basically loathe?

There is a paradoxical quality to Americans' interest in politics. Mostly we don't bother and we take our democratic processes for granted. At the same time we ardently believe in the democratic ideal—probably one closely resembling the populist ideal. There is a highly attentive stratum of the population that lives up to the ideal in some respects, taking full advantage of the available opportunities to get involved and influence this most permeable of political systems. Sometimes these active citizens represent the views of those less attentive, but that only happens either by chance or when the less attentive ones are contributors to a group that lobbies for them.

The only reasonable conclusion: Americans—those strong believers in democracy—for the most part want easy options. Deliberative forms of democracy are never easy; plebiscitary forms are much more so. It is simply much easier and more realistic to implement instant democracy than it is to bring ordinary people into policy discussions. Plebiscites are basically a passive form of participation; it only requires the activism of a few to put ballot measures before the voters—and there is no doubt that interested groups are ready and willing to supply the energy. Utopian schemes to get people involved in agenda setting and policy formation run into the roadblock of chronic apathy.

Probably the best that can be expected in the way of discussion democracy is something along the lines of the Jefferson Center's policy juries or Dahl's minipopuluses. These would incorporate ideas of coerced service—the jury concept—that Americans are used to, and they could, if properly constituted, achieve something like a representative sample. It is simply unreasonable to expect a large voluntary turnout; the only realistic alternative is to compel a representative few. The ability to participate from home that could be afforded by computers might make the burden of this kind of participation more feasible for time-strapped people. Those who would like to see more citizens than just a representative few participate in policy-making would be disappointed in such a development, but these ideas might be the best and fairest approach to deliberative direct democracy. In the long run, minipopuluses could conceivably be sanctioned to make recommendations for policy change and even to set agendas for legislatures or for ballot propositions.

In the end, it is much more likely that advanced technology will be employed in the service of instant democracy. The Internet may be used to make petition-gathering easier and less expensive for the ordinary citizen, thereby dramatically expanding the number of ballot initiatives decided by people in the states. Perhaps one day national questions will be brought to a vote—after all, most people support the idea of a national referendum. Sometime in the future people may sit at home and review material on the myriad issues brought to their attention and cast votes by computer.

From the standpoint of the Constitution, plebiscites are only allowable as supplements to representative decision-making in the states.[56] It would probably require a constitutional amendment to implement a procedure for a binding national plebiscite. But if such an event did come to pass, it would be hard to draw the line to limit their use, as experience has shown in the states. National referenda might start as a means for a popular veto on laws that are passed by Congress, or they could just be used as an advisory mechanism at first. Perhaps they would initially be limited to questions on taxes or some other discrete set of issues. But the rationale behind them—that a plebiscite more accurately represents the true will of the people than decision-making by representatives—would make it hard to resist the rapid expansion of their use.

Some suggest that ultimately legislatures and maybe even the Congress will be reduced to the traditional role of the House of Lords in Great Britain. The House of Lords does not propose or pass laws, but by custom is permitted to offer amendments to and delay decisions made by the House of Commons, where the real action is. In the United States a sort of "Internet House of Commons" might evolve if putting measures on the ballot becomes easier and computer voting is put in place.

Though the "House of Lords" scenario might seem far-fetched at the federal level, the experience in California indicates it is anything but that at the state level. Today in that state legislators and bureaucrats await the results of ballot propositions, commonly avoiding legislating and decision-making on difficult issues until after the inevitable plebiscite. Numerous measures there have also effectively tied the hands of legislators and other official policy-makers. In the case of the controversial property tax limitation initiative in 1978, Proposition 13, the effects continue to be felt more than two decades later.[57]

Californians are testing the limits of direct democracy. Even so, it is probably impossible to replace legislatures entirely. But the future might hold a greatly diminished role for elected representatives. Perhaps some accommodation might be reached whereby legislatures deal with extremely technical questions or matters of security,[58] while leaving most matters to be determined by plebiscite or through policy recommendations by sanctioned minipopuluses that meet by computer.

In effect, legislatures could become exalted law-writing offices. In the Congress and state legislatures across the country, members who come up with an idea for legislation must get that idea fleshed out and translated into legislative language. Is it possible that in the future this will be the primary function of our representative assemblies—translating policy determined by the people into technical and legal language?

Summary

One thing is certain: Politicians' interest in responding to voters' wishes and the inexhaustible energy and resources of the thousands of groups lobbying in Washington and in state capitals around the country that represent millions of citizens ensure that there will be a proliferation of technology-enhanced opportunities for citizen involvement in participatory formats. And from a practical standpoint, there is very little in the way of implementing an expanded version of plebiscitary democracy in many of the states. It is not out of the question that at some point initiatives or referenda will be put in place at the federal level. Instant democracy is sure to thrive because of its practicality, popularity with citizens, and popularity with active lobbies looking for ways to influence and bypass legislatures. Much greater obstacles stand in the way of more discussion-oriented formats, including the lack of a culture of that kind of participation and the demonstrated apathy toward and distaste for the process of legislating on the part of most Americans.

4

Direct Democracy Versus Representative Democracy

As referenda and initiatives flourish and the impetus for more forms of direct democracy grows in the United States, a vigorous debate is taking place on the opinion pages of major newspapers and magazines among journalists, activists, politicians, and academics. In this dispute, pro–direct democracy populists are pitted against modern-day constitutionalists, who continue to defend the virtues of representative democracy.

In this chapter, we look first in detail at the contemporary populists' criticisms of representative democracy and the various prescriptions they offer, from ambitious and comprehensive new forms of direct democracy to streamlined and modified constitutional arrangements to more modest plans to use plebiscites to implement specific reforms.

Today's populists can be roughly divided between those on the left, who tend to believe that increasing citizens' engagement with the political system is a good thing in and of itself and will usually lead to more progressive policy if structured properly, and those on the right and in the center, who tend to want to use direct democracy to rein in big government and the influence of special interests. All populists come to a meeting of the minds on one thing: representative democracy as practiced in the United States is not working. I conclude that populists of the center and right, far more than their counterparts on the left, have their finger on the pulse of Americans' discontent with politics as usual. Their agenda for citizen lawmaking (if not their policy agenda), with its emphasis on building on existing and flourishing institutions of direct democracy such as initiatives and referenda, is much more likely to influence the future direction of American politics than the constitutionalists'.

Subsequently I examine five of the most contentious questions that arise in the debate between advocates of direct and representative democracy:

1. Are voters informed enough for direct democracy?
2. Which is more special interest–driven, direct or representative decision-making?
3. What level of scrutiny should plebiscites be given by the courts as compared to laws made by representative institutions?
4. Does direct democracy threaten the rights of vulnerable minorities more than representative democracy?
5. Which contributes more to responsible governance, direct or representative democracy?

In trying to answer these questions, we will consider the relevant scholarly findings and the arguments made by participants in the debate. Advocates on both sides can draw on a wealth of recent research, as well as on experience, to bolster their positions; even so, some of the questions are difficult to answer definitively, given the current state of the evidence. Others depend a great deal on subjective judgments, for example, concerning the issue of just how well informed voters need to be to vote on policy, or what exactly constitutes responsible governance. For each question, I lay out the best arguments on each side and attempt to come to some reasonable conclusions as to which way the evidence points.

Even though the bulk of the evidence seems not to support the populists' position, the weight of popular opinion in this debate is clearly with them. Their argument is simple and persuasive. They believe that the majoritarian principle is at the heart of democracy. They argue that ordinary people are best able to judge what is in the public interest (especially when one considers the corruption rampant in representative institutions); polling the people is thus the only way to determine the popular will and something approximating the public interest. Further, they contend that the claim made by constitutionalists that representative institutions are better able to determine the public interest is elitist and fundamentally undemocratic.

But a great deal hinges on the method populists wish to use to identify what the people want in public policy—the vote. Can voting achieve what populists intend it to achieve? The answer is, surprisingly, an emphatic no! In Chapter 5 I develop a critique of the populist theory of voting, on which I subsequently build to construct a broader defense of representative institutions relevant to a twenty-first century when we are likely to see increasing pressures for more direct democracy.

The Modern-Day Populists on the Left

The Radical Transformationists

Populists on the left range from so-called "radical transformationists," who seek to restructure the political system to promote fully equal participation in policy-making by all citizens, to a more moderate group that seeks to find ways to complement existing institutions with more citizen input in lawmaking and more opportunities for contact with elected officials. Some in the latter group seek also to implement changes in those constitutional arrangements that they believe lead to deadlock and government inaction on pressing matters.

The guru of the transformationists is the political scientist Benjamin Barber.[1] Barber and others, including most prominently Theodore Becker,[2] attack representative democracy and the party system and outline an approach to a much more participatory form of democracy designed ultimately to replace many of the functions of representative institutions. Both aim to take full advantage of new technologies in their proposals to transform American politics.

Representative democracy is a "thin democracy," as Barber puts it. Actually, his criticisms are far more devastating than what is implied by that term; Barber suggests that representative government is really more akin to monarchy than to democracy. It destroys participation and citizenship and encourages a passivity among voters who cede their sovereignty to experts who proceed to bureaucratize, overorganize, and shunt over to the court system much of the policy-making on issues of importance.

The core reason that representative systems are not democratic, according to Barber, is that ordinary people are not permitted to make collective public judgments. Their participation is limited to a vote that they make in private, that is expected to be based on private interests, and that is influenced by manipulative ad campaigns largely paid for by corporate entities. The elected representatives, in turn, proceed to govern by self-interested bargain and exchange, not by a search for the public good.[3] In our system, writes Barber, this private-interest ethic is so pervasive that it even seeps into plebiscitary decision-making, where such measures are permitted. During initiative and referendum campaigns conducted in the states the public has no reasonable opportunity to learn about the issues that are foisted on them to decide; instead, they are subjected to an endless barrage of ads funded by private interests. Voters then proceed to vote on the basis of their private judgments, not after a healthy public debate involving interaction and democratic participation. In Barber's view, "public opinion" in a representative system is really a misnomer; public opinion is really the tallying of private opinions influenced by elites in

government and in the media and by slick corporate-sponsored market-
ing campaigns.

Barber thinks, further, that the theory of representative democracy assumes the worst of men and women: deemed unfit to make decisions for
themselves, they need to be protected from themselves. People are never
allowed to be inventive, or to participate in producing a communitarian
political decision. Representatives, bureaucrats, and judges determine
what is "just" in society, not the people. The people are assumed to be interested only in private gain, not in public ends.

At its best, Barber says, representative government is a search for great
leadership. But this search turns the people into passive watchdogs. In
Barber's words, representative government aims for "prudent rulership
not participation, private rights not public purpose, limited government
not active citizenship."[4]

According to Barber, a representative democracy is essentially "incompatible with freedom," because people willingly give their freedom over
to elected representatives and the bureaucracies they create; it is "incompatible with equality," because those with the most resources invariably
win the day in the give and take of legislative politics; and it is "incompatible with social justice," because real justice can take root only in a participatory environment in which people make informed decisions as
equals in a deliberative context.[5] Representative democracy is about control, keeping citizens apart and limiting their participation to the voting
booth. Such a system is deadening to people's souls, because there is none
of the interaction that is consonant with the truly interdependent nature
of people's lives and their yearnings for fraternity.[6]

The solution? Barber advocates a strong democracy that focuses on
participation, citizenship, and civic competence.[7] Strong democracy connotes a system in which people govern themselves at all levels at least
part of the time, and certainly on the major hot-button issues and on matters involving the use of a great deal of power by the government.

Barber believes that our "freedom is not the precondition for political
activity[;] rather [our freedom] is the product of [vigorous and active cit-
izenship]"[8]—a vigorous and active citizenship that is not a part of a representative system. Americans are bored and without purpose in antiseptic modern life; meaning can be found in self-government within the
framework of participatory institutions that reflect and celebrate equality.
Public judgment after deliberation and as a precursor to more discussion
will elevate politics above the private interests and market forces that
dominate representative democracy.

Barber's strong democracy is "politics in the participatory mode," as he
puts it. We must create a "political community that transforms dependent

private individuals into free citizens and partial and private interests into public goods."[9] Strong democracy provides a theory of citizenship that is utterly lacking in representative democracy. He defines strong democracy as "politics in the participatory mode where conflict is resolved in the absence of an independent ground through a participatory process of ongoing, proximate self-legislation and the creation of a political community capable of transforming dependent, private individuals into free citizens and partial and private interests into public goods."[10]

How to put this into practice? Barber prescribes the creation of deliberative institutions that would fully engage people in self-government, enabling them carefully to consider policies that would be good for the whole community. Barber is fully aware of what a radical break this would be from what people are used to. He acknowledges that initially there would be a need for civic education and transitional leadership to facilitate the move from undemocratic hierarchical decision-making structures (so familiar and essential a part of representative democracy) to structures in which citizens can participate on an equal basis. People would need to be indoctrinated in civic communitarian values as an antidote to the existing private-interest ethic.

Ideally, strong democracy would be characterized by ongoing talk that would foster a "spirit of reasonableness."[11] Community decisions would not necessarily be cast in stone; instead, they would be subject to more discussion and possible revision. To make all of this possible, it would first be necessary to set up neighborhood assemblies to discuss issues and create agendas. Advanced technology would obviate the need for representative assemblies at regional and national levels, as neighborhood groups could be connected via interactive television and computer. To the extent smaller regional and national deliberative institutions were needed, representatives could be chosen by lot.[12]

Ultimately many issues at the local, state, and national levels would be subject to a vote, but referenda would be conducted in ways that would facilitate a community decision instead of the counting of private judgments as we have today. Neighborhood assemblies would hold discussions on the issues that would come up for a vote. The government would commission independent filmmakers to make balanced videos on the issues, and voters would be given multiple options on the ballot to express their degree of support for a given policy. They also would be given the option to choose more discussion on the matter.

Barber describes the kind of scenario he envisions this way:

> Imagine a situation in which the State of California wished to offer a referendum to its citizens on a law banning Sunday retail commerce. Normally,

the private sector would go to work on voters, plying them with expensive advertisements portraying the loss to the economy of Sunday closings, and churches and the retail industry would indulge in a war of publicists. Voters, having passively received this bounty of misinformation, would eventually be constrained to vote their prejudices (religion versus convenience) and the matter would be "democratically" resolved. Yet with the assistance of the new technologies a very different scenario can be imagined. Every township and municipality in California might, for example, call a town meeting to discuss an issue initially. The State might fund a neutral documentary maker to produce a one-hour special on the issue, which might be shown on television prior to a debate by proponents of each side. A second set of town meetings would follow this, including a video hookup (teleconference) of urban and rural meetings to let different parts of the State understand how the issue was being discussed elsewhere. This could be followed by a final debate on television coupled with an interactive hookup permitting home viewers to pose questions to the "experts." Such a multiple-phase process involving information, adversarial debate, and direct engagement by citizens within their local communities and among the communities and the experts would offer genuine civic education. More public-regarding ways of looking at problems could emerge, and the final decision on the referendum would be both informed and more public-minded. The cumulative effect on the political competence of the electorate of a series of such procedures, replicated on different issues over several years, would be immense.[13]

In sum, Barber's strong democracy involves a complete transformation of the role of the citizen. The citizen, in effect, would be educated to the importance of participation by all in an equal environment. An array of institutions would be put in place that would facilitate politics in the form of an ongoing discussion, and ultimately decision-making by the community on the major issues of the day.

Both Barber and Becker see great potential in electronic means to enhance a transformed polity. Of course, advanced technology can be used for both good and ill; it might produce a Tower of Babel, or, if properly regulated, a more democratic and informed discussion of the issues involving all citizens.[14] If we are wise we will employ the new technologies for the purpose of increasing opportunities for democratic deliberation, not just for giving more citizen access to representatives and certainly not just for already well-placed and influential citizens to put their case before the people in initiatives. In other words, the new technologies will either confirm representative processes that take away people's freedom and increase the reliance on plebiscitary decisions by uninformed citizens who are influenced by slick ad campaigns, or they will be used in the service of strong, participatory democracy, including both officially sanctioned deliberative processes and informed plebiscitary ones.

Complementing Representative Institutions

James Fishkin's proposal for "deliberative public opinion polls" and Robert Dahl's "minipopuluses"[15] are based on a more moderate critique of representative institutions than that offered by Barber. Fishkin and Dahl intend not to transform the political system but rather to complement existing representative arrangements with democratic and popular ones.

Fishkin claims that "only a majoritarian vision of democracy is considered legitimate in the public eye."[16] Dahl says that the greatest shortcomings in American democracy revolve around the lack of political equality and opportunities for collective political self-determination.[17] Freedom is most meaningful, he says, when people decide matters of public import for themselves. According to Dahl, in representative democracy there is an insufficiency of equality largely because specialists—who are overwhelmingly of a higher socioeconomic class and who tend also to be white men—make *public judgments* for the whole society. There is no reason, he continues, to conclude that specialists are better able to identify the public good than ordinary people, particularly in view of the demographic skew in the political and policy class. Direct participation is the surest way for the people in a democracy to protect their shared interests; moreover, people develop as moral agents when they are responsible for the public good. When it comes down to public policy decisions, it is not as though there are definite right answers on complex questions. Specialists may be better able to lay out options than the layperson, according to Dahl, but there is no reason to put faith in the specialists' ability to determine the correct path for the society.

The problem comes in putting these ideas into practice. Although the technical impracticalities that used to prevent direct participation on a large scale are no longer or will soon no longer be major obstacles, Fishkin and Dahl imply that there is another practical question: Is it at all realistic to expect regular participation by millions in policy discussions as Barber and Becker propose, even with advanced technology? In fact, most people most of the time are simply too busy to participate in the way that some theorists might think is best. Of course there is another way to get large-scale participation—the initiative or the referendum. Neither Fishkin nor Dahl categorically rejects their use, but Fishkin is critical of them because of the dearth of opportunities for meaningful discussion and deliberation during the campaigns. The key, then, is to get ordinary people involved in a deliberative context.

The innovative proposals for reform offered by these two scholars meet the necessary criteria. Neither would burden too many people and they could potentially involve a cross-section of ordinary citizens in policymaking. Ideally, Dahl's minipopuluses would take on the status of a citizen obligation, perhaps analogous to jury duty, regularizing the idea that citizens belong in a deliberative policy-making process that should not just be the province of a select few.

"The Rational Public"

Two prominent and respected scholars, Benjamin Page and Robert Shapiro,[18] advance the notion—perhaps controversial to some—that citizens already do deliberate on issues of the day. They claim that the views of experts and elected officials filter down to ordinary people through the media, the people soak up some bits of information or take cues from their friends and perhaps respected people in their community, and they discuss issues that matter to them in the neighborhood, at church, and in other venues. Page and Shapiro make an interesting and paradoxical claim. They say both that a sizable number of people hold ill-informed, contradictory, irrational, and/or random viewpoints,[19] and that the public when looked at in its entirety tends to hold rational, consistent, and stable views.

How do they explain this paradox? Many people as individuals tend to make pretty good judgments, they say; the more people you consider, the more likely the good and sensible judgments will come through in a poll or some other systematic and scientific form of measurement. There are a couple of reasons for this. Even basically uninformed people can be quite good at taking cues from those they respect. In addition, randomly taken, or even irrational, viewpoints tend to cancel each other out.[20] The bigger the sample the more confident one can be that the outcome of the tabulation of opinion will reflect those who make good judgments on the basis of either their own research or their ability to take cues from good sources. The big-picture result of a poll, then, is likely to reflect measured, sober, stable, and even rational evaluations of policy.

The problem with policy-making, they say, is that the policy-makers don't pay enough attention to polls that actually reflect the good sense of the public. If public opinion as measured in properly administered polls really has the qualities Page and Shapiro suggest it has, and we are committed to democratic processes, the logical conclusion, according to the authors, is that the public, not the elite, should decide the big issues. It follows that either politicians should be more sensitive to public opinion or the public should press for wider use of initiatives and referenda.

Modifying the Representative Institutions

For at least a century there has been an impulse among liberal intellectuals to modify the constitutional arrangements that thwart majority rule. The journalist Daniel Lazare describes the system of checks and balances as antiquated and antidemocratic throwbacks to a time, the seventeenth and eighteenth centuries, when the public was thought of as *the beast*—essentially an unruly mob whose influence on policy must be drastically limited so that the better sorts could determine it.[21] Political scientists from Woodrow Wilson to James Sundquist have advocated some modifications of the constitutional arrangements to lessen deadlock and to increase the chances of one party controlling both branches of government in a kind of modified version of the British parliamentary model.[22] Essentially, the view of these liberal reformers is that the people cannot get their will done in a system so encumbered with checks and balances.

These intellectuals are not critical of representative government per se. Rather, the problems are the specific form of representative government outlined in our Constitution together with the tradition of federalism, which tends to decentralize political parties—the institution that might most easily be marshaled to carry out the majority will. Sundquist warns that our all too common experience with divided government is a failure; inaction and stalemate on pressing matters is far too common. He writes that we need to modify our institutions to increase the chance that one party can control both the executive and the legislative branches of the government and thus be in a position to act and be held accountable for those actions.[23] He suggests allowing for special elections when the branches are at an impasse; ending off-year elections for the House of Representatives and having the House and the president stand together at four-year intervals; and allowing members of Congress to serve in the cabinet, among other reforms. The theory is that it is democratic and desirable for a majoritarian position to be more easily identifiable, and subsequently for that position to be implemented into policy.

Although populists on the left have a wide range of criticisms of representative government and several prescriptions for reform, as we have seen there is general agreement that representative government as we know it in the United States is not as democratic as it should be. Some say it is crucial that a more democratic cross-section of the citizenry be involved directly in policy-making; there is no particular reason to defer to the judgments of elite experts. In fact, the process of doing just that is fundamentally undemocratic. Others suggest that the decentralized party system and the constitutional arrangements thwart decisive and democratic action by government. Whether or not representative government should be substantially replaced is a matter of some contention among these populists; there is no disagreement that the current arrangements are not working.

Modern-Day Populists of the Right and Center

Populists of the right and center take aim at the same target as those on the left, representative government, but their objections and motivations are often different. Many of these critics focus almost exclusively on the corruption they perceive to be permeating the political establishment—particularly the power wielded by the special interests. Only a thorough cleansing of the political system can eradicate special-interest influence and restore the proper relationship of the people to their government. The conservatives are not looking to transform the system into something new, *a la* Benjamin Barber and some of the others on the left; rather, they intend to return to a time when government observed proper limits. It is the case, however, these populists claim, that radical means might be needed to effect this restoration. Eric O'Keefe, president of Americans for Limited Terms, expresses the sentiment well:

> The biggest impediment to political change in America today, and the biggest myth in American politics, is the widespread belief that we have representative government at the federal level. The myth is promoted by a political class using the power and money of government to entrench and promote themselves. When that myth is shattered, we will see dramatic political change. If we are fortunate, it will be a move to lock in term limits.[24]

The movement for term limits accurately reflects the outrage activists and ordinary citizens of the right and a sometimes nebulous center feel. Term-limits advocates believe that, for all intents and purposes, congressional elections are a fraud. The elected representatives perpetuate their positions of power by catering to the special interests that fund their campaigns, and they often support policies opposed by most of the people or, conversely, oppose ideas, such as term limits, that the people overwhelmingly like but that would threaten their very existence.

Direct democracy is a vital step in giving power back to the people. Initiatives and referenda, at both the state and federal levels, are precisely the radical prescription that will enable people to go over the heads of the unrepresentative political class to implement policies that the entrenched interests oppose. But most important, the initiative process allows the people to put in place term limits, which would end the corrupt linkages between interest groups, members of Congress or state legislatures, and bureaucrats, all of whom pursue policies that advance their narrow interests or their careers.

O'Keefe and others perceive a war going on over term limits. At the same time as the people are speaking out in no uncertain terms in support of this reform, the elite is doing everything it can to stymie the effort. The leadership in Congress, while paying lip service to the movement, failed to go the extra mile to get a term limits amendment through the House in 1995.[25] All across the country elected representatives are increasing the obstacles to getting term limits and other measures on state and local ballots.[26] Dane Waters, president of the Initiative and Referendum Institute, based in Washington, D.C., is campaigning to make direct democracy more accessible, for it is exactly these plebiscitary outlets that are necessary, in his view, to keep the career-obsessed representatives honest and attuned to the public interest.

No one has expressed the populist outrage of the right and center better than the conservative gadfly Kevin Phillips, who asserts that the "grassroots of America have been losing national influence to a permanent political, interest group, and financial elite located in Washington."[27] According to Phillips, the failure of the government to respond to the social and political tumult of the 1960s was proof positive of the entrenchment of an unresponsive elite. Compare what happened then to what happened in the late nineteenth and early twentieth century and in the 1930s, also times of great upheaval. In those periods, when resounding electoral majorities signaled the need for dramatic changes in the role of the government in Washington, the government responded.

But by the 1960s the federal government had become an immovable object, according to Phillips. The huge growth of the domestic bureaucracy, which began in the 1930s and accelerated during President Johnson's Great Society, and the national security state, which began to grow unchallenged during the Truman Administration, were largely unaffected by the decisive rejection of liberal Democrats in the presidential elections of 1968 and 1972. The public was sending unmistakable messages about criminal justice, forced integration, school prayer, and the welfare state, Phillips writes, but the elite was unmoved. Much of the problem resided in the bureaucracy and the courts. The elite who "knew better" perpetuated controversial interpretations of the Constitution that led to busing and new rules for criminal procedure, among other things, and worked with well-placed allies in the Congress to continue highly unpopular welfare policies. The bottom line, according to Phillips, was that Americans were no longer able to control their own government through electoral majorities. Faith and trust in government have been on a steep downward slide ever since.

What we have in Washington is a new sort of tyranny, writes Phillips. It is no longer the threat of a ruthless government infringing on the rights of vulnerable minorities. The threat today is from a government that is incapable of coordinating national policy as a result of the unresponsiveness and independent strength of the power centers in the capital. Separation of powers "is an eighteenth-century miscalculation."[28] He goes on: "Branches of government arranged to be mutually suspicious were once a valid defense against despotism or an overbearing executive. What they encourage now, however, is a different tyranny—an inability to coordinate effective government policy."[29] And there are more centers of power than ever before in the capital, with the proliferation of unaccountable independent agencies, most notably the Federal Reserve. The increased pressure from citizens for more participatory democracy and more direct democracy is the most obvious sign of disenchantment with the immovable centers of power in Washington.

In Phillips's view, what is needed is an assault on the two-party system and its hegemony in our representative institutions. It is necessary to mobilize the people through direct democracy to counter the dominance of the special interests in our politics. The parties are in league with the interests, and they are too strong to be challenged only by the formation of a third party, such as Perot's Reform party or the Green party. Thus, it is crucial that direct democratic reforms and other changes be implemented in order to break the hold of the parties and the interests on representative government. It took a constitutional amendment, in 1913, to put in place the direct election of U.S. senators in order to counter the influence of the special interests. Once again, today, the legitimacy of the system is at stake, just as it was early in the twentieth century. Direct democracy comes with many risks, acknowledges Phillips, but the inadequacy of the current system calls for the gamble represented by such drastic action. He describes the development of his thinking on this subject this way:

> Since the 1970s, I have had some sympathy for the populist devices of initiative and referendum, but until recently, I would not have supported them on the national level in the United States. Back in 1968, I had hopes for a more or less normal realignment in the U.S. party system, and I had some minor recurring hope for the multiparty election process in 1992. Now my doubts that the U.S. party system can overcome the bipartisan entrenchment of Washington have simply grown too great. Brian Beedham has reached the same point in his *Economist* essay "A Better Way to Vote; Why Letting the People Themselves Take the Decisions Is the Logical Next Step for the West." Then, just as I was finishing this book, I came across a column by the political scientist Everett Carll Ladd, who explained why he, too, was modifying his orthodox faith in the U.S. political party system he had written about for decades: "Politics as usual inside the (Washington) beltway really has become an insiders' game. The interests that dominate it differ from those the Progressives battled, but are no less insensitive to popular calls for change. The old Progressive answer of extending direct authority and intervention to the citizens may be the only answer to present-day shortcomings in representative democracy." I have reached the same conclusion.[30]

Plebiscitary demands are sweeping Canada (which had its first national referendum in the 1990s) and Europe, and Phillips believes it may just be a matter of time before the allure becomes irresistible in the United States. States and localities are increasingly turning to direct democratic means as a way to counter the control of the two-party-dominated representative institutions. Phillips contends that the institution of a national referendum would have the salutary effect of forcing Congress to address the people's concerns. He also suggests permitting members of Congress to cast roll-call votes from their home districts so that they would stay there most of the time and be more apt to consider constituents' views on controversial issues.

The bottom line, according to Phillips, is that the more the people are brought into the equation the more likely the hold of the special interests and the corrupt political parties can be broken. Whether it is term limits, referenda, a recall procedure for federal officials, proportional representation, or any of several other possibilities, policy-makers must be made to reckon with the wishes of the people first and foremost and not those of the special interests.

Debating Direct Democracy

Although populists vary a good deal in their prescriptions for curing the ills of the political system, they do agree that there is something wrong with representative government, and most believe that institutions of direct democracy are necessary and desirable. This is because they believe that representative democracy squelches the will of the majority, special interests are rendering government ineffective and corrupting the system, and people are better able to decide what is in the public interest than elected representatives. Furthermore, in Kevin Phillips's view, the biggest problem in our political system isn't any longer that the government poses a threat to minorities, which was the main fear at the Founding, but that the government doesn't carry out the people's wishes.

Some on the left level an even more devastating critique. Benjamin Barber alleges that representative government is by definition undemocratic. It creates a ruling class and thwarts the will of the people. The political system must be transformed with various forms of direct democracy, both deliberative and plebiscitary. Others on the left are critical of representative government as it is arranged, has evolved, and is practiced in the United States. The people's will is thwarted by antiquated constitutional arrangements, they say; government must be streamlined to end deadlock and promote party government.

Those on the right have a different prescription and a different vision. Phillips, like some liberals, believes that the separation of powers has outlived its usefulness, but he does not see party government as the solution. Parties are part of the problem today. Instead, government must be made more responsive by allowing for citizen lawmaking by referendum and initiative. Some on the center and the right, in particular the leaders of the highly popular term-limits movement, wish to see a restoration to a time when lawmakers respected limits and when government wasn't run by bureaucrats in league with the special interests and representatives beholden to them. This restoration can be achieved by returning to the days of citizen-legislators and providing for the wider use of initiatives and referenda, including the implementation of a national referendum process, to keep elected officials honest.

As we saw in the last chapter, ambitious schemes such as Barber's are not in keeping with American traditions of political participation.[31] The transformationists' talk of reinvigorating, revitalizing, and reinventing participatory democracy is based largely on a fiction. As Michael Schudson has shown, even the fabled New England town meetings suffered from low participation rates and had agenda controlled by the elite.[32] Americans want the *opportunity* for involvement in open processes, but this should not be construed to mean that most are interested in getting involved in the nitty-gritty of politics. Politicians are given leeway in public policy, but this is not a blank check, largely because the people do not trust politicians implicitly and will get involved at unpredictable and haphazard intervals when something they are concerned about catches their attention. Nor is there any reason to believe that Americans are looking for swift government action by responsible parties along the lines of the British model. Americans do not identify with the parties; in fact, they are seen to be part of the problem, just as Phillips says. The institution of direct democracy in the form of plebiscites is a more practical and realistic alternative to systemic problems in the American political cultural context. And it is already practiced on a regular basis by millions of citizens at the state and local levels.

Among elites, the debate on the relative merits of direct democratic and representative decision-making is raging in opinion magazines and newspapers and among television commentators and the politicians themselves. The discussion usually revolves around the wisdom of the prevalent plebiscitary style of initiatives and referenda. Academics in the social sciences and the law have also weighed in. What does the evidence show? Is representative democracy really more special interest–driven than direct democracy? Are minorities' rights at risk with plebiscites? I will summarize and synthesize the debates on these issues presenting both sides' cases. In the end, I will explain why the advocates of representative democracy are losing the debate, even though much of the evidence, particularly that coming from the experience with plebiscitary democracy in California, seems to be on their side. To summarize the controversy, I address five controversial issues that were introduced at the beginning of the chapter. For easier reference they are reproduced here.

1. Are voters informed enough for direct democracy?
2. Which is more special interest–driven, direct or representative decision-making?
3. What level of scrutiny should plebiscites be given by the courts, as compared to laws made by representative institutions?
4. Does direct democracy threaten the rights of vulnerable minorities more than representative democracy?
5. Which contributes more to responsible governance, direct or representative democracy?

1. Are Voters Informed Enough for Direct Democracy?

This question has probably generated more heat than any other controversy over direct democracy. Skeptics often contend that voters are uninformed, too easily swayed, overburdened, or confused by the proliferation of referenda and initiatives they are confronted with in some states. Others contend that voters, even those who are less informed, take cues that enable them to behave much as though they were as informed as the model citizen who studies the issues carefully. Some suggest that voters hash out ballot issues at the checkout line and in the bowling alley in a manner that approximates the sort of deliberating that takes place in legislative chambers.

Actually, it is impossible to answer this question with any certainty. Not only is the evidence inconclusive, but in fact, scholars and other observers are divided as to what criteria are appropriate for measuring voters' fitness. But relevant research does enable us to get a general sense of how voters approach ballot questions.

One thing we need to remember is that legislators and congressmen themselves often are not in a position to learn the details of important pieces of legislation. State legislatures push through dozens or even hundreds of bills in relatively short sessions, frequently leaving most of the activity to a late-session flurry during which lengthy and complex matters are dealt with in a matter of days or hours. In the U.S. Congress, it is a common refrain among members that they are too frequently forced to vote on huge omnibus packages without having an opportunity to consider almost any of the details. Obviously, members of Congress and state legislatures take cues from colleagues and experts and rely heavily on the input of paid staff as they reach their voting positions. Do voters behave similarly, taking advice from trusted and informed friends or people in leadership positions in their communities? Is that process, to the extent that it takes place, a reasonable facsimile of the informed advice legislators get from paid professionals who work for them and the legislative body?

There is no doubt that legislators have more reliable sources of information than voters usually do, even though voters increasingly have access to good information via the Internet. Congressmen, and to a lesser extent state legislators, have paid staff and official research services to do the digging for them. If anything, they experience an information overload. But from the populists' perspective, if voters have lost faith and are rightfully distrustful of representatives and representative institutions, the real issue is not whether legislators are more informed. It is whether voters are reasonably suited to make these decisions *after others have laid out the options for them*.

David Magleby, a scholar of direct democracy, has devoted a great deal of attention to the question of the fitness of voters.[33] He has found evidence of a variety of problems with having voters decide ballot measures. For one thing, voters most often have only one source of information when they vote on referenda and initiatives: television. This unwillingness to take advantage of the many other available sources of information casts doubt as to whether voters are prepared to decide complex questions. Magleby has also found evidence that in some initiative and referendum campaigns many voters are so woefully ignorant that they have difficulty translating their views into votes. In other words, many people cast votes that are inconsistent with their ideological predispositions because of their confusion concerning the matter in question—thus, they may actually vote against their views and wishes. In fact, many of the official explanations of issues that are distributed by the states are written at a level—often a college reading level—that is beyond the comprehension of many voters.

On the other hand, the legal scholar Lynn Baker[34] and the political scientists Page and Shapiro believe that there is considerable informal deliberation by the public on many public questions. This deliberation, they say, is based on a kind of distillation of expert opinion filtered through various media that is absorbed by voters. Viewpoints that are debated in the major media trickle down to the ordinary voter, who then is in a position to make a considered judgment.

The political scientist Arthur Lupia has found some evidence in a couple of California initiative campaigns involving complex regulatory issues that voters who are not well informed are adept at picking and choosing among the various cues and end up making judgments on issues that resemble those of better-informed voters.[35] In addition, some of the most recent research indicates that voters demonstrate a measurable level of ideological consistency in voting on ballot propositions.[36] This means that those voters who vote consistently in partisan candidate elections are more likely to vote in a pattern consistent with their ideological predispositions in plebiscites. So we can say with confidence that there is evidence that some voters are taking cues, perhaps from public officials or from interest group leaders, as a guide to deciding how to vote on initiative campaigns and that, at least at a modest level, many voters are casting votes consistent with their ideological proclivities.

In partisan candidate elections the public demonstrates these same abilities to make decision-making "shortcuts" to an even greater extent. For example, when choosing a Senate candidate voters may focus on the candidate's party, or on a high-profile position he or she has taken in the past, or on the candidate's performance in a previously high-profile job. These sorts of decision-making shortcuts, many scholars believe, lead to reasonable and consistent voting decisions, as voters judge candidates on the basis of party affiliation, their past record of accomplishments, or a show of character. For example, voters might be inclined to support a war hero as a man who has demonstrated courage under fire and might be a good bet to have the courage of his convictions as a member of Congress.

In primary elections, on the other hand, voters seem to have a more difficult time finding meaningful cues to guide their decision-making. Candidates are often less well known, and they may have many of the same issue positions as their opponents of the same party. In these circumstances, how does a voter reach a decision? Unless they engage in exhaustive research, voters are stuck responding to less meaningful cues than those available in general elections. One might choose to go for the candidate who "looks" honest or courageous, or whose ads happened to catch one's attention. In short, primary voters are a bit more whimsical or even random in their vote choice than general election voters because the more substantial cues that characterize the general election contests—party affiliation, issue differences, etc.—are less commonly evident and less pronounced in primary contests.

A useful way to think about a typical voter's decision-making process when confronted with an initiative or referendum is to compare it with that used in different kinds of candidate elections. The voter's decision-making process on a ballot measure is much more likely to resemble the primary-election than general-election situation. At the very least, it is reasonable to assume that the vote choice in a plebiscite tends to be less structured and more random than in a general election between major-party candidates. There are a lot of reasons to think this. There is no overt party cue for voters to go on with many initiatives and referenda, and it may not be clear to a voter exactly what the consequences of his or her vote are. In addition, the policy questions may not be of interest to the voter. As a result, she might not want or be able to take the time to think about or research the measure. Compare that with a campaign between candidates who have positions on a wide range of issues. The voter who, for example, likes to support the pro-choice candidate can usually find out what the candidates' positions are on that issue and arrive at what for him would be a meaningful vote choice. The groups and individuals doing the endorsing in an initiative campaign may not be terribly familiar, either, making it more difficult for voters to gather reliable cues and make sense of them. Though there is no definitive evidence on the subject, what Magleby found regarding the sources of information voters rely on suggests that people may be more likely to fall back on television advertising in plebiscite campaigns than they are in general elections between opposing party candidates.

Still, when all is said and done, the real question might be not whether voters are suited for plebiscitary democracy but whether they want it and feel they need it because representative processes have become so corrupt. So, even with the demonstrable difficulties many people have in making sense of ballot issues, a large number of people—a majority, if the polls are any guide—believe that direct democracy is highly desirable as an avenue to go over the heads of representatives who are either too beholden to special interests or afraid to tackle issues the voters would like to have addressed. Direct democracy, its advocates say, is an invaluable tool for keeping elected officials mindful of the power of the people.

2. Which Is More Special Interest–Driven, Direct or Representative Decision-making?

Much of the criticism of representative institutions boils down to the charge that special interests have taken control of public policy. Direct democracy is seen by some as a corrective to this situation. But there are those who believe that with *direct* democratic institutions, the influence of special-interest groups actually becomes a bigger problem. Which is more special interest–driven, legislatures and electoral processes or initiative campaigns run by the same interests that fool voters into supporting the interests' pet proposals?

On the surface the answer seems obvious: with lobbyists teeming in the hallways of state legislative buildings and through the U.S. Capitol and adjacent office buildings, with special interests helping to pay for the reelection campaigns of the members, and with members almost obsessed with saving their seats, the potential that policy-making in representative institutions is dominated by those interests appears to be great. Meanwhile, the decision-makers in direct democratic institutions, the voters, are not buttonholed by lobbyists, nor do their jobs depend on interest-group contributions. It seems logical to assume that special interests dominate representative decision-making and have a relatively insignificant role in direct democracy.

The reality is much more complicated than that. In fact, it has become almost an article of faith in the journalistic and political community that plebiscites are vehicles for special interests and are every bit as susceptible to manipulation as legislative processes.[37] Many prominent journalists and the political elite are highly critical of the process of initiative generation by special interest advocates who propose and oppose ballot propositions and then conduct campaigns either for or against the proposals.

Charles Mahtesian of *Governing* magazine makes a compelling case that the so-called grassroots populist tool of initiatives has become a vehicle for politicians in power or striving for power and a method by which already influential interest groups try to circumvent the inevitable compromising involved in the legislative process.[38] Groups can put before voters policies that express exactly their interests rather than having to compromise with competitors in order to succeed in the state legislature. And initiatives have become a tool for entrepreneurial politicians as well. When he was governor of California (1991–1999), Pete Wilson used initiatives to bolster his position on the right wing of the Republican party. Proposition 226, put on the ballot in May 1998, which would have restricted the use of union dues in political campaigns, gave Wilson the opportunity to advocate a viewpoint that might enhance his future presidential prospects.[39] According to Mahtesian, to Wilson it mattered little whether 226 won or lost (it lost)—he just needed to be seen fighting the good fight. Similarly, Bill Sizemore in Oregon and Ron Unz in California are two wealthy political entrepreneurs who have used proposition campaigns as stepping-stones to bids for high office. In addition, many plebiscite campaigns pit well-placed and well-funded groups against one another both in the initiation stage and in the campaigns. As Mahtesian puts it, "If this is grassroots democracy, it is being played out on artificial turf."[40]

The political scientist Daniel Smith makes a similar point. In a study of tax initiatives in three states, Smith comes to the conclusion that what is going on with these people's tax revolts is really a "faux populism."[41] The propositions were initiated and funded by wealthy political entrepreneurs. He found little or no groundswell at the grassroots, contrary to the favored depictions of these campaigns as modern-day equivalents of the Boston Tea Party brought about by the protests of ordinary homeowners or taxpayers rebelling against overbearing government taxation. In reality, the people are involved in these campaigns only on Election Day.

Alan Rosenthal, a scholar who specializes in state legislative processes, suggests that voters are subject to manipulation by the special interests in initiative campaigns. Rosenthal says that the media campaigns that aim to influence voters in initiatives are "designed to intimidate, not to communicate."[42] Elected representatives, on the other hand, are tied closely to the people by the electoral connection, he maintains. As a result, they are unlikely to stray from the constituents' interests very often.

Elisabeth Gerber, a political scientist, has done some of the best empirical work on interest groups and direct democracy in recent years. She has found that direct democracy often enhances the influence over the legislatures of the very groups that already have the ear of legislators.[43] Even if a proposition favored by a group loses, it can show a significant level of support and serve as a kind of a threat to get the legislature to start paying attention to the group's concerns. Sometimes just demonstrating the potential to go the direct democratic route may enhance an interest group's clout. Citizens or groups with few resources simply are not in a position credibly to wield influence in this way.

But the picture is not quite as stark as one might conclude from Mahtesian's and Rosenthal's depictions. Although the wealthy and well-connected may be the ones frequently proposing and bankrolling initiative and referendum campaigns, they don't necessarily always get their way, nor do they always propose policies that favor narrow group interests. Certainly it is not the case that groups can lavishly fund an initiative and fool voters into supporting it.[44]

In fact, the evidence is overwhelming that the initiative process is a fairly conservative policy-making instrument. Voters have regularly demonstrated that they are not dupes. They seem inclined to vote no as opposed to taking a leap into the unknown. When voters are confused as to the meaning of a proposition, either because of their lack of research or through efforts to write the proposal in a confusing way, they tend to oppose it. In addition, money spent in opposition to initiatives has far more impact than money spent in favor of them. In short, the status quo is often preserved, either because groups are adept at finding attack points in propositions and wage sophisticated campaigns to oppose them, or because they are able to develop clever counterproposals and get those on the ballot. These proposals often include so-called "kill clauses," which provide that the proposition on a similar topic that gets the most votes will take precedence if both or all receive majority support.

As pointed out previously, it is not always accurate to characterize initiatives as vehicles for advancing narrow group interests, regardless of whether they actually have been brought to the voters' attention by an interest group. The majority of initiatives in California in the last decade or so address diffuse interests. Furthermore, those initiatives that address diffuse interests are considerably more likely to pass than those that are more narrowly focused.[45] It is fairly rare for proposals that benefit narrow interests at the expense of the broader community to be successful. This does not mean that these narrow interests are losers—as mentioned before, the aim of some groups or entrepreneurs is not necessarily to win, but may be to raise an issue's profile or the profile of the entrepreneur. Nevertheless, it is true that the ability of narrow interests to get what they want through direct democracy is often overstated by critics.

In fact, in the debate on the relative power of interest groups in direct democracy versus representative democracy, both sides overstate their case. The populist claim that direct democracy is the way for citizens to take back their government from the interests is patently ludicrous. Interest groups are highly influential in plebiscite campaigns and have much more of the ready resources to put measures on the ballot than ordinary citizens; furthermore, the despised politicians are becoming increasingly adept at the politics of direct democracy to further their careers. It is also probably fair to say, as many critics do, that the concerns of ordinary citizens are rarely addressed by ballot propositions.[46]

On the other hand, no one who looks at the numbers can claim that the people are easy to fool into supporting propositions that are not in their interest, and no one can seriously deny that special interests are influential in representative government. But at least, as M. Dane Waters, the president of the Initiative and Referendum Institute, says, the interest group politics in ballot proposition campaigns is out in the open, unlike the efforts of lobbyists in legislative politics. The legislative process in which lobbyists participate is often arcane and confusing and sometimes still conducted out of the public eye. With ballot initiatives, the public can freely make a choice in an open process.

Is the process of direct democracy more or less susceptible to interest group influence than ordinary legislative politics? That is probably impossible to measure. Alan Rosenthal believes legislative politics is much less controlled by interest groups than is claimed by populists. He makes a good case that at least legislators are accountable to their constituents, and they certainly seem to go to great lengths to listen and follow the wishes of people in their districts.

The evidence suggests that direct democracy is a great deal more susceptible to interest group influence than populists claim; at the same time, the public is much less prone to manipulation by ad campaigns than critics say, if only because of the public's demonstrated tendency to shy away from supporting propositions they don't fully understand.

3. What Level of Scrutiny Should Plebiscites Be Given as Compared to Laws Made by Representative Institutions?

There is a vigorous debate, primarily among legal scholars and some activists, on the appropriate level of judicial scrutiny for citizen lawmaking. Traditionally the courts have given a considerable amount of leeway to representative institutions, rarely delving into the procedural aspects of lawmaking, even if they do occasionally rule a law unconstitutional. But the process by which propositions arrive on the ballot (the petition gathering, etc.) is frequently subjected to judicial scrutiny, and courts are more likely to scrutinize the actual substance of citizen-made law than that passed by legislatures. The main points of contention are whether it is appropriate for direct democracy to receive more scrutiny than representative democracy, whether the presumption in favor of representative decision-making should remain, and whether the substance of initiatives should be reviewed for their constitutionality before they are put in front of the voters.

In 1998, the Colorado legislature passed a law making it illegal for out-of-state activists to gather signatures to put for initiative and referendum campaigns on the ballot in Colorado. Supporters of the measure claimed that representative institutions—state legislatures, in this case—had a privileged place in the system, and auxiliary checks such as these designed to reduce fraud in the process of putting initiatives and referenda on the ballot were legitimate. But the Supreme Court ruled that such a law violated citizens' First Amendment rights.

Despite this loss, legislative bodies at the state and local level remain active in placing obstacles in the way of initiative campaigns and the people who conduct them. There are numerous ways of doing this. State legislatures have passed laws to make it illegal to pay signature gatherers by the signature (Maine); to implement restrictions on extraneous markings on petitions (Massachusetts); to restrict signature gathering at grocery stores (Washington); and rigorously to enforce exact signature matches (Nebraska). Direct democracy proponents challenged all these measures in court in the last half of 1999.[47]

The most common efforts to rein in direct democracy usually involve raising the number of signatures required for ballot access, calling for strict enforcement of the "single-subject rule," or requiring preelection review of a measure's constitutionality.[48] The single-subject rule is the most important and controversial. Most states restrict plebiscites to one subject to avoid logrolling—the trading of votes by legislators to secure support for their favored legislation—and general confusion. But the interpretation of what constitutes a single subject is a matter of bitter dispute. For example, in Florida an initiative campaign that would put on the ballot a statute outlawing any preference on the basis of race and sex is being challenged at this writing on the basis that race preferences and gender preferences are two separate subjects. Such a strict interpretation can be used very effectively by opponents of citizen lawmaking to prevent measures from appearing on the ballot.[49] The question of whether initiatives should be subject to preelection review to determine whether the measure violates provisions in a state's constitution can also be an effective delaying tactic. There are, however, some critics of direct democracy who feel nevertheless that courts should wait until initiatives are actually passed before intervening in the process, if for no other reason than that most measures do not pass and early involvement is unnecessary and potentially wasteful.[50]

Populists do not believe that such strict scrutiny of direct democratic procedures is appropriate. They point out that the procedures used in representative institutions are rarely if ever subject to these kinds of scrutiny. Furthermore, they say, the courts accord the finished legislative product of representative institutions much greater deference than citizen-made law when constitutional challenges arise.

Some advocates of direct democracy, in defense of their position on judicial scrutiny of initiatives and referenda, point to evidence that direct democratic outcomes more often reflect the views of the people than the outcomes of the legislative process. There is a great deal of controversy surrounding this contention. (This debate is covered more fully in the response to Question 5.) In addition, some scholars are critical of the quality of deliberation in representative assemblies and suggest that the way people discuss issues informally is as meaningful as what legislators engage in, if not more so. Thus, there is no particular reason to give more deference to the legislative product of representative institutions than to the product of direct democratic ones.

To some populists these issues are essentially beside the point. If the people are truly sovereign, they argue, then it is pretty obvious that direct democratic procedures and outcomes should be given as much deference by the courts as representative institutions, or more. At the very least, they believe that the courts should strike down excessively onerous signature requirements, relax the strict single-subject enforcement doctrines that exist in some states, and refrain from reviewing ballot propositions for their constitutionality before people have had a chance to vote on them.[51]

The response to these arguments from representative government advocates is probably best stated by Julian Eule, a professor at Yale University.[52] Eule points to the constitutional basis for giving privileged status to representative processes. Article IV, Section 4 of the Constitution guarantees "to every state of the Union a republican form of government." Thus, there is a constitutional justification for a more privileged treatment of representative processes than of direct democratic ones. Some populists acknowledge this point. The direct democracy activist Tracy Westen has proposed amending the Constitution by modifying Article IV to put direct democratic procedures on an equal footing with representative procedures.

But Eule does not base his argument solely on this constitutional provision. He notes that there are good reasons for the presumption in favor of representative processes. The republican form of government is a filtering process that functions to sift out bad legislation. There is no similar process in direct democratic institutions. The legislative process at the federal level and in forty-nine of the fifty states involves bicameral consideration of legislation and, in most states, the potential of an executive veto. This process is a better, more careful way to consider legislation and is more likely to take into account the rights of citizens than direct processes. Consequently, it makes sense for the courts to defer to representative decision-making and to scrutinize the product of direct procedures carefully.

Representative processes are likely to continue to receive more deference than direct democratic institutions in state and federal courts as long as Article IV of the Constitution remains intact. The debate about which institutions better serve the public interest will continue.

4. Does Direct Democracy Threaten the Rights of Vulnerable Minorities More Than Representative Democracy?

This question raises a fundamental issue in the implementation of direct democratic institutions: the rights of minorities. In a political system predicated on the principle of protecting individual liberty and the rights of minorities, any potential threat from majorities able to implement their will with few obstructions must be taken seriously. In the Founding era, people holding unpopular opinions were thought most likely to be vulnerable to tyranny of the majority; today, it is individuals in minority groups—African Americans, immigrants, or homosexuals—who are more likely to be thought of as vulnerable.

The legal scholar Derrick Bell believes strongly that direct democracy poses a danger to African Americans and other minorities.[53] He points out that in legislative bodies there are all kinds of checkpoints at which discriminatory legislation can potentially be waylaid; there are fewer such checkpoints with direct democratic institutions, particularly initiatives. As a result, in some states almost anything can be put in front of the voters. Within a legislature, however, minority groups can function effectively, building coalitions with other groups and securing positions of authority and power in a way that enables them, in effect, to veto certain types of legislation. With plebiscites, the strength of raw majority rule can win the day against a vulnerable minority. In the halls of the state capitol, a gay rights group might be one among many legitimate claimants engaging in the bargaining and negotiating that characterizes those institutions. But initiatives and referenda frequently are debated in stark moral terms—terms of debate that don't lend themselves to compromise.[54]

Others have written about the experience in California when Governor Pete Wilson stoked the fires of resentment against immigrants by supporting a proposition that denied illegal aliens education and other services. Many of those suspicious of plebiscites claim that even when initiatives that might discriminate against gays or illegal immigrants fail, great damage has been done simply by virtue of having made a sensitive topic a matter for public discussion. In fact, there is some evidence that the existence of ballot propositions on such sensitive issues has affected the social climate in some states. One of the most systematic studies of this question concludes that antigay sentiment has been amplified by plebiscite campaigns under certain circumstances.[55]

The journalist Peter Schrag, perhaps the nation's most incisive critic of direct democracy, takes these sorts of criticisms of plebiscitary democracy in California one step further.[56] He asserts that the big-money dominance of the initiative process at all stages and the emphasis on tying the hands of legislatures with limits on the property tax and other sources of revenue is, in effect, an effort by the white middle class to reassert its control over California politics. His charge is that just when ethnic minorities are finally able to wield some power in the legislature, the voting majority of whites is changing the venue of lawmaking better to suit its interests. The motive for this tactic is similar to that of some of the turn-of-the-century Progressives who saw their political power leeched away by the party machines in the cities, which often were dominated by first- or second-generation Irish, Italian, or other white ethnic politicians.

Some of today's direct democracy advocates counter these arguments of Schrag's, claiming that legislatures kowtow to minority interests and fail to represent the interests of the majority. Defenders of direct democracy say that the threat of majority tyranny with plebiscitary democracy is way overblown. In fact, it is the case that propositions that deal with questions of minority rights are less likely to pass than other sorts of propositions.[57] In addition, some claim that the extent to which legislatures work to protect minority rights is usually exaggerated. After all, there is a long tradition of professional politicians preying on prejudices in order to attract attention and secure votes. Some of these prejudices include the belief that homosexuals are inclined to convert children to their way of life, stereotypes of dangerous black criminals, or the image of Spanish-speaking immigrants leeching government money.[58] Populists also charge that representatives, due to their expertise and experience, are likely to be cleverer in writing legislation to deprive people of their rights than the amateurs who create initiatives. Furthermore, they say, the courts serve as an effective check on plebiscites that might deny groups of constitutionally protected rights, an assertion bolstered by the fact that it is not uncommon for referenda or initiatives to be subject to injunctions or struck down outright on just that basis.

Probably the most ambitious effort to defend institutions of direct democracy against the charge that they are more likely than representative institutions to deprive minorities of rights was made by the Arizona State University law professor Lynn Baker.[59] One of her findings is that it is in fact theoretically possible for a bicameral legislative majority, elected with the support of far fewer than half of the voters, to pass legislation that is injurious to minority rights,[60] whereas it always requires more than half of the voters to pass an initiative.

She also charges that defenders of representative democracy fail to grapple with the logical consequences of their own assumption that representative institutions provide veto points that minorities can use to stop disadvantageous legislative proposals. She does not accept this assumption, but even if it were so, she points out, the logical corollary is that representative institutions are also tough places to pass legislation *advantageous* to a minority group. If veto points are available to blacks and other vulnerable groups, they are also available to racist, xenophobic, or homophobic factions within legislatures that can put a stop to legislation advantageous to the vulnerable. Accepting the constitutionalist's own logic, then, does not lead to the conclusion that representative institutions are always a more favorable venue for vulnerable minorities. Following that logic, Baker concludes that a proactive agenda would be more likely to succeed in a plebiscite, and a reactive agenda would dictate focusing on representative institutions.

But the core of her argument is that the institutional arrangements meant to protect minorities in American representative democracy do not even work in the way intended. The checks in the lawmaking process— bicameralism, open voting, the executive veto, logrolling, and deliberation by informed members—do not provide adequate protections for minorities. For example, she says, representatives often do not deliberate carefully, logrolling is often just a way to ignore the merits of an issue, and members often play on prejudices during open proceedings because most have more interest in getting reelected than in protecting the rights of minorities.

Baker is right when she points out that defenders of representative democracy often overrate, even to the point of mythologizing, the deliberative qualities of legislatures. She is also on the right track in focusing much of her attack on the institutional arrangements of representative democracy. After all, advocates of representative democracy do not rely on the goodwill of the people in elected office to protect minority rights; it is the institutional arrangements that are meant to act as safeguards against tyranny.

On the whole, however, Baker's arguments have been effectively discredited. The political scientist William Riker has shown that minorities trying to prevent discriminatory legislation from passing truly are in a better position to do so in a legislature because of a bias in favor of the status quo in parliamentary procedures that does not exist in direct democratic institutions.[61] Also, he makes the point that vulnerable minorities are rarely in a position to promote legislation to benefit them at the expense of others; if the minority group is truly vulnerable to majority tyranny, then the prospect of passing advantageous legislation is dim and the strategic focus will be on stopping disadvantageous proposals. In addition, it should be noted that logrolling, though sometimes used as a means to avoid dealing with the merits of proposals, just as Baker suggests, is often the *only* way that truly vulnerable minorities can get something advantageous to their interests passed into law.

Julian Eule pointed out another flaw in Baker's attack on the checks in the legislative process meant to protect minorities.[62] Baker looks at each one of the checks individually and never considers their cumulative effect. Furthermore, she neglects to consider the impact of the parties and committees in the legislative process. These units arguably offer more effective opportunities for savvy legislators to protect minority interests than any of the other checks considered by Baker.

These disputes may be impossible to resolve definitively, but one measure of the strength of the opposing arguments provides an unmistakable result. Consider this question: Which venue do vulnerable minority groups prefer? There is not a single such group—representing homosexuals, African Americans, or immigrant groups—that would take its chances with a plebiscite. Representatives of these groups firmly believe that if they have any effective representation at all, it is easier to water down, kill, or defeat potentially abusive measures in a legislature than to pursue their aims through a plebiscite. And, as mentioned before, logrolling can be employed to accommodate minorities' concerns.

Ultimately, defenders of direct democracy have a pretty tough sell in arguing that representative democracy is a greater threat to minority rights than direct democracy. Even if measures threatening minority rights are less likely to pass in a plebiscite than other types of measures, some do pass that might never have seen the light of day in a legislature. Initiative advocates such as Baker often betray a startling level of ignorance of legislative procedures. People familiar with legislatures are aware of their cautious nature and the tendency of members to protect even unpopular minorities in their districts in the hope of getting at least some of that group's votes in the next election, or at least of discouraging them from funding a viable opponent. Legislators know, intuitively if not always consciously, that majorities in electoral and legislative politics are almost always coalitional and that the interests of the various components of that coalition are sometimes at odds with one another. Losing a few key supporters here and there can spell defeat.

Political parties in legislatures, the entities that organize these institutions and hold a great deal of power within them, are themselves unwieldy conglomerations of minorities that often will work to protect the vulnerable within the coalition in the interest of maintaining majority control. And the byzantine nature of parliamentary procedure has famously been used by minorities of all kinds—from slaveholders in the early to mid-nineteenth century to African Americans in the late twentieth—to protect their interests. The committee system has also been instrumental to that end. Committee and subcommittee chairs automatically receive deference throughout the legislative chamber. Even members not on a particular committee will defer to its chair, because at some point they are likely to have some matter of interest and importance to their constituency come before that committee. In recent years we have seen that African American representatives serving as chairs or ranking members of powerful committees use their prerogatives just as segregationists did from about 1930 into the 1960s.

The fact is that blacks were denied rights not just because they were members of a minority but, more important, because they were not often permitted to vote or run for office in some regions of the country. As such they were never permitted access to legislative politics. That is no longer the case, and African American representatives are now among those best placed to gather seniority and wield power in committees and on the floor in state legislatures and the Congress.

In the end, the fallback position of direct democracy advocates is a strong one: the courts are there, at the state and federal level, to check the wishes of the majority when plebiscites violate minorities' constitutional rights. One can quarrel about the merits of this or that particular case, but the principle that minorities' rights are sacrosanct is not in question today. There is irony even in this point, however. Populists are most adamant in questioning the right of unelected, elitist judges to go against majority opinion on issues that involve controversial interpretations of the Constitution,[63] while at the same time citing these very same courts as a corrective for direct democratic institutions when they go too far.

5. Which Contributes More to Responsible
Governance, Direct or Representative Democracy?

In order to answer this question, we must define what constitutes "responsible governance." A precise definition can be the subject of legitimate disagreement, but it is reasonable to say that responsible governance is characterized at least by the following qualities: a big-picture view of public policy—how one policy might affect another or be integrated rationally with other policies; fiscal responsibility—essentially the idea that government should live within its means short of catastrophe or emergency; taking into consideration the interests of all citizens, whether they are well connected or not, in the making of public policy.

One of the most damaging criticisms of initiatives and referenda relates to the first quality. The piecemeal process of bringing disparate issues to the public's attention through the initiative or referendum process does not give voters the chance to consider the whole picture. Voters are not required to integrate issues, or even to consider whether expenditures that might be required with the passage of a given proposition should be made. An example would be "three strikes and you're out" legislation that would result in the need to build more prisons. What revenues might need to be enhanced to build the prisons? Or where should cuts in other programs be made to pay for it? In other words, with ballot initiatives voters are not asked to set priorities and make necessary trade-offs. Neither are they in a position to have to reconcile conflicting or incompatible measures that might appear on the same ballot.

Let us say that voters are confronted with a proposition that will put severe restrictions on the ability of the legislature to raise taxes at the same time as they are asked to vote on whether to dramatically increase the state's commitment to education. Legislators often operate under the constraints of a comprehensive budget process and the knowledge that by law (in the states) they may not run annual deficits. But voters are not required to consider the budgetary consequences of their actions on Election Day. The main point of having people in leadership positions in legislatures is to have them do that which citizens are in no position to do—construct some sort of rational whole out of a given year's budget. Of course, legislators may often not do a good job of making these kinds of decisions, but at least, say critics of direct democracy, they can be held accountable for their failures. No one is accountable for the decisions made at the ballot box in plebiscites that ignore budgetary realities.

Opponents of direct democracy cite myriad other weaknesses in the process. There is little systematic deliberation during the formative stage of the generation of an initiative that could lead to more carefully crafted legislation. Also, politics often requires leadership, defined as the ability to anticipate and move on issues that will confront a state or the country in the future. Alan Rosenthal charges that the initiative process enfeebles leadership by making legislative action subject to reversal on the whim of an unaccountable entrepreneur who has the wherewithal to put a measure on the ballot.[64] Legislators end up reacting instead of leading in states where ballot measures are common.

In addition, the importance in a democratic polity of consensus building is lost with direct democracy. Legislators have to work together on a wide range of issues over time and usually learn to work with one another to build a consensus on one issue in order to be able to work together better on future issues. More constituents are served by policy made by consensus than by policy that is passed by a slim majority vote in a plebiscite. In fact, such consensus-crafted policies can be better even for those who are not represented by an interest group involved in the process. Advocates of representative institutions assert that the cumbersomeness of legislative politics, particularly with bicameral legislatures and the executive veto, minimizes the amount of bad legislation that will be passed, which contributes to responsible governance.

On the other hand, advocates of direct democracy point out that legislatures often write bad laws, just as initiative generators do, and the motivations for all the compromising in the legislative process are rarely pure. Not only that, the endless bargaining and compromising in legislative session may distance the final public policy output from the wishes of the voters.

In fact, some scholars have found evidence that plebiscites are frequently more likely to reflect the views of the median voter on important matters of public policy.[65] For example, the economist John Matsusaka has shown that after many other factors are taken into account, direct democracy states have lower spending than other states, which by some measures is in keeping with what voters want.[66] Furthermore, it is not at all uncommon for legislatures to pass individual measures that would not pass if put to a vote of the people.[67]

One could argue that if the aim of direct democracy is to restrict the growth of government spending, which is thought by many fervent supporters of direct democracy to stifle economic growth and to pose a threat to individual and property rights, then there has been considerable success. Direct democracy states have fewer broad-based taxes and more user fees and charges than states without direct democracy, a policy approach popular with the broad based of middle-class voters. Through term limits, supermajority requirements for tax increases, expenditure limitations, and other changes, moderate and conservative populists have succeeded in changing the way government does business in several states. If government has gotten too expansive and too flabby, then direct democracy seems pretty clearly to be a corrective of sorts.

One of the reasons some populists want to see direct democracy at the federal level is that it is the federal government—the only government that may run deficits—that historically has been unable to live within its means. In the space of just the last twenty years—during peacetime, at that—the federal government has abused its privilege by running up the national debt from one to five trillion dollars, putting an oppressive interest burden on future generations.

The successes of direct democracy in limiting taxes and spending have had a downside, however, and these successes present a curious paradox. Some critics point out that direct democracy states tend to have less progressive tax policy than other states. In addition, some states suffer from greater indebtedness because of continued pressures for spending from the public and interest groups just as the sources for revenues are limited by plebiscites initiated by tax rebels.[68] The paradox is that voters, by putting into state constitutions supermajority requirements for raising revenue, may be making it extremely difficult or impossible to realize other desires they have such as increases in spending for education or other popular programs. The fact is that people often express conflicting views on what they expect from government, frequently indicating a preference for tighter budgets and lower taxes at the same time as they prefer more spending in a variety of specific areas.[69] The populist ideal that prescribes putting into law the wishes of the voters can be stymied if supermajority requirements for tax increases make it impossible to commit expenditures in areas the public wants.

There is another unintended consequence of successful efforts in direct democracy states to reduce spending and taxes. Direct democracy states tend to be those with a heritage of weak political parties and relatively strong interest group influence. This is a vestige of the populist-Progressive tradition that was strong enough in some states to both weaken the political parties and institute provisions for direct democracy.[70] Parties are the main vehicle for the expression of the interests of groups in the population with fewer resources; interest groups are vehicles for just the opposite, the better-off. When states institute stringent spending and taxation limits by initiative, there often ensues a furious scramble for scarce resources that are allocated by the legislative process. In these states what seems to happen is that those who have the ear of the legislators—usually the well-heeled lobbies—get their share of the take. The poor and underrepresented do worse. Thus, the influence of the special interests, the avowed enemies of populists of all stripes, may be enhanced in states with institutions of direct democracy.

These are the sorts of results that have led Peter Schrag to argue that the initiative process is at root a power grab by the white middle class against the increased influence minorities have managed to acquire in legislatures in recent years.[71] In California, not only have the poor been shortchanged, Schrag says, but everyone is upset with the government because the mishmash of unrelated propositions over the last couple of decades has tied the hands of legislators as they try to deal with the issues they were elected to address. California's infrastructure, particularly public education, has suffered grievously. As a result, Schrag concludes that direct democracy in the state has generated greater dissatisfaction with the performance of the government.

The conservative journalist George Will opines that direct democracy is also an invitation to demagoguery: although conservative populists are happy with some of their accomplishments in limiting the expansion of state governments and in putting into place tax limits, conservatives, he says, "have struck a Faustian bargain, advancing their agenda by a process that infuses public discourse with vulgarity and volatility, the prevention of which should be a primary purpose of conservatism."[72]

The best argument in favor of direct democratic institutions is that they have successfully reined in some excessive spending and taxing at the state level. Who could say that the federal government wouldn't benefit from some of the fiscal discipline imposed by these institutions? However, this advantage is partly counterbalanced by the tendency toward greater indebtedness in direct democracy states and the inability of institutions of direct democracy to take in the whole picture and effect rational budgetary trade-offs. Another unfortunate side effect is the tendency of institutions of direct democracy to enhance the bargaining position of special interests in budget politics.

Advocates of direct democracy acknowledge that these plebiscitary institutions need some tinkering; they are in their nascent stage, particularly in the context of the high-tech era, and it might be necessary to implement some changes and safeguards. Advocates maintain that it is especially important to make sure that ballot measures are written clearly, that voters receive easy-to-understand information regarding the consequences of their voting decision, and that a limited number of measures appear on the ballot during each election cycle.[73] Ideally, according to populists, institutions of direct democracy can serve as something akin to a fourth branch of government. The unfiltered voice of the people is needed to check the inherently corrupt processes of representative government, regardless of how blunt an instrument the plebiscite is.

Conclusion

The highlights of the comparison of representative and direct democratic institutions are the following points:

1. There is some evidence that voters have trouble making sense of ballot issues; on the other hand, voters do show some measurable ideological consistency on them. It is harder for voters to find reliable cues to guide their choice in plebiscite campaigns than it is when two major party candidates are running against each other. Though voters surely are not as informed as legislators are when voting on policy, they are also rarely duped into voting for measures they don't fully understand. Direct democracy is essentially conservative in the sense that voters tend to maintain the status quo when they are not certain what to do. Direct democracy advocates claim that, regardless of how informed voters are, they are more likely to consider the public interest than professional politicians who are prone to making policy to protect their careers.

2. Special interests are influential in state legislatures and the halls of Congress, but they are also very influential in plebiscite campaigns. However, narrow interests don't often succeed at the expense of the general public, and plebiscites that serve the interests of the diffuse public are more common than is frequently asserted by critics of direct democracy. Although it is impossible to tell whether special interests are more influential in legislatures or in plebiscites, it appears that direct democratic institutions may *increase* the influence of interest groups within state legislatures.

3. Courts in most states scrutinize the procedures used to put measures on the ballot as well as the content of those measures much more carefully than they do legislative procedures and laws that legislatures pass. This is likely to remain the case as long as the Guarantee Clause remains in Article IV of the U.S. Constitution.

4. It is relatively rare that plebiscites infringing on the rights of vulnerable minorities pass; some plebiscites have, however, been shown to increase animosity toward minorities even if they don't pass. Minority groups such as gays and African Americans are skittish of direct democracy and choose to protect their rights in the legislative process, probably because gaining power within the political parties and the committee system affords even small minorities the opportunity to prevent legislation they find noxious from ever becoming law. Direct democracy advocates rely on the courts to protect minorities from majority tyranny, which is ironic because these very same courts frequently are the objects of their derision.

5. States with direct democratic institutions have lower spending than other states and rely more heavily on user fees for revenue. Sometimes these states tend toward greater indebtedness, as the pressure to spend on popular programs remains strong even when tax revenues are not there. Though plebiscites may rein in excessive spending and lower taxes, voters deciding policy at the ballot box are not in a position to see the big budget picture and thus are not in a position to make rational trade-offs when funding is scarce.

Ultimately, the pivotal question is this: Which set of institutions better serves the public interest? Populists argue that elected representatives have a lot of things in mind other than the public interest when deciding how to vote on legislation. Many if not most representatives focus a large portion of their energies on saving their seats and promoting their political careers. Pursuing these ends may sometimes coincide with the pursuit of the public interest, but it may also frequently be the case that the public interest would be served if representatives did something that would likely lead to electoral defeat.[74] Some voters may also look at a ballot issue from a purely selfish perspective, but in most cases and for most voters there will not be a personal stake in the outcome. For that reason, populists contend, voters are more likely to consider the public interest first and foremost in casting a vote; certainly, according to populists, there is no particularly good reason to believe that a representative is in a better position to act on, or even have a grasp of, what is in the public interest than an ordinary citizen.

Defenders of representative decision-making make a more complicated argument. They claim that it is the *web of institutions and norms* in the legislative process that result in a more careful consideration of the public interest than the often ill-considered judgments of voters on Election Day.[75] At the federal level, the Senate and House terms of office are designed so that members consider legislation from different time perspectives: senators with their six-year terms take the long-term view; members of the House, who have to stand for office every two years, take the short-term view. Also, the makeup of their constituencies is different, another factor that influences their take on issues. In addition, only rarely does legislation become law without the signature of the president, who brings yet another perspective to the table. The fact that no bill can become law without making it through this cumbersome process means that legislation has to take into account various interests and perspectives, producing an outcome that is more likely to serve more people better.

Bernard Crick, the political theorist, argues that the public interest in a complex, heterogeneous democracy is better represented in the clash of interests, some of them irreconcilable, that must be negotiated and worked through face-to-face in representative institutions, than by taking a vote.[76] The public interest is principally a matter of procedural fairness, say the political scientists Elizabeth Theiss-Morse and John Hibbing: if the public business is conducted in a fair and open forum, then the public interest is served, even though the people may find those normal democratic processes messy and unattractive, fraught as they are with bombast, disagreement, compromise, and uncertainty.[77]

The legislative scholar Alan Rosenthal defends the qualities and value of the individual legislator:

> Legislators have their own rationales, and their own peculiar calculations, for figuring out what benefits their constituencies and the state as a whole. The procedures they use are neither scientific nor holistic. Legislators tend to see things in terms of increments and fragments. Moreover, they recognize the group basis of politics and the inevitable conflict among various interests and points of view. Their model of political democratic reality is being challenged today by those who claim to represent the public at large.[78]

Representative institutions are organized internally in such a way as to consider the aggregate effect of different policies. Direct democracy tends to break policy down into small fragments; each plebiscite determines whether a particular program or a particular tax is popular—and that's the end of the analysis. But legislatures consider the whole picture; budget committees, policy-steering committees, and party leaders are charged with considering how different policies integrate with one another. Sometimes unpopular concessions are required and trade-offs have to be made. The process is far from perfect, acknowledge the constitutionalists, but it is necessary to have an institution that can be held accountable for the big picture.

Even if one is persuaded by the constitutionalists' arguments, it appears that the simplicity of the populist position usually wins the day. Populists believe that the majoritarian principle is at the heart of democracy. Ordinary people are best able to judge what is in the public interest, especially in light of a legislative process infected by special interest considerations that are portrayed as antithetical to the public interest. Taking a vote is thus the best and most democratic way to determine the popular will, which should be implemented into policy. The claim made by constitutionalists that elected representatives are better able to determine what is in the people's interest is elitist and fundamentally undemocratic. According to Lynn Baker: "If the ordinary citizen cannot be trusted to make the laws by which she will be governed, why should she be given the responsibility of electing the representatives who will make those laws? Indeed, why should we leave the important task of lawmaking to representatives elected by the masses when an appointed bevy of Platonic Guards is available to do the job?"[79]

Of course, most Americans' position is not quite as extreme as Baker's. People in the United States display a reverence for the Founding, the Constitution, and the idea of checks and balances, while at the same time believing in populist principles and supporting institutions of direct democracy. Though alterations in the system of checks and balances do not receive widespread support, an amendment to provide for a national referendum procedure is popular. Some of the prescriptions of populists on the right and in the center are consistent with this ambivalence. These conflicting impulses lead to a desire for the restoration of a much less corrupt representative democracy of citizen-legislators, a desire that the term-limits movement taps into, with plebiscites as a safety valve to make sure representatives remain honest and responsive. Essentially, Americans want to have it both ways. They want to have their revered separation of powers and checks and balances, but they rather like the idea of having initiatives and referenda as complementary institutions.

I do not believe that these two impulses can produce a workable arrangement; they certainly haven't where the use of initiatives and referenda is widespread. For better or worse, plebiscitary democracy is corrosive of the principles of representative democracy, principally because it removes the accountability for policy from the shoulders of elected representatives. In addition, the incentive for members of representative institutions to put the time in to craft good legislation and to put together workable budgets is undermined by direct democracy. Notwithstanding these downsides, there is no doubt that the recourse citizens and groups have to the initiative process in the states in which it is available is highly popular for exactly the reasons cited by populists.

So is the public interest better expressed through the counting of votes at the ballot box or through the clash of interests and the various forms of deliberation in representative assemblies? For populists in America today, everything hinges on the method used—usually voting—to determine what the people want in public policy. In the next chapter, we will see that it is actually impossible for voting to do what populists say it can: determine in some kind of coherent and meaningful fashion the wishes of the electorate. This brings the very premise of populism into question.

5

Dispelling the
Populist Myth

As we have seen, ever since the late nineteenth century, American populists have expressed a deep-seated suspicion of representative institutions. They charge these institutions with being unrepresentative, unresponsive, and inhabited by professional politicians who cater to special interests instead of serving the public interest. Some modern-day populists go so far as to question the need for these institutions; after all, with technological advances it is no longer impracticable for people to rule themselves directly.

Populists say the people's views on policy, as expressed in polls or at the polls, should be implemented into public policy. This position is predicated on a very simple notion, the populist theory of voting: the results of a plebiscite or an election represent or reflect the will of the people. Since voting is the central participatory act in a democracy, this theory of voting amounts to the foundational premise of populism as it was defined in Chapter 2: "the belief that a legitimate democratic political system should be arranged to ascertain the popular will, usually by the majority-rule principle, and then implement that will into public policy."

The simple and seemingly obvious notion that the results of a vote accurately reflect the views of the people actually does not hold up under scrutiny. This point is counterintuitive for most people, but it is a very important one because it undermines the populist view of democracy. The main idea I develop in full in this chapter is that institutions of direct democracy have intrinsic and serious shortcomings. We can never assume that the people's views are represented by the outcome of a vote, whether the vote is set up as an election or plebiscite between two choices (a two party election or a yes-or-no vote on a constitutional amendment or a statutory initiative) or the public is asked to choose from among more than two options. Let us see why this is the case.

Introduction

The field of inquiry known as "public choice," which was mentioned in Chapter 1, is concerned with the mechanisms of political and economic decision-making. It has been an important subfield in the disciplines of political science and economics for several decades now, particularly since the publication in 1963 of the second edition of *Social Choice and Individual Values,* by the economist Kenneth Arrow. Specialists within that field, called social-choice theorists, study how the preferences of individuals are counted and then translated into an enforceable decision—really the essence of democratic politics. This involves looking at how votes are counted, decisions are made, and results are interpreted in elections, committees in a legislative body, and in those legislative bodies as a whole.

Scholars in this field have made many important discoveries about elections and group decision-making and have produced dozens of articles and books, in which they almost always use highly technical jargon and relatively sophisticated mathematics to explain their findings. This is unfortunate, because some of these findings are quite relevant, particularly in relation to the question of direct versus representative democracy, and, in many cases the basic principles are relatively simple and straightforward. The sad truth is that many political scientists and economists have been aware of them for years, but no one has bothered to translate these findings and principles into plain English, even for the most informed and attentive strata of the public.[1]

The modern study of social decision-making could be dated back to the rediscovery in the mid-twentieth century of a mathematical paradox originally recognized two centuries before by the French social philosopher the Marquis de Condorcet.[2] Kenneth Arrow, Duncan Black, and others dubbed this basic discovery the "paradox of voting." The paradox shows that the results of a vote can make no sense, even when all individual members of a society hold rational and informed opinions. In other words, there can be a curious and counterintuitive result when tabulating votes—one can add up the individual preferences of the public, even a hypothetical public made up of perfectly rational individuals, and arrive at a result that is literally incoherent. In short, individual rationality does not necessarily translate into group rationality.[3]

Recently some mathematicians have started their own investigation of this paradox using computer simulations to confirm what these earlier scholars found. In a report published in 1998, two mathematicians, Dr. David A. Meyer of the University of California at San Diego and Dr. Thad A. Brown of the University of Missouri, in the journal *Physical Review Letters,* presented formal proof that collective decisions can be chaotic, even when the views of all participants are known and a standard voting rule is strictly applied. The *New York Times* reported their principal conclusion:

> When a group of decision-makers must choose between three or more options[4] by comparing two of them at a time, the collective outcome often depends on the order in which the choices are presented. The outcome can cycle chaotically, the mathematicians found. Even non-human decision-makers—the computers that buy and sell commodities according to programmed rules, for example—are subject to chaotic uncertainty, a situation in which prediction becomes impossible.[5]

Public choice scholars have spent much of the last few decades building on the basic insight provided by the paradox of voting. If it is in fact possible that a group of well-informed people cannot arrive at a meaningful decision by taking a vote, how often is this the case and under what conditions does the paradox appear? Are there ways of counting votes that get around this problem? Are there fair ways to narrow choices down to two for the purpose of arriving at a clear majority decision? The scholars' relevant findings are summarized below, starting with the basic paradox of voting:

1. Whereas an individual can make a rational, logical, and coherent ordering of choices presented to him or her, it is often impossible for a group, even one made up of well-informed and rational individuals, to order their choices coherently.
2. Majorities in party politics are really unstable coalitions of minorities that rarely if ever carry clear and comprehensive policy instructions.
3. Different legitimate and widely used methods of decision-making often produce different winners.
4. Decision-making processes may be manipulated by strategic voters.
5. We can never be sure that the popular will is reflected in the result of a decision-making process.

Do the results of elections or plebiscites reflect the desires or will of the people on questions of public policy? The answer from scholars in the field: sometimes no, and we can never be sure. These findings are a devastating blow to populism and direct democracy. Elections between candidates for office and plebiscites on policy often cannot be interpreted to reflect any coherent viewpoint at all, and they can never be interpreted with any certainty or precision. Elections and plebiscites cannot serve the purpose that populists invest them with. Instead, they are very blunt instruments that can at best be interpreted only in the most general way. In this chapter we will see exactly why this is so.

The next three sections of the chapter are designed to illustrate the points listed above. First we investigate the problems associated with interpreting the results of elections between parties or candidates for high office. The inevitably coalitional nature of mass politics, as well as the tendency of some citizens to vote on constitutional principles instead of along the lines of the populist model, renders futile the effort to interpret comprehensive policy mandates from these elections.

Next, I develop a hypothetical scenario in which a community is asked to decide how to use surplus public monies. We will be privy to the views of all the voters, which enables us to take a micro-level look at group decision-making. By doing that we can gain some insight into the uncertain and arbitrary nature of any process that is used to determine a winner from among three or more options. We shall see exactly why we can never be sure that the desires of the public are reflected in the outcome of a vote.

Scholars of public choice have more recently applied their analytical tools to the particular case of the direct democratic institutions common in the United States, initiatives and referenda. The so-called "paradox of multiple elections" illustrates some of the peculiar, even sometimes illogical, outcomes that can result from these forms of plebiscitary democracy. Using some hypothetical examples, we will be able to see precisely some of the problems inherent in making public policy on the basis of initiative and referenda results.

The fact that elections cannot serve the purpose populists want them to serve obviously does weaken the case for plebiscitary democracy substantially. But is the decision-making process in representative institutions any better? I think yes, and at the end of the chapter I suggest some reasons to support this view. Those will be fully developed in Chapter 6.

The Old Populist Paradigm and the Myth of the Mandate

The traditional answer to the question of how best to identify the popular will was to hold an election according to the responsible party model. In parliamentary systems that operate under that model, the public makes its choice on Election Day between or among parties with distinct platforms. The party that secures a majority in the legislature gets full control of the government, gaining the ability to implement its platform relatively unobstructed. That party is then held responsible for its actions at the next election. Great Britain is one of the better examples in the world of this sort of system.[6]

   The American system of separated powers is designed—deliberately so in some ways—*not* to achieve the populist ideal. Instead, the system is based on the liberal democratic model; this involves cumbersome checks and balances between the branches of government as a protection for the liberty of the citizens. The theory is that unobstructed majorities at the national level pose a threat to citizens who hold unpopular viewpoints. The legislative body is made up of two chambers with roughly equal power, the Senate and the House of Representatives. One of them, the Senate, was originally and to a great extent remains about as antipopulist a democratic institution as one could intentionally devise.[7] The House, on the other hand, is characterized by responsiveness to demographic changes. These legislative chambers are likely often to be at odds, given their different constituent bases and constitutional prerogatives. In addition, there is a separately elected executive to compete with. By contrast, the head of government in the typical parliamentary system is not separately elected; he is the leader of the majority party in the legislature, and he forms a governing cabinet from among the members.

   To the extent that anyone claims a mandate in American national politics, ordinarily it is the president and not the congressional parties. The president is the only person elected by the whole country, which makes it in most cases more credible for him to claim a mandate to implement his platform. The president is also often held responsible by many voters for the state of affairs in the country, even though he is typically stymied in the enactment of his agenda by the Congress.

   Though these constitutional arrangements militate against unfettered majority rule, the American system does have one distinctive quality that might seem to facilitate it. This is the existence of a relatively stable two-party system for nearly the duration of the republic, with the Democratic and Republican parties dominating national politics since the 1850s. The result is that one of the most diverse and fluid countries in the world has the most stable party system.

   There are endless academic squabbles as to exactly why the system seems to lend itself to stable two-party politics. Indisputably one of the important reasons that the Democrats and Republicans maintained their hegemony in the late nineteenth and early twentieth centuries was that other parties were actually or effectively outlawed in many states. In more recent years, the two parties have opened their doors to groups previously left out of the parties—both now have an open door policy in most states. The parties have proved incredibly adaptable, especially in the face of the threats to their legitimacy during the tumultuous 1960s and early 1970s.

   Despite the cumbersome representative institutions outlined in the Constitution, we in the United States seem to have stumbled upon what at first blush appears to be a neat and easy way to derive policy instructions from elections: a stable two-party system. When there are only two choices in an election, we can be sure that the winner of the election is the choice of the majority of the people voting. In Great Britain, the existence of a stable and fairly popular third party usually makes the attainment of a popular electoral majority impossible—even though one party has managed to gain a majority in the House of Commons in recent elections. Even the 1997 Labour landslide was achieved with fewer than half of the popular vote. How can such an election be interpreted as reliably reflecting the wishes of the majority of the people? In the United States, if the parties' candidates have presented clear platforms, it does not seem to be too much of a stretch to say that the winning party should be able to implement its program unhindered by antidemocratic constitutional restraints. Populists contend that we could streamline the system by having all members of Congress come up for election at four-year intervals together with the president, who would be charged with articulating an overarching vision. In that way, it is more likely one party could capture both the legislative and executive branches and carry out a mandate to enact the people's will, overcoming the obstacle of separate powers.

But this scenario ignores a crucial issue: How does the political system neatly narrow the choices down to two parties and two presidential candidates? In a free society, there are more than two plausible candidates for president. Is the narrowing done democratically? If not, then how can one say that the people's will is reflected in the final choice?

In fact, until 1972 the Democratic and Republican parties never claimed that the choice of presidential nominees was arrived at democratically, according to populist principles. Up until that time the leadership of the parties claimed the legitimate power to nominate candidates they considered fit for office. There was no pretense that the public would determine the nominees; rather, party leaders considered themselves (and were considered by many) to be legitimate representatives of their constituent groups empowered to make decisions in the name of the rank and file. Frequently they stifled debate and employed other methods of power politics to get their way.

There are good arguments for having a system with two strong parties controlled by leaders ultimately accountable to their rank and file, and there is no question about what was happening. Elites in the political system engineered two candidates for Election Day. Not only that, they went to great lengths to discourage the formation of viable alternative parties. Ordinary people did not have any direct input in deciding the candidates and generally did not have a fair opportunity to organize and present third or fourth choices. Thus it could not reasonably be said that the electoral results produced by such a system reflected the popular will. The people simply passed judgment on two choices presented to them by party leaders.

The party system today is very different. As we have seen, the two parties, in their quest to remain viable, opened their doors in the 1970s to just about anyone willing and able to get involved and active. They both hold primary elections that in most states are effectively open to all voters to determine the nominees for all positions up to and including the presidency. The parties thus are claiming a sort of populist or plebiscitary legitimacy in the selection of candidates—the rank and file are choosing the candidates instead of the leaders.[8]

The opening up of the parties was thought by populists to be a way to legitimize a two-party system that had become dominated by unresponsive elites. Once the parties had committed to populist democratic processes at the nomination stage, the thinking went, the general election would become a true reflection of the will of the people. We will see later exactly why any process of narrowing options to two, such as that used by the parties to determine their nominees for president, cannot be relied upon to contribute to such a result. But for now, for the sake of argument, we will accept the assumption that the process of determining presidential nominees does reflect accurately the will of each party's rank-and-file voters. In that case, can we say there is a policy mandate for the majority winner of the general election?[9]

One of many reasons to be skeptical of the concept of the mandate is this basic insight about the nature of electoral politics: voters are as likely to vote against one of the candidates as to vote for the other candidate and his platform. For example, Jimmy Carter's election in 1976 probably was due mostly to a reaction to the desultory performance of the economy during President Gerald Ford's tenure in office and the controversial pardon of Richard Nixon by Ford. Obviously most voters preferred Carter to Ford, but the idea that his election reflected anything specific about what policies the public wanted is far-fetched, especially since Carter did little during the campaign to develop a clear policy platform. In fact, if anything, Carter tried to make a virtue of his fuzziness on the issues, according to the journalist Jules Witcover.[10]

Another reason to be skeptical of the idea that an election is a mandate is the nature of the broad-based, big tent, umbrella parties that have always dominated American politics. This quality means that even when a candidate receives a resounding majority in the 60 percent range, as did Lyndon Johnson in 1964, Nixon in 1972, and Ronald Reagan in 1984, the society's choice on the issues of the day may not be interpretable from the election results.[11] For example, consider the reasons different segments of the population voted for Reagan in his reelection campaign of 1984. Some were responding to the improving economy, others primarily to his tough negotiating stance with the Soviet Union, still others to Reagan's personal bonhomie, and others to his conservative rhetorical stands on social issues. Whatever mandate one could derive was murky at best; in fact, many public opinion polls indicated stronger support for his Democratic opponent, Walter Mondale, on many of the major issues of the day, including deficit spending, the tension in Nicaragua, and arms control talks with the Soviet Union.

One of the best examples of an effort to use an election to validate a concrete policy platform in American history was the congressional election of 1994. The House Republicans went to great lengths to advertise their Contract with America, a specific ten-point program. Republicans went on to capture the House of Representatives for the first time in forty years in what was one of the most surprising election outcomes of the century. (The Senate also went Republican by a decisive margin. Many GOP Senate candidates were sympathetic to the Contract's provisions.) If any American election could be said to be a reflection of the popular will on a clear policy platform, it had to be that one.

But the idea that the American public expressed an endorsement of the Contract with America on Election Day that year did not hold up under scrutiny. Every competent observer of House elections noted that most of the Republicans who won previously Democrat-held seats did so more because they successfully exploited the weaknesses of their opponents and were able to compete financially with Democratic incumbents accustomed to token opposition than because they trumpeted the Contract.

What we are stumbling upon here is a more profound perspective on democratic elections contested by mass parties than that held by populists. Majorities in elections are better thought of as *coalitions of minorities* with varying and sometimes conflicting interests than as a coherent group holding one view.[12] James Madison understood this concept more than two hundred years ago, and it was an important part of the foundation of his political philosophy. He regarded majorities as temporary and fleeting and held out the hope that elected officials would recognize this and not wield their power over the losing parties in elections; the wise politician would recognize that in the fullness of time he would be in the minority and would not wish to have his rights trampled on. Of course Madison wasn't naïve enough to depend on the goodwill of politicians to preserve the liberties and rights of losers in politics. That is why he advocated the institutionalization of obstacles to the abuse of power, particularly checks and balances and separated branches of government which are the bedrock of our constitutional system.

Most politicians understand the point about coalitions of minorities instinctively. If they end up on the losing side in an election, or even on a particular policy they are committed to, they don't give up. They realize that the reason they lost may be that they failed to come up with an issue to split the majority coalition on the winning side. Why do losing politicians keep campaigning? Why do losers in the legislative process keep offering amendments or trying to get their idea considered in a different committee or attached to a different bill? They are not all tilting at windmills. They are in constant search for a new issue or a more persuasive argument or a different venue that will upset the prevailing balance of power. In common parlance, they try to drive a wedge between groups that make up the majority that favors the other party by focusing on a new policy option that appeals to one group.

An example from recent American politics of this wedge approach illustrates this point well.[13] In the middle decades of the twentieth century the Democratic party enjoyed hegemony in American politics that had its basis in the highly popular welfare state policies implemented during the New Deal. How could the Republicans possibly upset the winning coalition the Democrats had assembled, made up of southern segregationists, northern industrial union members, the elderly, Jews, Catholics, and blacks, in support of the guarantee of economic security implicit in Social Security and other programs? What it took was the ingenuity of some of the more entrepreneurial politicians of the 1950s and '60s. Taking his cue, ironically, from the Alabama Democrat George Wallace, the Republican Richard Nixon first destroyed Democratic hegemony by stressing law and order in the face of the crime wave of the 1960s. He decimated the Democratic presidential coalition, reducing its share of the vote in the 1968 election to 43 percent from the heights of 61 percent in 1964. Nixon himself only managed a slim plurality in that election,[14] but between 1968 and 1972 he consolidated a strong majority on the basis of associating his party with social conservatism, against Democratic social liberalism.

What Nixon did was bring a second salient issue dimension into the political arena. Hitherto the fight between the parties had been largely over big government—and it was a fight the Democrats had won.[15] Nixon threw into the mix another issue, social questions, sometimes with a racial tinge, which served to disrupt the Democratic coalition of minorities. A crucial segment of voters who generally tended Democratic began to vote with the Republican party on the basis of crime and cultural issues instead of pocketbook issues.[16] Mary and Thomas Edsall have shown how Ronald Reagan brilliantly built on Nixon's introduction of social issues as wedge issues by using these issues to discredit the welfare state.[17] Essentially, the Edsalls argue that Reagan linked big government to unpopular programs that helped racial minorities—affirmative action, busing, and especially Aid to Families with Dependent Children (AFDC)—and built a case for reducing taxes in order to shrink the welfare state. The introduction of these new issues and the realignment of segments of voters made it next to impossible for a Democrat to win the White House for nearly a generation. Even the popular President Clinton, who finally ended the presidential drought for the Democrats, was not able to secure a majority of the popular vote in his two winning presidential campaigns.

Clearly, seemingly stable majorities in electoral politics are always temporary, because they coalesce on the basis of the issues relevant during a specific time. Meanwhile, politicians are earnestly working in the wings to capitalize on new issues or develop new ways to sell old issues. To see politics as static in a free society is to be a fool—and a loser. In free countries, there are always people looking for an issue to exploit in order to satisfy their ambitions or to advance a cause. The more open the political system is, the more unstable the party coalitions are likely to be.

In the end, two-party elections may be a good thing. There is rarely doubt as to the legitimacy of a person or party that takes power as a result of a true majority vote. In that sense, we may be lucky in the United States to have had majority winners so regularly owing to the dominance of only two parties. But majorities can be and often are construed to reflect the popular will on issues of the day, even though electoral majorities in mass politics usually are constituted of diverse and sometimes divergent minority interests. These coalitions are always vulnerable to the introduction of a new issue that will upset the balance in favor of the other party as it attempts to wedge off a group of voters from the previous winning coalition. A coalition obviously can be fractured when its winning position becomes less popular; but this can also happen even when a winning position remains popular if a new issue emerges to replace it as the most salient concern for a substantial segment of voters. For example, large segments of the welfare state have remained popular, but in the 1960s and '70s social issues and race emerged as more salient issues for many voters, and these broke apart the Democratic coalition.

There is yet another factor that is frequently ignored by populists wishing to interpret election results as pointing to policy prescriptions. Many Americans vote for *constitutional* reasons. They cast their vote for the presidential candidate whom they trust more to carry out the major constitutional functions of the presidency, which have little to do with policy platforms and everything to do with the conduct of foreign affairs, the protection of America's interests in the world, and the duty faithfully to execute the laws of the land. Populists think that voters should come into the voting booth with a checklist of issue positions by which to judge the candidates. But this, to many voters, is a narrow-minded way of deciding a presidential election; instead, many make a judgment on the basis of character and trust.

None of this is to say that a winning candidate or party shouldn't try to implement its program or platform. That is often the point of winning—not just to gain power but to use that power to put in place the policies of the party. But if we understand what majorities really consist of, we understand something more profound about politics than populists do. A comprehensive policy mandate is very unlikely to be reflected in the outcome of an election between mass parties, and we should be suspicious of claims to a broad mandate for policy initiatives. To the extent that they exist they will be temporary and fleeting. There may be parts of a winning party's platform that enjoy strong support, but even positions that are popular on Election Day may become less so subsequently if opponents can come up with persuasive new arguments or more attractive alternative positions. A majority of votes cast for the candidates of a certain party indicates only one thing for certain—more than half the people prefer one candidate or party to the other(s). Nothing more and nothing less.

Testing the Populist Theory of Voting: A Micro Look

One of the many intuitively appealing aspects of populism is its straightforward simplicity. If you want to have people rule themselves, lay out the options and take a vote. If elections between mass parties rarely convey a clear policy message, then let the people make policy directly by plebiscite.

Naturally, there will almost always be more than two policy options to choose from on any policy matter that anyone cares about. But this does not seem to pose an insuperable obstacle.[18] Arrangements could be made to permit people to vote on multiple policy options at once—this is what happens in a primary election among candidates for a party's nomination—and either award the victory to the first place finisher or, if no candidate or option receives greater than 50 percent of the vote, have a runoff between the top two finishers.

There is another way to deal with multiple policy options in plebiscites. Simply have voters consider each option in turn with the choice of voting yes or no on each one. (A "no"-vote usually means maintenance of the status quo.) A rule, called a "kill clause," can be instituted whereby the option with the most votes, assuming it received a majority, is the winner.

In all cases, the method is simple, and it seems as though the people's will can be done. Of course, as I have said, the interpretation of the results of elections and plebiscites is nowhere near that simple. In fact, the most preferred choice probably loses out fairly often and there are times when the policy preferences of a group are not coherent. We will see exactly why in this section.

But first, we need to lay the groundwork for analysis. First, we will look at some simplified scenarios. A group of people is deciding among three policy alternatives.[19] We will consider scenarios of two kinds. In one, the decision-making rule dictates narrowing the choices to two for the purpose of identifying the final winner. In the other the voters will determine the winner by choosing from among all three options on one vote. We will also do something that is impossible to do in the real world of politics: we will be omniscient observers, privy to the true feelings of voters regarding all of the options presented to them in the hypotheticals.

To do this, we need to define what would constitute a group's most preferred choice—its "will," in populist jargon. If there are only two choices, it is easy to define what the public's preferred choice is: the option that receives more votes. But how do you determine a preferred choice in a multi-option field? The following guideline receives widespread support from experts in the field of public choice: "The people's choice in a field of alternatives greater than two is that alternative which would beat all others if they were paired against each other in one-on-one contests."[20]

This is an obvious and reasonable solution to the problem of defining the most preferred choice of a group. If one alternative can beat all others when paired off against them, it stands to reason it is the most preferred choice. This is no different in principle from saying that the professional football team that can beat all of its rivals is the best in the league.

Example 1: The Paradox of Voting

The city of Surplusville has twenty voters. (This could be thought of as 20,000, 200,000, or 2 million, but it is easier to picture the situation with just twenty.) Surplusville has collected a windfall in tax revenues this year and has enough money to fund a major capital improvement. There seems to be significant public sentiment for building new lanes on the major commuter thoroughfare, which has become congested of late, as well as for putting in a new runway at the airport. Unfortunately, the surplus money in the budget can pay for only one of those projects. There is also some support for returning the money to the taxpayers in the form of a tax rebate. Surplusville is a town with a strong populist heritage that decides issues like these by plebiscite. Furthermore, all of the voters of Surplusville are model citizens—they are rational and fully informed about public issues. So the voters of Surplusville must decide from these three options:

Airport renovations (A)
Road improvements (R)
Tax rebate (TR)

As omniscient observers, we know the following about the voters' preferences, including their second-choice preferences. As it turns out, nine of the twenty voters (V 1–9) are regular commuters; they prefer the road improvements option (R) to the others, with the airport runway renovations (A) second, and a tax rebate (TR) third. Six voters (V 10–15) travel by plane a good bit but are staunch economic conservatives. Because of that, they favor the tax rebate (TR), with airport improvements (A) second and the road improvements (R) the least desired of the three. Five voters (V 16–20) are strong supporters of airport renovations (A); they don't drive much, so the tax rebate (TR) is second and the road improvements (R) the least preferred option. All the voters, being rational, prefer their first choice to their second and their second choice to their third; they also prefer their first choice to their third. Their preferences are "transitive" in the mathematical sense that if A is bigger than B and B is bigger than C, then C is logically bigger than A.

In our experimental situation let us see which option would win in different cases, using two different voting rules commonly in place in the United States.

RULE I (plurality winner): Each voter casts a single vote for his/her first choice; the option with the most votes wins.
RULE II (run-off): Same as Rule I, except that in the case that no option receives more than 50 percent of the vote, a run-off is held between the top two finishers in which the top vote getter wins.

Employing Rule I produces a victory for adding new lanes to the commuter highway. This option receives the votes of nine people; the tax re-

TABLE 5.1 Surplusville's Voter Preferences on Use of Surplus Revenues

	First Choice	*Second Choice*	*Third Choice*
V 1–9	R	A	TR
V 10–15	TR	R	A
V 16–20	A	TR	R

bate gets six votes and the airport improvements get five votes. But nine is not a majority of the twenty votes cast. So if Rule II is in effect, a run-off must be held between option R and option TR. In this case, the supporters of the airport improvements, with their first choice out of the running, would vote for their second choice, the tax rebate. The tax rebate would carry the day, 11–9. Thus, the two different methods of voting produce two different results.

Rule I: Option R wins with 9 votes, to 6 for TR and 5 for A.
Rule II: Option TR wins 11–9 in a run-off against R.

The citizens of the city, being committed to identifying the true will of the people, might be confused at this point. Which option, R or TR, is truly the more preferred option? The preferred option, as we saw at the top of the section, is the one that can beat the other in a one-on-one contest. Obviously, then, TR should be the winner, as it defeated R when they were pitted against one another in the run-off. Thus, the winner by Rule II, the run-off rule, better reflects the people's views than the winner by Rule I.

It might seem as though TR represents the "popular will." But there is one very important reason to think otherwise. As omniscient observers, we know that more voters (the R supporters and the A supporters, fourteen of the twenty voters) prefer airport renovations to a tax rebate. If airport renovations could ever have been paired against the tax rebate, the airport plan would have been the winner. But neither of our rules provided for that matchup.

We have uncovered a very odd fact about the preferences of the voters in this particular scenario. As a group they favor road improvements over airport improvements, which are favored over tax rebates, which, in turn, are favored over road improvements. Each individual has logical, transitive preferences, but the group does not. For example, V 1–9 all like R better than A and A better than TR (depicted as R>A>TR), and they like R, their first choice, better than TR, their last choice, as we would expect. But the group as a whole, while also liking R over A and A over TR, *likes TR over R* (or R>A>TR>R). The fact that rational voters with transitive preferences can produce an irrational—intransitive—result like this one is called the paradox of voting. Here is a summary of the results of that paradox comparing the transitive preferences of the voters and the intransitive preference of the group:

Individuals' Preferences Compared to Group Preference.   All individuals are logical

V 1–9: R>A>TR, with R>TR, as expected with logical preference ordering

V 10–15: TR>R>A, with TR>A, as expected with logical preference
ordering

V 16–20: A>TR>R, with A>R, as expected with logical preference ordering

The group is not logical

V 1–20:

R>A>TR>R

This is a cyclical phenomenon, unlike the individual orderings. No
matter where we start we can go around and around. If we start with A,
we have the same result:

A>TR>R>A

Or if we start with TR, we have:

TR>R>A>TR

In this situation, since the group preference really doesn't make sense, it
cannot be said that there is a "popular will." The citizens of Surplusville,
as a group, do not have a coherent viewpoint; they most certainly do not
have a most preferred choice, since each choice can be defeated by one of
the others when they are paired off against each other. Unfortunately for
populists, some variation of this kind of scenario is not uncommon.
Computer simulations make unmistakably clear that as the field of choices
increases, the chance that a group of people does not have a most preferred
choice increases.[21] In these sorts of cases, the selection of a winner may be
entirely arbitrary and dependent on the type of voting method used.[22]

The problems with interpreting these plebiscite results can be made
much more complex with the addition of a human component: political
savvy. In the real world, voters and legislators frequently do not vote according to their true preferences in a strategic calculation. They do this either to enhance the chance that their first choice will ultimately prevail or,
at the very least, to damage the prospects of a despised option. Of course
voters in the real world do not know the true preferences of all the other
voters. But many people make strategic calculations on the basis of informed opinion—maybe tracking polls or news stories; legislators especially make use of conversations with colleagues.

To examine a scenario taking such calculations into account, let us imagine that Rule II, the run-off procedure, is in effect. What if several of the V 1–9 voters, the road improvements advocates, had a good sense of the political landscape and were wary of their prospects of defeating their last choice, the tax rebate, in a run-off. (As we saw above, the tax rebate would defeat road improvements in a run-off if the voters expressed their true preferences at every stage.) They much prefer the airport renovations to the tax rebate, so they are strongly interested in defeating the tax rebate option. If six out of the group V 1–9 decided to vote for their second choice, airport renovations, in the first round, the airport plan would win the day without a run-off.

Outcome with Strategic Voters Under Rule II.

R: 3 votes (V 1–3 vote for R; V 4–9 vote strategically for A)
TR: 6 votes (V 10–15)
A: 11 votes (V 16–20 and V 4–9, who cast votes for their second option)

This result would probably be interpreted as a strong endorsement of airport renovations and a reflection of the popular will. It is a majority vote, after all, over 50 percent. Of course, as omniscient observers we know otherwise. (In fact we know that the voters of the city as a group do not have a preferred position.)

The important point illustrated by this example is that even a majority vote can be deceiving. The potential actions of strategic participants *always cast doubt on the nature of the outcome of a group decision.* Decision-making processes involving more than two choices are manipulable, as can be seen in this example—the problem is that in the real world we never know exactly how or when.

This is not to say that the result of this election with strategic voting was in any sense "illegitimate"; the outcome would be and should be regarded as legitimate. Every voter had the same fair chance to try to achieve his or her ends. Voting strategically is not the same thing as cheating. But to say that there is a legitimate winner (there was), and to say that there is a clear most preferred choice (in this case there wasn't) or anything resembling the "popular will" are two different things. We can derive agreed-upon legitimate decision-making procedures; it is, however, impossible to conclude that the winner—even a majority winner—reflects the public's true preferences. We need to keep in mind that election results are often artifacts of the decision-making rules and strategic calculations, not perfect reflections of the group's preferences or the "popular will."

Example 2: Decision-making When
There Is a Preferred Choice

Lots of times a group will have a clear choice—one choice that can beat all the others when they are paired against it. But problems sometimes arise anyway. Different election rules can produce different results, and the outcomes can be manipulated by strategic participants who favor options that are not so popular.

We will assume the same political dilemma for Surplusville, and we will also assume that most of the voters have the same preferences. The difference: the group most supportive of the road improvements (V 1–9) favors a tax rebate over airport renovations. Here is the new distribution of voter opinion:

If we employ Rules I and II, we will end up with the same results as in the first scenario. Option R would win the plurality vote with Rule I. Option TR would win with the standard run-off.

But the difference in the views of the voters in this situation has profound implications. Going by our definition of a most preferred alternative, we now have one. Consider all the possible matched pairings of alternatives:

TR versus R: TR wins 11–9 (gaining votes of A supporters)
R versus A: R wins 15–5 (gaining the support of TR voters)
A versus TR: TR wins 15–5 (gaining the support of R voters)

TR defeats the other two options when competing against them. TR meets the criterion for the most preferred alternative of the citizens of Surplusville. The group preference is transitive and rational, just like the individual preferences. It is TR>R>A, TR is favored over A. The first choice defeats the third choice this time. Of course our two voting rules came up with different winners, but perhaps we can settle on the run-off as the superior method since it identified the most preferred choice, TR,

TABLE 5.2 Surplusville's Voter Preferences on Use of Surplus Revenues (slightly altered)

	First Choice	*Second Choice*	*Third Choice*
V 1–9	R	TR	A
V 10–15	TR	R	A
V 16–20	A	TR	R

while the plurality winner method didn't. Studies do, in fact, indicate that the run-off system is better for identifying the true preference of a group when such a preference exists. It is not infallible, unfortunately.[23]

But in the real world of politics we must, again, consider the potential for strategic calculation by some of the voters. We assumed voters expressed their true preferences in this most recent example. As previously discussed, people in our hypothetical town may endorse the idea *in theory* that a decision-making process should identify the popular will, but in practice at least some people will do what they can to make sure that they get their first choice or avoid the selection of their least favorite alternative. In the following example, just two crafty supporters of road improvements alter the outcome in their favor under Rule II, the run-off voting rule.

Operating under Rule II, a few supporters of R are insightful enough to see the writing on the wall. They feel confident they will make the run-off, but they are concerned that their likely opponent, the tax rebate, would defeat them in the final vote. (As we saw earlier, the most preferred option, the tax rebate, would in fact defeat road improvements in a run-off.) But they feel their chances would be much better if only they could face airport improvements in the final.

If we look at the preferences of the voters, we can see that it would only take the defection of two strategic voters from among V 1–9 to give A seven instead of five votes. R would be reduced to seven, losing two of its supporters (the ones who defected and voted strategically for A in the first vote). TR would stay the same at six. The run-off would now be between A and R, the most preferred choice, TR, having been eliminated because of strategic voting. In that scenario, as we can see, tax rebate supporters prefer road improvements to airport renovations. The R supporters who voted strategically would come back to the fold. R would emerge the winner by a resounding 15–5 vote.

Run-off Outcome with Strategic Voting.   First round

   A: 7 votes (receiving 2 extra votes from strategic R supporters)
   TR: 6 votes
   R: 7 votes (losing its 2 strategic voters)

Run-off

   R: 15 votes (regains its strategic defectors and gains support of TR
      people)
   A: 5 votes

Conceivably, no one would be the wiser, and it would appear that R was the clear choice of the public. But, in fact, we know that the outcome was manipulated by just a few savvy participants who managed to manipulate the process such that the community's most preferred option lost. There may be better and worse motivations for strategic voting, but the fact is that the incentive to vote strategically is frequently strong when the field of options is greater than two.

What Do We Make of This?

Unfortunately for the populist theory of voting, interpreting the outcome of decision-making processes that attempt to pick winners from among more than two options is fraught with problems. Sometimes a group of people cannot express a coherent viewpoint, as we saw in the paradox-of-voting example. Decision-making rules may be arbitrary, sometimes resulting in the selection of the wrong option, as we saw in Example 2, and almost any decision-making arrangement, particularly those that involve narrowing options down to two, can be manipulated by strategic voters.

The most important point stressed by public choice scholars is the *indeterminacy* of the outcome of any decision-making process. Even majority votes, as we saw, may be subject to manipulation. Without omniscience, we can never know for sure whether outcomes reflect the views of the people, whether they were manipulated, and whether a group of people even has a most preferred choice.

Initiatives and referenda are frequently held on complex issues for which there are three or more viable alternative approaches. Though any single initiative or referendum is conducted in a way similar to the final vote in the legislative process—a "yes"-vote indicates support for a proposal, and "no"-vote is a vote for the status quo—multiple options sometimes do come to a vote in a curious way in plebiscites. And, just as in the examples we have looked at, the outcomes may not make sense.

Initiatives and Referenda:
The Paradox of Multiple Elections

Recently, public choice scholars, particularly Steven Brams, Marc Kilgour, and William Zwicker, have extended the lessons of social choice theory to the results of initiatives and referenda.[24] The principles about elections and plebiscites that were illustrated in the examples above still apply, and in addition, some new, relevant lessons can be drawn about the public policy consequences of initiatives and referenda.

What is significant is that several plebiscites often appear on the same ballot. As the number of these measures increases beyond just a few, it may be that only a small number of voters, or even none at all, will approve of the overall outcome—the combination of measures that pass and that fail. Brams, Kilgour, and Zwicker have presented considerable evidence for the existence of outcomes with multiple elections that may go against the wishes of the public. In fact, they have pointed out that if there are numerous items on the ballot it may turn out that no voter supports the particular combination of measures that ultimately passes.

The problem is most serious when voters link two or more measures in their minds. For example, let us say that voters are confronted with a measure that permits riverboat gambling to add to general state revenue and one that creates a lottery to fund educational scholarships. A voter who saw gambling in any form as a moral problem would link these two measures in her mind. Such a voter would probably like to see neither measure pass, but she might very well rather see both pass than just one. Her thinking might go something like this: "If there must be gambling, we might as well have a lot of it to raise more money for good causes." The middle-ground approach—passing one measure and not the other— might be the least-preferred overall outcome for someone with a moral reservation regarding gambling. In other words, her preference on one measure is contingent on the outcome of the other. The problem is that voters do not cast their vote on one measure knowing what will happen with the other.

The following examples serve to illustrate the paradox of multiple elections under three different scenarios.

The Kill Clause Dilemma

Let us imagine a state with three initiatives on the ballot regarding state policy toward racial and gender preferences. The current state policy includes a broad range of preference programs for African Americans, Hispanics, and women. The kill clause is in effect. If more than one measure passes with a majority, only the one with the most votes will become law.[25]

Proposition A calls for an end to all preferences based on race, ethnicity, and gender in state policy regarding government contracts, employment, and state university admissions. Proposition B also calls for the end to preferences in all areas of state policy, but includes a policy of outreach to African Americans, women, and Hispanics to increase their awareness of government contracting opportunities, opportunities for employment, university admissions, etc. Proposition C calls for implementation of a new preference program that would favor people below the poverty line, but would also disallow preference on the basis of race, ethnicity, and gender. The highlights of the different propositions are as follows:

Proposition A: Ends all preferences related to race, ethnicity, gender, or anything else in state policy toward contracting, university admissions, employment, etc.

Proposition B: Also ends all preferences in state policy, but includes an outreach program designed to inform African Americans, women, and Hispanics of the availability of government contracting opportunities, opportunities for employment, university admissions, etc.

Proposition C: Implements a new preference policy in contracting, employment, and admissions for people below the poverty line irrespective of race, ethnicity, or gender.

This state has three voters, Susan, Tom, and Sharon. These three have the following preference order for the three initiatives.

Let's get into their heads. Susan and Tom are particularly interested in seeing either A or B passed into law, and both think B is the best choice. They are lukewarm toward C, but think it is better than the status quo race/ethnicity/gender preference programs and plan to vote for it. Their disdain for the status quo will cause them to vote for all three. Sharon, however, is only interested in seeing C pass—it is the only measure she prefers to the status quo. She prefers the status quo to the more strongly antipreference measures, B and A. However, she does slightly prefer B to A, since it includes outreach. Here is how the three will vote (Y is a "yes"-vote and N, a "no"-vote).

TABLE 5.3 Voters' Preferences on Affirmative Action Propositions

	First Choice	*Second Choice*	*Third Choice*
Susan	B	A	C
Tom	B	A	C
Sharon	C	B	A

TABLE 5.4 Affirmative Action Vote Subject to Kill Clause

	Proposition A	*Proposition B*	*Proposition C*
Susan	Y	Y	Y
Tom	Y	Y	Y
Sharon	N	N	Y

As we can see, all three propositions gained a majority, but C will be the state's policy on affirmative action because it won unanimous support and will kill the others that received only two thirds of the votes. But, as we saw from the distribution of preferences shown earlier, B is favored over C by two voters, which is more than the one voter who favors C over B. In fact, two of the C supporters were pretty lukewarm on it. In this case, then, the winning alternative is reasonably popular, but it is not the public policy option that is most popular with two thirds of the voters.

The Sensible Center Loses the Day

Let us imagine that three voters are considering three pro-environment propositions that appear on the ballot at the same time. Since none of the propositions conflicts with any other, the kill clause rule is not in effect. Any measures that gain more than half of the votes will be put into law. Propositions A and C are both moderate in approach, putting some regulations on businesses in the state. Proposition B is the most extreme, measure; it proposes several new stringent environmental standards.

The voters, Kevin, Nisha, and Chris, have the following views. Kevin and Chris are moderately pro-environment and would like to see one of either A or C enacted into law. They think enacting both would put an undue burden on business in the state. They are opposed to B because it is too extreme. Nisha is the strongest environmentalist and supports B most of all, and plans to vote for A and C as well in the hope that at least one of the measures passes. Kevin, after careful consideration, thinks A is the wisest of the propositions, and plans to vote only for it. Chris concludes that C is better than A; he votes only for it.

TABLE 5.5 Voters' Preferences on Environmental Propositions

	A	B	C
Kevin	Y	N	N
Nisha	Y	Y	Y
Chris	N	N	Y

The results as depicted above: Propositions A and C both pass 2–1, and B goes down to defeat. Thus, the result is YNY.

Note that Kevin's choice was YNN, Nisha's was YYY, and Chris's was NNY. The winning combination, YNY, was supported by none of the voters. In addition, the majority of the voters, constituted of Kevin and Chris, wanted *either* A or C to pass, *not* both. In short, the referendum process did not permit the voters to coalesce around what a majority of the voters thought was a coherent policy position.[26] The result was not consistent with the views of the voters, even though all the voters were thoughtful and made careful judgments regarding the issues at hand. But they had no mechanism to work out their differences (in this case the majority had only minor differences).

The Center Wins the Day ... but Shouldn't

Suppose a state holds two referenda on the topic of criminal sentencing; Referendum A requires a mandatory life term for possession of a certain substantial amount of crack cocaine; Referendum B requires a mandatory life term for possession of a certain amount of ordinary cocaine. Our three voters, Mary, Tim, and Ina, have the following preferences for how they would like to see the referenda come out. YY indicates both referenda passing; NN, both failing; etc.

TABLE 5.6   Referenda on Criminal Sentencing

	First Choice	*Second Choice*	*Third Choice*	*Fourth Choice*
Mary	YY	NN	YN	NY
Tim	NN	YY	NY	YN
Ina	YN	YY	NY	NN

Mary and Tim have different first preferences—one wants both to pass, the other wants neither to pass—but both see the two measures as linked. In their minds, it would be unfair to penalize one of the offenses harshly without also penalizing the other harshly. This is not an unusual stance regarding these two issues, as many people interested in the issue have alleged that the generally lighter sentences received for cocaine possession reflect a racial bias. Ordinary cocaine is a "white man's" drug and crack a "black man's" drug, they say. Ina, on the other hand, sees crack as the more serious issue, because of the violent crime associated with its use and sale. She feels that the mandatory life term is probably too extreme in the case of cocaine, but she definitely wants the crack criminal put away for life, regardless of what happens with the cocaine referendum.

We can see from these preferences what would happen when the vote is taken. The crack referendum would pass 2–1, with support from Mary and Ina. The cocaine referendum would fail, for only Mary would vote for it. Now if Tim knew that the crack measure would pass, he would have changed his vote on the cocaine referendum, as the fairness question links the two measures in his mind.[27] But given that plebiscites on

particular issues are decided one at a time and not as a package, the outcome in this case is quite unsatisfactory to the majority of voters. This
"middle ground" result—one tough measure passes while the other does-
n't, is exactly what Mary and Tim, constituting the majority, did not want
to see happen.

Plebiscites involving the kill clause as well as those involving noncon-
flicting measures on the same general topic present new problems in ag-
gregating voters' preferences. The paradox of multiple elections may well
render the corporate judgment unsatisfactory to a majority a significant
portion of the time. Obviously, this raises serious questions concerning
the proliferation of ballot measures in the states.

Conclusion

Adding up the preferences of groups of people to arrive at a social choice
is nowhere near as rational a process as is generally assumed. Many observers simply accept the idea that the outcome of a vote will reflect the
true wishes of the voters, particularly if the voters are reasonably informed and rational. For example, a leading scholar of direct democracy
wrote the following after concluding that individual voters are, on the
whole, fairly consistent and rational in deciding how to vote in
plebiscites:

> When voters make choices on a large number of initiatives, it is reasonable
> to expect that outcomes "make sense" after all the votes are counted. That is,
> it might be relatively unlikely that a majority of voters would approve two
> policies that are logically incompatible with each other given the sort of [ide-
> ological consistency] demonstrated here. This is not to say that inconsistent
> outcomes could not happen on occasion [owing to voter irrationality], but
> we should not expect it to be common.[28]

The findings of public choice scholars yield a strong qualification: voter
rationality is in many ways *irrelevant* to the quality of the outcome of a
plebiscite. *The outcome of a vote may be irrational, even when all of the participants are rational and informed.* And when the group does have a preferred
choice, it is not necessarily the case at all that the decision will reflect that.
Decision-making processes can be arbitrary in the sense of being completely dependent on the method used to determine the winner and can
be manipulated by strategic voters; outcomes can be downright wrongheaded; and frequently groups have no clear preference at all. Even the
most decisive-appearing results may be deceptive—produced by strategic calculations instead of being the true expression of the voters' preferences. And of course we never know for certain when strategic voting has
occurred, nor whether nor how that voting influenced the outcome. The

potential for manipulation always casts doubt on the validity of the final decision. These weaknesses apply whether the voting method narrows multiple options down to two for the purpose of producing a majority decision or voters choose from among more than two options.

In addition, it is hard to glean from the results of elections between mass parties any sort of broad policy mandate. In a society with any diversity of opinion and interests at all, majority coalitions formed to elect candidates and put parties in power are inherently unstable owing to the changing political landscape and the efforts of clever politicians to exploit that landscape. The more open the political system, the more unstable the coalitions. As for initiatives and referenda, their proliferation can lead to results that fail to square with the views of the public, even when voters are informed and thoughtful. The essential point is this: *Electoral arrangements, including initiatives and referenda that determine public policy, are intrinsically flawed and can never be relied upon to identify the will of the people.*

The analysis of plebiscites yields another valuable insight. We have seen that it is very difficult in some cases to capture the nuances and complexity of people's views on some issues with these institutions of direct democracy. Think about the moderate views the majority held on environmental questions in the hypothetical regulatory plebiscites. Or the complex views on sentencing for drug crimes the majority held in that example. There was no practical way for people to express those positions within the framework of these institutions.

So where does this leave us with the populist theory of voting and, more broadly, the populist conception of democracy? Elections are blunt instruments that simply cannot serve the functions that populists intend for them. Their theory of voting fails the test. The populist conception of democracy really does not make sense.

However, this conclusion does not necessarily prove that institutions of direct democracy are inferior to representative decision-making processes (particular if the latter are as corrupt as populists claim). An important distinction needs to be made, that between *outcome* and *process*. We have shown that the populist project to identify the popular will from election results is futile. Furthermore, if election results can be wrongheaded at worst and can never be interpreted with any certainty or precision, then it is patently ridiculous to say that the public interest is reflected in these outcomes. But proving that the public interest *as an outcome* cannot be identified with any precision by elections or plebiscites does not mean that the public interest defined *as a process* might not be better served with direct democratic institutions than with representative institutions. Institutions of direct democracy such as initiatives and referenda do provide a reasonably practical way to determine policy, however imperfect electoral institutions are. Perhaps the *process* of permitting people to determine public policy directly is desirable and preferable to representative processes, even if the outcomes cannot be construed in the way populists would ideally like. And many argue that, at the very least, direct democratic institutions can usefully complement representative institutions.

The question comes down to whether representative or direct democratic institutions better serve the public, and whether direct democratic institutions can act as useful complements to representative institutions. These are the subjects of the next chapter.

6

Curing the Mischief
of Plebiscite

The tension between populism and constitutionalism in American political culture has been with us since the Founding. The fundamental difference is manifested in opposing ideas about how the political system derives its legitimacy—the populists believing that legitimacy comes from popular majorities and the constitutionalists maintaining that the people express their sovereignty by subscribing to republican principles.

In the first century and a half of the republic, the conflict between these ideas was bridged by Thomas Jefferson's brilliant accommodation. His insight was that constitutionalism was desirable at the federal level, because it was the federal government that posed the threat to the people's liberties. At the state and local level (where the action was at that time), however, Jefferson said that populist principles should prevail; people should keep close tabs on elected officials at those levels, and even govern themselves directly when and where feasible. At the beginning of the twentieth century President Theodore Roosevelt recognized that many of the most important political issues and problems were national in scope and could not be neatly confined to state or local jurisdictions. State and local self-government was less important than it had been for the simple reason that people could not control their lives at those levels. Jefferson's accommodation became still more untenable in the 1930s during Franklin Roosevelt's New Deal, when the federal courts began to permit the Congress to intervene in states' affairs previously considered off limits.

The conflict between populism and constitutionalism is manifested in different ways today than in the past. The core of the debate is whether American representative institutions are responsive enough to the popular will. Populists contend that elected officials in representative institutions are out of touch with the people and fail to express the people's will in legislation; constitutionalists counter that representative institutions are *too* responsive to public opinion polls and popular pressure more generally, which leads to an abdication of leadership and irresponsible public policy.

There is little question which side most Americans are on in this debate. Polling indicates in no uncertain terms that Americans want their representatives to abide by majority opinion in the district when deciding public policy. And people are actually even more populist than that. Americans in direct democracy states strongly support the institutions of initiatives and referenda, and in some polls people respond favorably to the idea of a national referendum process. The advent of constant polling over the last few decades and the potential for direct democracy promised by dazzling new technologies make the allure of populism even greater. Activist populists look to petitioning for initiatives over the Internet or even to on-line voting as models for future direct participation. As the number of Americans connected to the Internet increases every day, instant democracy becomes more feasible and more attractive to people.

Scholars are just beginning to grapple with the issues surrounding the use of new technologies in American politics. In particular, as direct democracy becomes feasible, they are asking what exactly will become of representative institutions? Will elected representatives be able to perform their legislative duties adequately as plebiscitary democracy becomes more common? At the extreme, can they even survive the onslaught of new forms of direct democracy and the continuing popularity of existing ones? Should they?

Some academics on the left side of the political spectrum, most notably Benjamin Barber, are enthusiastic about the potential for change afforded by new technologies. They feel that enhancing and widening the scope of face-to-face interaction over interactive television or computer—involving more citizens in the discussion and formation of policy—would be healthy for the political system. Truly popular deliberative institutions could be a democratic utopia, they say, combining the benefits of discussion and careful consideration with mass participation. New technologies could serve this worthy end. But it is far from clear that that will be the path taken.

First, there are precious few indications in the experimental uses of advanced technology in politics and policy-making that people are willing to participate in great numbers. The participatory tradition (New England town halls, etc.) that the advocates of deliberative styles of direct democracy point to as a model never really existed in quite the way they suppose. Even the most practical methods of involving representative samples of the population in deliberations on public policy, such as

Dahl's minipopuluses and Fishkin's deliberative polls, would not or did not achieve what their creators envisioned. Fishkin managed a mere 36 percent response rate for his effort, despite the fact that the participants were remunerated. The fundamental problem in devising a truly popular deliberative institution is that any deliberative process meant to be open to the public would in practice exclude people who may not be well educated or otherwise intellectually equipped to participate and understand the details of public policy.

Perhaps most telling is the fact that the best studies seem to indicate that most people are strongly turned off by the inevitable clash of people with irreconcilable differences and the messy haggling over policy that characterize politics and governing. Ultimately, populists of the left fail to face the reality that the American people are inclined to be monitorial rather than regularly or constantly active in politics. They pay attention when they need to in order to protect their rights (and certain government programs they feel entitled to); there is no deep-seated need and no tradition to draw upon for sustained attention to and participation in the details of politics and policy-making. Citizens are not inclined toward participation in the nitty-gritty details of policy, and they are not going to sit still in order to be retrained according to some academics' conception of what their civic responsibilities are.

The only practical way to sustain popular interest and involvement in the details of public policy would be to create a powerful incentive. House Majority Leader Dick Armey (R-Texas) devised a plan in the mid–1990s that might just do that. He suggested ending the post-World War II practice of withholding federal income taxes from each paycheck. Citizens would be required, each month or each quarter, to pay their tax bills just as they pay their telephone, electric, water, credit card, and gas bills. The theory is that if people had to budget for their tax bill, they would pay a great deal more attention to what the government is spending its money on. My guess is that such a scheme would achieve that end. Of course, Armey's ulterior purpose—which he made no effort to hide— was to get people to protest their tax bill and push for reductions in government spending. Perhaps for fear that Armey's intentions might be realized, none of the advocates of popular involvement in policy-making on the left has endorsed his idea. Nor is it particularly popular with almost anyone else. When it comes right down to it, people across the ideological spectrum do not really want to get that deeply involved in policy-making.

It is much more likely that the new technologies will lead to the wider use of plebiscites. There are two major reasons for this. One is that interest groups and citizen groups find initiatives and referenda a useful way to make their mark on public policy. There are also some groups that have the expressed intention of expanding the use of direct democratic institutions. They are working to make access to the ballot easier and to promote voting by computer from home. The other reason is that ordinary Americans *are* interested in influencing public policy—as long as they have easy options. Plebiscitary forms of democracy are much easier and less time-consuming than those that require discussion and deliberation.

Though citizens want and like direct democracy, especially in the states that use these institutions the most,[1] it is not clear that citizens are well equipped to participate in some plebiscites. Reliable voting cues are less available in initiative and referenda campaigns than they are in general elections between major party candidates. Voters struggle in some states with several sometimes confusing and complex ballot measures. Probably most people are able to vote in a way that reflects their actual intentions, but there is some evidence that some voters are confused enough so that they end up voting against their intentions. On the whole, citizens have more difficulty finding good information or reliable voting cues in plebiscites than in general election races between major party candidates.

Populists' most frequent criticism of representative institutions is that they are too heavily influenced by interest groups. No one who follows legislative politics in the states or at the federal level would quarrel with this contention, even if some would qualify it a bit. However, it is by no means clear that direct democracy has the effect of reducing that influence. With the initiative process, interest groups can actually get their ideas put in front of voters in an undiluted form. In addition, some ballot measures that have been passed into law have had the perverse effect of increasing the stakes in the legislative process and also the volume of lobbying. In California and other states, voters have passed referenda and initiatives limiting the spending and taxing powers of public officials. This has the effect of raising the stakes in fierce late-session battles over scarcer resources, an environment that is particularly hospitable to well-connected lobbies.

Perhaps the toughest criticism of direct democratic institutions is the allegation that they place vulnerable minorities in jeopardy of majority tyranny. Populists have put forward elaborate arguments to make the case that legislatures are just as apt, or more apt, to discriminate against minorities than the people are in a plebiscite. This goes against the conventional wisdom, including that of the leadership of the vulnerable minority groups themselves—most notably African Americans, gays, and immigrant groups—who are far more comfortable using the legislative setting to protect their rights than direct democracy formats. The truth is that there are myriad ways in representative institutions to stop legislation deemed undesirable by a vulnerable group, particularly in committees and through the party organizations. In American history, minority groups such as African Americans were much more vulnerable to majority tyranny through legislative action *before they were permitted to vote in many states.* Nowadays, representatives who are themselves black or who have large numbers of minorities in their constituencies have risen to powerful positions and are able to wield influence that may even enhance their impact on the legislative process.

Most important are the actual observable results of direct democracy. In California, the experience with democracy by plebiscite is not encouraging. Peter Schrag, in *Paradise Lost,* has described in compelling detail the results of two decades of frequent statutory and constitutional plebiscites in California. His book depicts a dystopian polity. A tangled web of tax restrictions and conflicting and inconsistent mandates, some of which play on the native-born citizens' worst fears about immigrant groups, has led to a government that can't govern responsibly and a deteriorating infrastructure—in particular, a weakened public school system. The very process that is supposed to reconnect citizens to their government, the plebiscite, has resulted in a seriously dysfunctional public sphere. Even though Californians say they want direct democracy, there is no evidence that its frequent use has reduced their alienation from the political system. If anything, the consequences of plebiscitary democracy might be contributing to that alienation.

Despite all this, populists are adamant that representative institutions perform worse than direct democratic ones. The populists' point is a simple and generally persuasive one: representative institutions reflect the narrow interests of the career-minded public officials that inhabit them and the interest groups that fund the politicians' campaigns, not the public interest. The special interests and the politicians team up to produce an undemocratic and unresponsive electoral and policy-making process. Whatever the quality of plebiscitary decision-making, at least the process of permitting people to decide policy at the ballot box is out in the open and democratic—with voters more apt to consider the public interest than legislators—and it is a method that forces legislators to respond to concerns voters have. In short, populists admit that institutions of direct democracy may need to be tinkered with and reformed, but the principle of having the people decide for themselves should prevail.

There is some validity to the populists' position, but the crux of their argument, that representatives are beholden only to the special interests and as a result are unresponsive to the clearly expressed wishes of the people is largely not valid. No informed observer of the legislative process at the state or federal level takes seriously the charge that elected representatives are unresponsive. If anything, they are overly responsive. Legislators border on being hyperkinetic in their rush to address the latest fad issue. They tend to be obsessively responsive to all sorts of groups in their districts or states, and the trend is in the direction of more responsiveness, as citizens become increasingly sophisticated in their means of contacting and influencing elected officials and bureaucrats, and politicians become more dependent on poll data. Most scholars and journalists who have observed these patterns are quite critical. The consensus among those who are familiar with the legislative process is that members ought more often to take a step back, to exert some independent judgment and attempt to tackle the difficult and controversial problems. These observers usually agree with populists that representatives are too careerist; it is just that they believe that the careerism is oriented more often than not to pleasing constituents, not some ill-defined special interest cabal. In addition, much of the criticism of special interests amounts to self-criticism; today the majority of Americans one way or another are represented by active and effective lobbies in Washington.

Although there is evidence that legislators often vote against the wishes of the people on specific issues, these instances are sometimes unavoidable. Budgetary exigencies sometimes require unpopular solutions—revenue enhancements that a majority of the public opposes or cuts in popular services or transfer payments. After all, when are the people going to be for an increase in the gas tax or cuts in education spending when these options are viewed in isolation from the overall budget or policy picture? Sometimes revenue must be raised and choices have to be made.

This is not to say that representative government does not have its flaws. There is ample reason to believe that these institutions are not performing as well as they should and are in need of reform. The problem is that populists have conjured up inflated and sometimes bogus arguments in support of institutions of direct democracy that have not performed well in actual practice. Initiatives have not become tools for the people to challenge the interests; as often as not they are used by the interests to increase their leverage in the policy-making process. And they most certainly have not functioned to reconnect the citizenry to its government; instead they have probably contributed to cynicism and alienation from government.

What is more, the analysis in Chapter 5 undermines the very premise of populism: that votes can identify what the people want in public policy; that the result of a plebiscite produces the best representation of the public interest, since ordinary citizens are more apt than representatives to consider what is good for the whole community when pondering the issues. In reality, elections and plebiscites are very blunt instruments that are not reliable means for achieving the purposes populists have for them. Plebiscitary decision-making processes may produce results that literally make no sense, even some that go against the wishes of the majority, and they are always subject to strategic manipulation. The results of a plebiscite or an election simply cannot be interpreted with any precision.

The analysis in Chapter 5 goes further than just undermining the premise of populism. It also contributes to a broader defense of representative institutions as we enter a new century in which the populist impulse is likely to be stronger than ever. The findings of public choice scholars underline the fact that properly constructed representative institutions better serve the public interest and are in fact *more* democratic than institutions of direct democracy. The main aim of this chapter is to develop this defense.

But that is not the end of the story. Representative institutions in the United States *are* ailing. For them to serve their purpose in the political system they must be truly representative, and they must be accountable to the people. Making sure these institutions are sufficiently representative and remain accountable is an ongoing challenge requiring constant tinkering and reform. I address these problems at the end of the chapter.

Representative Democracy and the Public Interest

The populist instincts of Americans and the popularity of direct democracy in the country, just at the time when technology can greatly expand the use of institutions of direct democracy, brings into question the purpose of representative institutions. Why rely on them in a democracy if it is feasible to replace many of their functions? The tangled web of separated powers and checks and balances were instituted to protect people from government. If we can now govern ourselves, the argument goes, we don't need that protection.

On the contrary, as we have seen in this book, recent discoveries in the social sciences tend to weaken the argument for direct democracy. These discoveries also bolster the case for representative institutions. The following five-part defense of representative institutions shows, among other things, why they are more democratic than direct ones, why they better reflect the public interest, and how they can give citizens more control over policy-making.

The Complexity of Public Opinion

We saw in the examples in Chapter 5 the problems that cropped up when trying to interpret specific policy instructions from the results of elections. We know, as demonstrated in the paradox-of-voting example, that there are times when a group of people simply does not have any sort of coherent preference on an issue. More often, however, the problem in interpreting elections may not be the incoherence of the people's views but their complexity. Most questions of public policy that matter to people are by their very nature complex and don't lend themselves to simple solutions.

In the environmental policy plebiscites we looked at, the reasoned and moderate views of the majority could not be captured with the direct democratic institution that was used, and in fact those views were not reflected in the final election results. Similarly, in the plebiscite concerning crack and cocaine, the majority of voters, who linked the two sentencing measures, were not able to see their preferences realized. The voters in these examples, not unlike many voters in the real world, had nuanced, carefully considered views that are not easily captured by institutions of direct democracy such as those in place in the United States.

Let us consider two examples of hot-button issues that voters are sometimes asked to consider in plebiscites, abortion and affirmative action. If it is desirable for people to be well informed on issues that they are asked to decide, these two would be model topics for citizen lawmaking. Both have been controversial for decades now, and "don't know" responses in polls are rare where they are concerned. The problem is that some of the issues that receive the most attention and are the most controversial are also the very ones that are difficult or even impossible to characterize in any simple shorthand. For example, a majority of Americans support choice in abortion, but Americans are also supportive of greater restrictions like parental consent and waiting periods. To further complicate the matter, polls regularly indicate that the vast majority of Americans think that many of the reasons people give for getting an abortion—such as convenience or wanting a child of a particular sex—do not in fact justify getting an abortion.[2] In general, people prefer choice, but if the question about abortion is worded in a way that asks whether abortion should be permitted for "convenience" or for "gender selection," the response is quite different.

On the question of affirmative action, too, many people are conflicted. Most oppose racial preference in principle but do support race-based outreach programs, which may sometimes be indistinguishable in actual practice from preference. In addition, in some polls there is evidence that people support race as a criterion in hiring for police forces in some cities on the theory that policing a community requires sensitivity to the concerns of certain segments of a community—sensitivity that cannot easily be learned by people not of that community. And there is considerable support for the use of race or ethnicity as a criterion in hiring public school teachers, again, on the theory that, say, African American teachers may be better able to connect with and educate African American children. It is simply impossible to make any simple declaration of the public's views on the matter of affirmative action.

If public opinion is complex and nuanced, then which policy-making process better captures that reality? Public choice findings show that the result of a plebiscite in many cases does not reflect even the relatively simple nuances we considered in the various examples in the last chapter. On the other hand, properly functioning representative processes lend themselves well to attempts to achieve resolutions to difficult issues that can incorporate sometimes conflicting and complex viewpoints. This is because lengthy deliberation, compromise, and consensus are frequently the hallmarks of policy-making in legislatures. The fact is that most political issues that anyone cares about are highly complex and require extended deliberations.

Social Security is another example of a complex issue where people's opinions are nuanced. The Congress may take up the volatile issue of Social Security reform in the coming years in the context of the new budget surplus policy environment. The consideration of this issue will be subject to endless debate, and numerous proposals have come forth. Should most of the surpluses go to shore up Social Security? Should half go to tax cuts, and half to Social Security? What about three fourths to tax cuts, and one fourth to Social Security coupled with some minor benefit reductions to assure the program's long-term solvency? These ideas barely scratch the surface of possible options. If reform is to be achieved, it will come only after all major factions have had their input into the reform package. Any satisfactory result will be highly complex and involve controversial policy trade-offs.

Referenda and initiatives do not operate with such sophisticated understandings about the nature of political choices and public opinion. In fact, stark choices are often put up for a vote. The public is asked to make either/or decisions on environmental questions, affirmative action, abortion, gay rights, assisted suicide, taxes, and a raft of other high-profile—and some low-profile—issues. The interests of minority factions and potentially vulnerable individuals are sometimes at stake.

It should be noted that when legislative bodies finally vote on a given matter, the members are confronted with an either/or choice just as voters are in a plebiscite. When the roll call of members is taken, as in the Senate, or votes are recorded electronically, as is often the case in the House, they vote "yea" (for the proposal) or "nay" (to maintain the status quo). And, if one looks at the end product of the legislative process as a plebiscite of sorts, the outcome can be said to be subject to all the shortcomings that plebiscites are subject to, such as possible incoherence, manipulation, the identification of the wrong winner, etc. Legislative bodies engineer an either/or choice for the floor vote, a process that may work to exclude a more popular option at an earlier stage, either by strategic manipulation or by chance.

In spite of surface similarities, there are good reasons to think differently about the legislative process than we think about plebiscites. For one thing, the outcome of a measure up for a vote in the U.S. Congress and in state legislatures is often pre-ordained to a great extent—which is to say that the important votes and decisions that lead up to the final vote are made in committee and in consultation with interested parties and dozens of members. In other words, public policy in representative institutions arranged as they are in the United States is the product of institutional arrangements and informal practices—committee hearings, conferences with members of the executive branch, meetings with lobbyists, meetings with members—that take into account a wide variety of interests. Representative institutions operate under a different premise than direct democratic institutions. In our representative institutions, public policy is the result of compromise, negotiation, and consensus. With direct democratic institutions, policy is made on the basis of the vote of a (sometimes uninterested) populace. With direct democracy, *the vote itself* is thought to produce the best resolution in the interest of the public. With representative institutions, the process of negotiation is thought to produce the best resolution.

The contrast is clear. Legislatures are better able to consider complex questions and have the potential to reflect more accurately the complex nature of public opinion on some policy questions. They tend to be flexible, fluid, and contingent, not rigid and devoid of compromise.[3] In the inevitable and messy process of bargaining, negotiation, and compromise, legislatures, in the process of crafting legislation, are more apt to take into account more interests and provide a forum for competing interests to bargain.

Representative Institutions Are, Well, More Representative

As we have just seen, the populist conception of public opinion is oversimplified. People cannot adequately express their views on contentious, complex issues by plebiscite. Such issues require sustained consideration and deliberation in order for policy alternatives to be crafted. It is equally important to note that people's interests, not just their viewpoints, involve far more than just the expression of an opinion on issues that capture their attention or that are placed in front of them on Election Day.

Our communities, our careers, and our values, among other things, make up what are called our "interests." If a person is a teacher, a hunter, a feminist, and a union member, her interests will be at stake in a wide range of issues, many times in ways that she may never be fully cognizant of. Such a person's interests are much more than just the expression of an opinion—such a person is not well represented merely by having the opportunity to express an opinion by casting a vote in a plebiscite.

Tallying opinions on Election Day is a clean, antiseptic way of resolving complex issues in a diverse society. Taking a vote is not in and of itself a satisfactory way of dealing with divergent and even irreconcilable interests, values, and viewpoints in such a society. The most important thing for individuals or groups with strongly felt convictions is to be represented, to be at the table when difficult questions are being worked out that affect them and the community as a whole. It is better and fairer to hash out controversies face-to-face. Institutions of direct democracy do not afford people that opportunity.

The key is to devise institutions that can represent diverse interests, values, and viewpoints in a fluid, ever-changing society. The best that humans have done so far is to create a manageable set of institutions that is representative of and accountable to the people, that give the people a stake in the decision-making process. In the American political system, the theory is to represent the people locally through the House of Representatives, by state through the Senate, and nationally through the presidency. On first blush, the presidency, as the only nationally elected office, would seem to represent the people the best. But the presidency is designed to do many things, perhaps the most important of which is to consider the national interest in relations with other countries. In domestic politics the president may have a more national perspective than anyone else, but even so, he may have received the bulk of his support from certain parts of the country toward which he may be inclined to be particularly sympathetic. Citizens are represented in a much more intimate and immediate way in their communities by members of the House of Representatives, who are likely to be sensitive to people's local needs. The federal system of states in the United States makes it so that each state has particular interests as well; the members of the U.S. Senate represent people from that perspective.

Certainly these three essentially geographical forms of representation—national, local, and state—do not exhaust the ways in which citizens should be represented. The member of the House does not just represent the tangible economic interests of her constituents; she also represents their values and sensitivities, some of which she may well share by virtue of having grown up in that area. Senators and presidents do not serve that function as well, but they serve the critical function of balancing out many more interests in their much larger constituencies. The principle of having a manageable (albeit barely so, sometimes) set of institutions representing us in a variety of ways, representing different perspectives on each matter of controversy, requiring these diverse interests to sit down together to work out differences in order to come up with legislation, reflects the people's interests much more effectively and comprehensively than a simple plebiscite.

And that is the heart of the matter. Populists have a naïve and dangerous conception of the public interest. The very concept of "the public interest" is, of course, a slippery one. Populists tend to elide the public interest with the popular will—"If the people say they want it, it must be in the public interest." (This notion poses some problems of its own, as we shall see below.) But, as we have seen, there is literally no way to determine with certainty precisely what the people want on a complex policy matter. In any event, the public interest cannot be defined *a priori*, except, perhaps, in the rare cases when the security of the country is at stake. In a democracy that accepts the legitimacy of differing and minority viewpoints, the public interest can only properly be thought of in terms of process. A fair and representative process that takes into account people's diverse interests and permits clashing interests to confront one another, sometimes working things out, sometimes not, serves the public interest better than an institution that simply tallies people's opinions on important and controversial matters.

Minority Rights

Representative institutions operate on the principle that deliberation leads to better legislation. In the American system, with the bicameral legislature and an independently elected executive, compromise and consensus seem to be the dominant style of doing business within the deliberative framework. The distinguished political scientist David Mayhew provided good evidence for that assertion. In *Divided We Govern*,[4] he showed that nearly all major legislation at the federal level since World War II has been the result of bipartisan compromise and numerous concessions. Most of these measures ultimately passed the Congress by overwhelming majorities and received the support of the president.

There are many reasons for this. Most notably, American legislative institutions are complex entities that have many veto points—committees, subcommittees, floor procedures, the party organizations, etc. The only way to be sure that a significant piece of legislation will wend its way successfully through this byzantine process is to build overwhelming support for it from members of both parties. A committed minority often may be able to engineer a strategy that kills a bill it doesn't like. Anyone who really wants to accomplish anything in this system must bring minority interests into the equation in order to achieve success.

Minority interests can also be served by the party system. American political parties are unwieldy coalitions of diverse, and sometimes conflicting, interests and groups. The congressional parties reflect these qualities, which makes it difficult and sometimes impossible for the leaders of the parties to keep the rank and file in line. As a result, small groups of members can hold large amounts of power in negotiations on major legislation, especially when the margin for error is small. Republican House leaders in the 106th Congress (1999–2000) found that out (the GOP had only a five-seat working margin over the Democrats), having been whipsawed by both the moderate and most conservative factions of the party. A moderate faction within the party, sometimes numbering as few as eight or ten members, has forced action on several measures the leadership would rather did not see the light of day.

Another factor that causes members to be sensitive to the interests of even small minorities is the fact that many members feel vulnerable in their districts. Even members in seemingly safe seats do not ignore minority concerns; after all, you don't want to alienate any group—whether that means gun collectors or a racial or ethnic group—that might promote and fund a challenger in the next election. All politicians run scared to some degree. There are too many examples of seemingly safely ensconced congressmen who took their reelection for granted and received a rude shock. To the extent that members of Congress have safe seats, it is *because* they run scared, it is because they go out of their way to address the concerns of their constituents in order to stave off the threat of a challenge in future election cycles.

The upshot of all of this is that very few represented groups are left out when major legislation makes its way through the Senate and House and on to the White House for presidential consideration. There is a downside to this picture, by some people's lights. Compromise and consensus lead to logrolling and some wasteful pork-barrel spending in our legislative institutions. But this is probably the price that must be paid for a legislative process that protects minority rights. In addition, it should be noted that logrolling is often the only means by which potentially vulnerable minorities can do more than just stop disadvantageous legislation; logrolling sometimes offers opportunities for minority groups to get something advantageous to them passed as part of a larger package that might not see the light of day if it were considered in isolation.

The ability of minorities to use the legislative process to block popular legislation that they feel is threatening can be very frustrating at times. But liberal democracy is not meant to serve only the interests of the majority; it is meant to provide some protection for the rights of minorities as well. The alternative is a strict 50-percent-plus-one majoritarianism that runs the risk of leaving vulnerable minorities out in the cold. When contentious social issues come to the fore, plebiscitary politics can be a zero-sum game, and winning a majority may involve inflaming public passions. The fact is that the values of consensus and compromise that are characteristic of representative institutions provide very real safeguards against this kind of politics.

Limited Government

The twentieth-century political philosopher Isaiah Berlin provided a useful formulation that can be applied to the ways populists and constitutionalists think about liberty and the role of government.[5] Berlin posited two types of liberty, "negative" and "positive": "freedom from" versus "freedom to." For the populist, liberty is "positive," that is, truly free people act corporately, using their government to reach their aspirations or achieve their will. For the constitutionalist, liberty is "negative"; that is, freedom is thought of in its purest form as the absence of government coercion. (In fact, the idea of positive liberty is believed by constitutionalists to carry within it the building blocks for tyranny.)

The distinction between the two types of liberty is a very important one. The populist position implies that a sovereign people has an unlimited right, by majority vote, to institute whatever policies it wants. Corporate action of this sort is thought of as a meaningful expression of freedom. But this viewpoint provides no principled foundation upon which to limit the scope of government activity. By poll or plebiscite, the populists say, the people should, by right, get their way.

Many of the contemporary populist advocates of direct democracy have a different take on the purpose of citizen lawmaking. Though maintaining the right of the people to act corporately, they say it would be wise to limit what can be considered in a plebiscite. Perhaps referenda could be restricted to measures involving taxes or to constitutional amendments that have passed muster with a state legislature or the Congress.

The reason is that many modern-day populists, particularly those on the right and in the center, are motivated by their ideological commitment to smaller government. As we saw in Chapter 4, the term limits and antitax movements—movements that include the most politically powerful populists in the United States today—are relying on direct democracy to rein in big government. They wish to use the plebiscite to restore the status quo ante of smaller government and federal principles resembling Jefferson's. They do this by using the initiative process to pass measures that tie the hands of legislators with supermajority restrictions on taxation and spending and by pushing for a national referendum process and a balanced budget amendment to the Constitution.

The cynic might suggest that these populists know that the people really do want more government spending on entitlements, health care, education, etc., and the only way to achieve their ideological objective of smaller government is to *prevent* majorities from expressing their will by passing measures to increase the public commitment to these sorts of programs. Of course the conservative populists counter by saying that the people do want these restrictions and that it is the elected representatives who ignore public opinion to satisfy their addiction to spending on a wide range of programs that are unpopular with the people but serve the politicians' electoral interests. As a result, they say, drastic measures, such as imposing supermajority requirements, are necessary to prevent representatives from thwarting the will of the people.

These populists are either naïve or disingenuous. For about seventy years Americans have enjoyed a big government at all levels that provides numerous benefits and subsidies. There is no evidence that either broad-based entitlements or more narrowly focused spending (on education, job training, environmental cleanup, unemployment insurance, to name just a few) are unpopular. Populists are probably right: the only way to rein in government may be to implement antidemocratic restrictions on its activity. But make no mistake about it, this is not what the people want. It is one thing for populists to advocate reining in the federal role in policy-making. This is entirely consistent with constitutional principles. But the view of Jefferson and many others that popular majorities are sovereign at the state level seems to be a position many modern-day populists are a bit uncomfortable with in their zeal to put in place barriers to more spending and taxes. They say that the people must be able to run their government by majoritarian plebiscitary means, but apparently they are afraid of what the ramifications of that might ultimately be. If sovereignty is believed to reside in popular majorities, then political institutions should permit people to put in place whatever policies they wish *as expressed by a popular majority*. In that case, arbitrary limits, such as supermajority requirements, are not technically legitimate.

Of course most modern-day populists also advocate the use of plebiscites at the federal level. This is also justified by the appeal to the idea that popular majorities are sovereign. But if popular majorities are really sovereign at the federal level, then there is no justification for reining in the federal role in the way Jefferson proposed. Obviously, contemporary conservative populists are caught in a bind. They cannot reconcile their desire for conservative policy outcomes (less spending and reduced taxes) with the fundamentally unconservative philosophy of populism they espouse. At whatever level, the notion that popular majorities are sovereign puts in place a mechanism to destroy barriers to the expansion of the role of government and presents a threat to liberty.

In the past, those opposing big government have relied on constitutional principle to rein in government and the passions of the majority. And with good reason. As George Will put it, populist conservatives are entering into a Faustian bargain by using plebiscites to do the work of controlling government. The separation of powers and checks and balances, as well as federal principles, are surer ways to safeguard the people in general, and especially vulnerable minorities, from overbearing government. The constitutionalist position implies something very different about the use of government power. If true freedom is the absence of coercion ("negative liberty," as Berlin described it), then, for a people to be truly free, government must be limited in what it is permitted to do. The populist ideal unleashes the potential for the people whimsically or intemperately to do *anything*. There is no principled justification for limiting what government can do.

Liberal constitutionalists, on the other hand, do not put the same stock in political participation. Free people, they say, choose for themselves where to derive satisfaction and meaning. This may be from politics, but it also may be from the enjoyment of the arts or recreational activities, or it may be from one's spiritual and religious life. Politics need not be an important expression of one's freedom. Liberals, in the classical sense of the term, have confidence that free people will choose to participate in public life when they need to. In essence, liberals have traditionally believed that it is coercive and, in fact, antidemocratic, to *force* people to participate in politics. True liberty is "negative"—fundamentally a matter of being free from coercion.

Thus, the belief that people should be free to participate (or not participate) as they see fit, as opposed to a more clearly defined expectation that citizens should participate fully in deciding policy, has important consequences for the formation of political institutions. The democratic institutions we set up must be a good fit for a free people, and they must not badly disadvantage those who cannot or will not get directly involved in policy-making.

A Different Theory of Voting

In a free and democratic society the fundamental dilemma in the development of political institutions is this paradox: *the people want to maintain control over their government and public policy-making; at the same time, they wish to be free not to be required to get involved in all the details of politics and policy-making.* The constitutionalist approach provides a workable solution to this dilemma.

We have already talked about the second part of the dilemma. Representative institutions, properly constructed, serve as forums for the expression of a variety of viewpoints in the process of formulating public policy. People need not be directly involved in all the details. But it is the issue of *control*, the first part of the dilemma, that poses the trickier problem.

This is where the constitutionalist's theory of voting comes in. Unlike the unrealistic and incoherent populist theory, which expects the results of elections and plebiscites to carry explicit policy instructions, the constitutionalists' theory has a very limited and achievable purpose for voting and elections. Elections are to give the people the power to hold public officials accountable for their actions. Nothing more. Accountability through elections is the foundation of representative democracy. If we want control, and at the same time believe we should be free not to participate at every stage of politics including the actual formation of policy, then our ability to hold the people making the decisions accountable is crucial.

This gives people control over the public sphere, without their having to be involved in policy-making. Sure, it's not perfect: The "kick the bums out" mentality may be exercised indiscriminately; sometimes the people decide to replace representatives for no good reason. And sometimes they may be unable to remove a clever elected official when perhaps he should be removed. (The quirks of election rules, as we saw in Chapter 5, may result in the reelection of someone the public does not prefer.) But as long as the *threat of replacement* is real, the vote can be used to hold representatives accountable.

This constitutional theory of voting is different in a fundamental way from the populist theory. Instead of using the vote to dictate policy instructions, the vote is employed to entrust elected officials with carrying out their constitutional duties (debating and writing laws for legislators, defending the national interest in foreign affairs and managing the government for the executive).

Pundits often lampoon the voting public for failing to understand complex policy questions or not knowing where candidates stand on the issues. But there is an entirely defensible way to think about voting that does not depend on knowledge of that sort. We can think of voters as charging politicians with carrying out their constitutional duties, and then judging them on Election Day on the basis of how well they have done. This is a manageable, realistic, and practical way to view voting. The populist method is much less so, because people simply are not going to immerse themselves in policy questions. Furthermore—and this may be even more important—the constitutionalist take on voting does not depend on trusting politicians' promises made during campaigns, as the populist view does. The populist expects voters to endorse this policy program or that one on Election Day, but the voters themselves are smarter than that. They know enough not to take campaign rhetoric too seriously. It may even be true that to the extent that people do take the rhetoric seriously, politicians become ever more promiscuous in pandering to them. The constitutionalist position is the wiser one; it depends only on voters' holding the ultimate power—as they should in a democracy—over who makes policy.

Populists are up in arms about "elite influence" in representative democracy. And there is no question that elites do have the policy-making power in the representative system. But it is important to keep in mind that, in a properly functioning representative system, it is *accountable* elites who have that power. But if we assume that people—because of their own free choice or because they may be poorly educated—cannot, will not, or should not be required to get involved directly in policy-making, there is going to be some elite or another that will gain more power than the rest of the population by involving itself actively in the policy-making process. Plebiscitary democracy has the unfortunate effect of promoting the power of *unaccountable* elites.

In initiative politics, unelected and unaccountable citizens and groups create statutory ballot measures and constitutional amendments to put before the voters. Then the public, which had little or no part in determining the options and which may comprise people who know almost nothing about the issue, passes judgment. The public, in effect, determines the outcome of a public policy question by choosing from among alternatives that, as far as they are concerned, come out of the blue. And then no official entity is accountable for the decision.

The stakes can be great, and, in the real world of mass politics the results can be distressing. Ron Unz, an initiative initiator himself, recently described the infamous Proposition 187 campaign in California in 1994.

The initiative banned all nonemergency government services for illegal immigrants and their children—a simple and reasonable-sounding proposal, until one realized that it would force the immediate expulsion of hundreds of thousands of immigrant children from public schools throughout California. The initiative had a number of clauses: one draconian clause stipulated that mothers who attempted to use false documents to keep their children in school would receive mandatory five-year prison sentences; another required teachers and doctors to report immediately to the Immigration and Naturalization Service any individuals they "suspected" of being illegal immigrants, thus raising the specter of a wave of ethnic witch-hunts. Reflecting its grassroots origins, the measure was poorly drafted and highly ambiguous, and was written in explicit defiance of a 1982 U.S. Supreme Court decision, *Plyler v. Doe*, requiring public education for all children, documented or otherwise.

None of these seemingly fatal flaws lessened the overwhelming popularity of Proposition 187.[6]

We must face the fact that, regardless of whether direct democratic or representative institutions are in place, elites of one stripe or another do the lawmaking. The practical question is whether that lawmaking should be done by accountable elites or unaccountable ones. Direct democratic institutions bring into the policy-making process a whole array of unaccountable elites such as maverick policy entrepreneurs, interest groups, and campaign consultants. This is not likely to change. Representative democracy involves elites making policy who are ultimately responsible and have to stand for election and reelection.

The potential for manipulation of the people is probably greater when unaccountable people are engineering initiative campaigns than when elected officials are crafting legislation. Elected officials must answer to their constituents on a regular basis at the polls and in informal settings. People who initiate ballot measures do not. The contrast is even more pronounced when one considers the interests of the poorest and most vulnerable members of society, who often are undereducated and ill equipped to cope with advanced technology or to understand complex ballot propositions. The poorly educated and the ignorant are better served with a manageable and practical form of democracy. The threat of electoral defeat, a credible threat regardless of the education level or the sophistication of those issuing the threat (after all, everyone has an equal say at the ballot box), gives all voters a meaningful form of control over agenda setting and policy-making, something not afforded by direct democratic institutions.

Thus it can be seen that direct democratic institutions are, in an important way, *less* democratic than representative ones. Elite decision-makers are accountable in representative democracy; with direct democratic institutions much of the policy-making and agenda setting is under the control of unaccountable entities with their own agendas. Ordinary citizens have more control over public policy through the punishment and reward system of elections than they do over the free-wheeling policy entrepreneurs who produce initiatives.

Summing Up the Case for Representative Democracy

The populist conception of democracy has a lot of shortcomings. The theory of voting that serves as its premise is not valid; elections cannot achieve the purpose populists have for them. In addition, the dichotomous either/or choices presented to the public in plebiscites engineer a majority that neither reflects the complexity of public opinion nor pays sufficient heed to the rights of minorities historically vulnerable to majority tyranny.

In the constitutional conception of representative democracy, by contrast, the vote gives ordinary citizens control over public officials by the use of the veto on Election Day, and in effect gives them a place at the table. It enables a vulnerable group to use the procedures of representative institutions to veto potentially damaging legislation. Direct democracy provides no similar safeguard.

Representative institutions provide a more varied and meaningful form of representation, far truer to the various and conflicting interests and passions of the public. In these institutions, productive compromises and deals can be worked out that can result in good public policy and that reflect consensus. Direct democratic institutions, by contrast, offer a zero-sum strictly majoritarian decision-making process. The experience with plebiscitary democracy in California has been disastrous, resulting in a dysfunctional public sphere and campaigns that have poisoned the social climate.

One argument frequently put forth in favor of plebiscitary democracy is that the initiative and referendum process provides an outlet for the public when the legislative institutions fail to address public concerns. In one respect, this is an unchallengeable point. There is no doubt that those people with the wherewithal to conduct a signature-gathering campaign have the opportunity to put forward legislation or constitutional changes tailored exactly to their particular interest in a way that is impossible to do through normal legislative channels. But this advantage, if it can be called that, must be weighed against the weaknesses of plebiscitary democracy catalogued above—particularly its failure to balance different interests in the drafting of legislation and to protect the rights of minorities. Furthermore, plebiscitary politics is corrosive of representative institutions because it undermines their ability to control crucial facets of legislating (budgeting, planning, etc.). This, in turn, takes from the people their ability to hold those responsible for legislative outcomes accountable. Direct democratic institutions are not and probably cannot be set up to budget and plan. The simple lines of accountability present in representative democracy give all citizens the means to exercise influence in politics. Plebiscitary politics gives more power to an unaccountable few and frees public officials from responsibility.

Ultimately, plebiscitary democracy might still be desirable in a closed political system in which there were not outlets for the public. But what has evolved in the United States is a participatory democracy in which the electoral process and even the legislative process are exceptionally permeable. Ordinary people have a multitude of ways to express their viewpoints and make their case to public officials. And public officials listen and more often than not heed the people's wishes—ignoring them only at their peril. The fact is that plebiscitary democracy gives more influence—including the power to have their wishes put before the voters in their purest form—to precisely those people and groups already well placed and influential within the political system.

It is important to reemphasize that representative institutions do not close the door on direct forms of participation—participatory democracy, as I have called it. Nor do they discourage people, politicians, groups, or parties from attempting to implement a policy program. In any free society, particularly one with the populist, distrustful-of-elites political culture that is so strong in the United States, people will contact politicians and will promote and try to implement an agenda. The crucial question is whether the institutions of government should be arranged to ratify these efforts in the name of all the people without due consideration.

It is wiser to have institutions set up in synch with the realities of democratic politics in a free society: that election results are always inconclusive, that free citizens—while rightly desiring control over policy-making—should not be *required* to participate directly in policy-making in order to have their case made, and that politics is conducted best and implemented most wisely after deliberation, discussion, and compromise.

Shoring Up Representative Institutions

I started this book by describing how Americans have lost faith in the institutions of government—the *representative* institutions. If representative institutions tend to be respectful of individual and minority rights and can give citizens control over policy-makers, then why have people lost faith in the political system, and why do they say that something is wrong with the institutions of government?

Some of the crisis of confidence in the representative institutions is attributable to the inevitable bickering among partisans that anyone can view on C-Span almost around the clock. People don't like to see that; they seem to think that acrimony between partisans means that there is something wrong with the system. That doesn't necessarily follow, for people with different viewpoints, sometimes irreconcilable, are going to fight hard for what they believe in. That is a part of democratic politics. Democratic politics in a vast and diverse country is not going to be clean, neat, polite, and orderly all of the time.

Some people say that the nastiness and partisanship are greater than in the past, but that is a debatable assertion. In comparison to the tactics of Senator Joseph McCarthy in the 1950s or the bitter arguments and even physical confrontations that occurred on the floor of the House of

Representatives in the nineteenth century, things are mild indeed today. But of course in the 1850s the people never got to see what was happening in the halls of Congress, and in the 1950s only on rare occasions were hearings televised. Now we get to see what is happening all the time. Furthermore, it is regular practice for self-serving politicians and activists to portray the political institutions in a bad light as a form of pandering to public suspicions.

But, as I suggested in the first chapter of the book, there is more to the criticisms of the political institutions than just perceptions and a lack of perspective. Many of the most well-respected members of Congress complain of the lack of comity in and the ineffectiveness of some recent Congresses. Though it can be argued that our representative institutions have compiled a good record in recent years on welfare, budgeting, health issues, and in other areas, there are serious problems with them that should be addressed before they fester. These institutions are delicate mechanisms, sometimes subject to the kinds of abuse alleged by populists, including excessive interest group influence, corruption, and gerrymandering and other efforts to rig election rules to protect incumbency and party control. If the keepers of these institutions—the elected officials themselves—are not mindful of the need for reform when abuse gets out of hand and the public loses confidence, in a sense they deserve simple-minded populist solutions such as term limits, calls for national referenda, and the balanced budget amendment. Sometimes elected officials have no one to blame but themselves; they have the primary responsibility to maintain the integrity of these institutions. In the final analysis, for representative institutions to work, they must be truly *representative*, and the electoral system must be maintained relatively free of corruption to ensure the institutions' *accountability*.

As for the question of representativeness, it is probably impossible for any institution adequately to represent every interest in a country as large and diverse as the United States. Not only that, it is literally impossible to achieve perfect descriptive representation—a perfect match between a population's demographic characteristics, such as race, age, economic status, gender, ethnicity, and religion—in a legislative body. It would require rigging elections even to approach that ideal. It should be noted that though many groups understandably and rightly feel it is important to elect people of their race or gender, effective representation doesn't require it. For example, political scientists have shown that African Americans have been represented just as effectively by white members of Congress as by members of their own ethnic group.[7]

Size also affects representativeness. It is sometimes suggested that congressional districts have gotten too large and populated for members to be able to represent well all the people in their districts. (The typical member now has well over 600,000 constituents.) In fact, the House of Representatives is one of the smaller bodies of its kind in the world. It might be wise to revisit the question of how large the body should be. A six-hundred-member House would reduce the size of the average district considerably, to below 500,000. Even then, though, the House would still be smaller than similar bodies in other countries—the British Parliament's House of Commons has 659 members.

But the most important question is whether voters are able effectively to hold their representatives accountable for what they do in office or, as often is the case, what they don't do. Much of the frustration and dissatisfaction with representative institutions boils down to the perception that elected officials in the legislative and executive branches are too often able to avoid accountability on the big issues—a perception that, if true, is symptomatic of a larger problem in these institutions. If people in office are able to use the institutions to avoid accountability, then the people's frustrations are grounded in something more than the ignorant desire that politics be nicer and more pleasant.

In fact there are some entirely legitimate reasons for discontent, most of which point to the fact that elected officials are able to avoid accountability for what government does, and particularly what government doesn't do. One problem is the tendency, which became pronounced over the last half of the twentieth century, of the Congress to cede essentially legislative power to unaccountable bureaucrats in the executive branch. The Congress does this either by default, in the case of lax oversight of the executive branch, or by passing intentionally vague and ambiguous statutes that permit bureaucrats and judges to, in effect, write the laws. Citizens have chafed at the endless rules and regulations promulgated by faceless bureaucrats at the Internal Revenue Service, the Bureau of Alcohol, Tobacco, and Firearms, or the Immigration and Naturalization Service. Members of Congress take the easy way out and blame the bureaucrats, when it is actually Congress's responsibility to oversee these agencies. The result is an understandably frustrated and increasingly alienated citizenry.

The same problem can crop up with so-called "judge-made law." The vague laws that the Congress often produces leave some judges with little option but to fill in the blanks. It is unhealthy for the system for an unaccountable branch to be performing essentially legislative functions. The people must retain control over the laws through elected representatives; they cannot do that when judges end up making the law.

One of the greatest failures of omission in recent years has been the unwillingness of the Congress to reform the tax code. To the extent that special interests really do take advantage of the legislative process, their favorite target is the tax code. This document is laden with special privileges designed to protect industries, categories of citizens, and even specific constituents of well-placed members. In 1986, the Congress (it consisted of a Democratic House and a Republican Senate at the time) achieved a remarkable *rapprochement* on tax reform with the Reagan Administration. A streamlined tax code was created that lowered rates, reduced the number of brackets, and eliminated dozens of special interest breaks. Ever since then, particularly in the Clinton White House-Republican Congress years, the politicians have re-larded the code with numerous breaks, both broad-based and narrowly targeted.

The code is, to put it simply, an abomination. Academic specialists, ordinary citizens, and even the tax attorneys who make their living because of the complexity of the code all agree with that assessment. The tax code may arguably be the single most important federal statute. The failure to produce one that is manageable and that doesn't favor the well-placed over the ordinary citizen may be good evidence for corruption; at the very least it is prima facie evidence of a lack of accountability in the system.

Another difficult issue in American politics today is the need to shore up the Medicare system and Social Security in anticipation of the retirement of the baby boom generation. These sacrosanct programs, the two biggest in the federal government by far, will place tremendous stress on the budget in the next century. In a couple of decades, spending on them may eat up nearly two thirds of all federal spending, requiring either large tax increases or substantial spending cuts in other areas. These unpopular and draconian exigencies can be avoided by action in the near term. Tinkering with the programs now will provide huge, compounded savings over the next few decades. There is a broad bipartisan consensus that something should be done. But, unfortunately, there is no solution on the horizon. Both issues have become political footballs and all reasonable proposals have been filed and forgotten amid the partisan sniping. The failure to act to ensure the viability of these broad-based entitlements is another sin of omission contributing to cynicism and distrust of the political system.

Fortunately, the outlook is not hopeless. In 1996, President Clinton signed a welfare reform bill that dealt with an issue that caused about as much cynicism as the tax code—government payments under Aid to Families with Dependent Children (a program often generically labeled "welfare") to people who weren't playing by the rules as most Americans interpreted them. The changes were and are immensely popular. The bill itself was practically a miracle, overcoming one of the most severe partisan divides in American politics in recent times. How did it happen?

Clinton, a Democrat, was willing to cross the aisle and embrace an approach—the elimination of the entitlement to welfare—that was too bold even for his conservative Republican predecessors George Bush and Ronald Reagan to propose. The "Nixon-goes-to-China" scenario is often a source of great policy innovations in U.S. politics. For both parties to benefit politically, both have to be on board. To achieve that end requires leadership, usually presidential leadership. But if the president won't take the important step for fear of political repercussions, then the system is stalemated. Dealing forthrightly with difficult issues *can* be made to work politically—it certainly worked that way with welfare reform—but it requires leadership and risk taking.

The difficult part for members of Congress and other politicians is that it is never perfectly evident when doing the right thing will prove to be popular. Democrats walked the plank in 1993 to cut deficit spending by increasing taxes and cutting spending, and they paid for it in the next election, losing the Senate and the House for the first time in forty years. But the policy seemed to calm the markets and contributed to the creation of surpluses five years hence, and perhaps played a role in the booming economy of the mid-to-late 1990s. The Democrats' profile in courage in 1993 should be commended, although it is unrealistic to expect that sort of performance on a regular basis. It is, however, realistic to expect members to see opportunities to work together that, while inevitably rife with political traps and dangers, are reasonably likely to be rewarded with electoral success—such as with Medicare, Social Security, and tax reform. When this does not happen, public confidence in the institutions plummets, and rightly so.

There is no magic bullet for restoring public confidence in the political institutions. The best bet is good performance along the lines of the welfare reform in 1996. If people see the parties working together to solve sticky problems that are not intrinsically partisan—I have suggested that tax reform, Social Security, and Medicare are the big three—it is at least possible that confidence will be restored.

It is my contention that the system, although not at a crisis point, is not working as well as it could, because it is all too easy for representatives to avoid accountability. The fundamental health of representative democracy depends on the public's ability to hold elected officials accountable for what they do or don't do. The point is a simple one: if people are able to hold elected officials accountable, they are much more likely to try to tackle the tougher issues. I offer some modest reforms below that are designed to move in the direction of that goal, as well as to restore some of the lost confidence in the political system. None of them is a panacea, but perhaps they would contribute in a substantive—not merely cosmetic—way to improving citizens' ability to control representative institutions and demand better performance.

National Gerrymandering Legislation

Citizens are rightly suspicious that gerrymandering to ensure incumbents' reelection and to secure partisan advantage is a widely—really universally—practiced process. Every ten years, on the basis of the decennial census, each state must redraw House district lines either to account for shifts in population densities (each district must have nearly the same population) or the addition or subtraction of seats because the population goes up or down. The stakes are great in this process. In fact, the party that controls drawing the House district lines in California after the 2000 census may have a decisive leg up in controlling the House of Representatives in the first decade of the twenty-first century: California is already the most populous state and will be adding still more House seats in the first decade of the new century.

Congress should move swiftly to require states to use nonpartisan or bipartisan commissions to draw House district lines. Some states already use these, subject to legislative and gubernatorial consideration. This step would not end gerrymandering entirely, it would put a stop to its most cynical manifestations and help to dampen an important source of criticism for members, who are (sometimes accurately) thought to rig their elections, denying the public the chance to hold them accountable.

Doing Business in the House and Senate

Parliamentary procedure, although often confusing and seemingly pointless to the casual observer, serves a variety of crucial functions in representative institutions. Having a clear set of rules of the game helps make the playing field reasonably fair for all involved when major issues are discussed and laws are passed. In addition, some rules, procedures, and protocols, both formal and informal, are designed to enable members who may not like each other to work together while going about the business of legislating. And last but not least, the very cumbersomeness of the legislative process gives committed minorities a chance to slow down or stop measures that they do not like. This may be considered "antidemocratic" in some sense, but, as we have seen, the process provides a crucial safeguard for minority rights.

The benefits of occasionally cumbersome legislative procedures notwithstanding, there are some practices on the Hill that either serve no useful purpose or are abused to the point where the very integrity of the institution can be harmed. In the Senate, such procedures include the use of informal holds on legislation, which allow individual members anonymously to prevent floor consideration of a measure and the promiscuous use of the filibuster, whereby forty-one senators may prevent a vote on a bill. Whereas once the filibuster was used sparingly, today the threat of one is invoked at the drop of a hat. At one time the filibuster was saved for use when particularly controversial matters were at stake; today senators must take into account the likelihood of its use on almost any piece of legislation they plan to bring to the floor. It has become too easy for the Senate to avoid floor consideration of important and controversial legislation. This undermines the accountability of the institution.

Both of these procedures were once important for protecting minority interests in the body. Today they are used so frequently that they amount to a means by which the Senate in effect hides from its responsibilities to confront publicly some of the major issues of the day. There are already sufficient checkpoints in the legislative process for the protection of minority rights to allow for the elimination of these sometimes secretive and overused means of stopping legislative action. The members should not have recourse to these methods of avoiding their legislative responsibilities.

In the House, the problem is different. It is a much more structured body whose agenda is controlled by the majority party. Agenda control may be the one most important perk of majority status. But the heavy-handed use of this power has the effect of preventing the minority from bringing almost any of its legislation to the floor for a vote. It would be in the interest of the reputation of the institution to relax the rules to allow the minority party easier access to the floor for the purpose of bringing some limited number of their proposals up for a vote. This would have a couple of benefits. For one, it would be viewed by the public as fair, perhaps reducing some of the frustration people have with the Congress. Also, it would force the House to be accountable for a wider range of issues, not just those approved by the majority.

Whatever the prospects for these proposals, the important point is to highlight that the people's representatives must be willing to go on record on the major issues. Hiding behind arcane and undemocratic procedures heightens cynicism and undermines citizens' confidence in their representative institutions.

Modest Campaign Finance Reform

The prospects for reforming the campaign finance system are not great, both because of fundamental constitutional issues that are at stake and because of the deeply partisan nature of the differences on the subject. For one thing, the First Amendment prohibits the sorts of restrictions and reforms some would like to see. And this is, in the main, a good thing. For a couple of reasons you simply cannot, and should not, take the money out of politics in a free society. First, overzealous finance reform threatens free speech. Second, opposing those in power is only practically possible if a person or group has the freedom to spend its money to spread its message, however contrarian it may be. In addition, the two parties have very different ideas about what would be appropriate limits on financing. Democrats stress corporate soft money abuses that favor Republicans (although Democrats have not avoided problems of their own in that area in recent times), and Republicans charge that unions improperly use members' dues to pay for partisan political activities and contributions. This difference is deep-seated and gets to the root of the philosophical and constituent bases of the parties. There may not be room for compromise.

But there are some modest changes that could be agreed to. The complexities of the system inevitably lead to all sorts of abuses and ethically questionable, if not technically illegal, practices that compromise the integrity of public officials. To combat this, the regulations on contributing need to be simple and understandable, and the public must have easy access to summaries and full information concerning the contributors. It is absolutely crucial that all expenditures on the publicly owned airwaves and all contributions to candidates be exposed with full information as to the affiliations of the contributor. People must have access to information that might imply a corrupt relationship between the money an official receives for his campaign and the policy positions he takes. The mystery surrounding campaign financing contributes as much as anything else to public cynicism, largely because of the numerous loopholes that permit plainly unsavory fundraising practices. Simplifying the system would be an important step in reducing that cynicism.

The "None of the Above" Solution

For many public offices voters feel they have no choices. And sometimes, for offices up and down the ballot, including in elections for the U.S. Congress, they literally have no option but to vote for the incumbent or not at all. Other times the party opposing the incumbent will have a token underfinanced, unattractive, and unqualified candidate on its line. These are not isolated circumstances. Most House races are uncompetitive, and many Senate races are. The financial barriers to running are high, and sometimes there is no one in a position to challenge an incumbent, who typically has access to a great deal of money. Voters have reason to charge that they have no choice. In some sense, citizens are helpless. They have no practical way to hold their representatives accountable for what they are or are not doing in office. I acknowledge that this complaint is mitigated somewhat by the fact that many representatives have safe seats *because* they serve their constituents well. Still, the lack of options and the uncompetitiveness of so many House races is becoming a serious problem and contributes greatly to the general dissatisfaction with the political system. This may ultimately require a radical solution.

Many populists believe that term limits would solve this problem. They make the valid point that forcing members out of office after six or ten years will open up more seats more often; open seats are the most competitive and give voters the choice they must have in a democratic political system. But there are two problems with the term-limits solution. First, though it opens up more seats in each election cycle, it does nothing to give voters the power to hold members accountable during their stint in office. In fact, if anything, members may be less likely to heed their constituents because they know that their hold on that office will be terminated by law in the near future anyway. Second, term limits rob the people of representation by worthy and responsible legislators whom they want to keep in office. Furthermore, the Congress is well served by members who know the issues and have institutional memory. In short, term limits is the wrong solution to this dilemma.

The "none of the above" solution would do far more to improve electoral accountability in the system.[8] This reform would allow voters to cast a vote for "none of the above" in the event that they are displeased with the incumbent's performance and also don't like whatever alternative, if any, has been served up by the opposing party. If "none of the above" were to win two straight House elections involving the same incumbent, then the incumbent would be removed from office. Party committees in the district would convene to select candidates, and a special election would be held in three months' time. The "none of the above" option would not be available to voters in open-seat races, nor would it be available in the special elections.

In the Senate, since members come up every six years, I propose that anytime the "none of the above" wins, a special election would follow. As with the House, open-seat races and special elections would not feature the "none of the above" option.

The rationale for this reform is as follows: Voters must be in a position to vote out the incumbent in order to have the control over public policy that is promised by a representative system of government. Just because the financial obstacles to running are so high as to make it extremely difficult to challenge incumbents does not mean citizens should not have a way to subject incumbents to the popular veto. The "none of the above" reform offers a practical way for citizens to exercise the most important power they have in representative democracy—the right to vote out of office an elected official. Unfortunately, a lot of the time this right can't be exercised. The simple "none of the above" reform would restore it. If the citizens held power of this sort over members of Congress, the pressure to address the major issues of the day would be much greater than is currently the case. This reform might be the single most effective way to begin the restoration of confidence in representative institutions and the wider political system.

Conclusion

As I have said earlier, the health of our representative institutions rests squarely on the shoulders of elected officials themselves. They must recognize the importance and dignity of their offices and especially of the institutions of which they are a part. In an age when distrust is rampant and new forms of direct democracy are proposed on a regular basis, it is up to these officials to offer the evidence, through legislation, oversight, and reform, that representative institutions can work.

The people, too, have some responsibilities. One of these is to understand that decision-making on hard issues on which people disagree vehemently cannot be done neatly and cleanly in a democracy. We cannot expect representative institutions that accurately or even roughly reflect our many conflicting interests to function smoothly and harmoniously all the time. Our differences are often sharp, and the debate on the great issues of the day is going to be harsh. There is no way around that. But the alternative to the messiness of representative institutions is much worse: direct democratic institutions that are insufficiently respectful of minority rights; that have produced and promise to produce more irresponsible and unaccountable governance.

In the end, for democracy to last, the center must hold. Debate only at the extremes leads to extreme measures and attempts to rule by force. Leadership from the center, able sensitively to reach common ground where possible and ameliorate differences where common ground is impossible, is a necessary ingredient to a working democracy. This kind of approach can be undertaken only in deliberative representative institutions, institutions that are open and permeable and whose members can be held accountable by citizens at the ballot box. Institutions of direct democracy are inimical to these aims.

Notes

Chapter 1: Introduction

1. Scholars have written a great deal about the effect of the franchise on political power for African Americans. See Bernard Grofman and Chandler Davidson, eds., *Quiet Revolution in the South* (Princeton: Princeton University Press, 1994); Bernard Grofman and Chandler Davidson, eds., *Controversies in Minority Voting* (Washington, D.C.: Brookings, 1992); and Thomas Husted and Lawrence Kenney, "The Effect of the Expansion of the Franchise on the Size of Government," *Journal of Political Economy* 105, no. 1 (1997): 54–82.

2. See Michael Nelson and Sidney M. Milkis, *The American Presidency: Origins and Development, 1776–1998* (Washington, D.C.: Congressional Quarterly, 1999).

3. Some scholars believe that television has contributed to an entirely new party system, one that is "candidate-centered" in which the parties' primary function is to cater to the needs of candidates as opposed to the more traditional functions of pursuing a policy agenda, serving constituents, distributing patronage, etc. See John H. Aldrich and Richard G. Niemi, "The Sixth American Party System," in Stephen C. Craig, ed., *Broken Contract* (Boulder: Westview Press, 1995).

4. See John R. Hibbing and Elizabeth Theiss-Morse, *Congress as Public Enemy* (New York: Cambridge University Press, 1995).

5. See David Broder, "Whose Government Is This?," *Washington Post*, July 13, 1999, A17.

6. In the era of budget surpluses that began in 1998 (albeit largely created by borrowed money from the Social Security Trust Fund and other trust funds), politicians are finding that constituents do not even trust them to provide a tax cut with the surplus funds. Voters seem to opt for debt reduction over new spending—even in popular areas like education—or tax cuts. See Michael Grunwald, et al., "At Home, Lawmakers See Debt-Cutting's Deep Appeal," *Washington Post*, 7 September 1999, A1.

7. See Jonathan Rauch, *Demosclerosis* (New York: Times Books, 1995), for a detailed comparison of America's wealth in the 1990s compared to that in 1960.

8. Middle- and upper-income Americans do particularly well. Neil Howe and Phillip Longman in "The Next New Deal," *Atlantic*, April 1992, 88–90, describe how Americans with incomes over $100,000 receive about twice as much from the government in direct subsidies and tax breaks as those below the poverty line. Recent changes in the tax code have added numerous breaks for middle- and

upper-income taxpayers, though lower-income citizens have also been helped by the expansion of the Earned Income Tax Credit.

9. In his book (New York: Simon and Schuster, 1992), Dionne argues that Americans are thoroughly fed up with politics, politicians, and the government because they accurately perceive that the politicians continue to hash out culture war issues of the sixties and seventies that have little or no relevance to their lives in the nineties.

10. Sundquist, in *Constitutional Reform and Effective Government* (Washington, D.C.: Brookings, 1992), warns that our experience with divided government is a failure and that we must modify our institutions to increase the chance that one party can control the government and be held accountable for the government's actions. He suggests allowing for special elections when the branches are at an impasse, ending off-year elections (so that the House and the president stand for election together at four-year intervals), and allowing members of Congress to serve in the cabinet, among other reforms. Phillips, in *Arrogant Capital* (Boston: Little Brown, 1995), calls for similarly thoroughgoing changes. See Chapter 4 for a full examination of Phillips's proposals.

11. Benjamin R. Barber, *Passion for Democracy* (Princeton: Princeton University Press, 1998); and Benjamin R. Barber, *Strong Democracy* (Berkeley: University of California Press, 1984).

12. Public opinion polls regularly indicate strong support for national referenda. In Thomas Cronin, *Direct Democracy* (Cambridge: Harvard University Press, 1989), Chapter 7 is devoted to national referenda.

13. James L. Fishkin, *Voice of the People* (New Haven: Yale University Press, 1995); James L. Fishkin, *Democracy and Deliberation* (New Haven: Yale University Press, 1991); and Robert A. Dahl, *Democracy and Its Critics* (New Haven: Yale University Press, 1989).

14. David R. Mayhew, *Congress: The Electoral Connection* (New Haven: Yale University Press, 1974).

15. Steven Stark, "Too Representative Government," *Atlantic*, May 1995, 92–106.

16. Rauch, *Demosclerosis*, and Anthony S. King, *Running Scared* (New York: Martin Kessler Books, 1997).

17. King, *Running Scared*, 55.

18. Populists often profess a near-mystical faith in the "popular will" as expressed by electoral majorities. The focus of Chapter 2 is the historical tradition of populism in the United States and the way that tradition is manifested today.

19. Thomas Friedman, in "The Critics Were Wrong," *New York Times*, 5 September 1996, A21, warns of what might have happened had Harry Truman consulted a focus group in deciding whether to push for the Marshall Plan. Derrick Bell, in "The Referendum: Democracy's Barrier to Racial Equality," *Washington Law Review* 54 (1978): 1–29, suggests that some of our greatest advances in the direction of racial equality were not at all popular at the time.

20. Anyone who has worked in the Congress can attest to how conscious members are of fundraising and electioneering, and how much time these activities consume. Members of Congress have precious little time to develop personal re-

lationships with their colleagues, relationships that are crucial for the sort of co-operation needed for responsible policy-making.

21. See Alan Ehrenhalt, *The United States of Ambition* (New York: Times Books, 1991).

22. Tocqueville traveled to the United States from his native France in 1831, ostensibly to study our penitentiary system. Ultimately he wrote *Democracy in America* on the basis of his observations, the first volume of which was published in 1835.

23. See James Madison, Alexander Hamilton, and John Jay, *The Federalist Papers* (New York: Random House, 1937), especially Papers 10 and 51.

24. See E. E. Schattschneider, *The Semisovereign People* (New York: Holt, Rinehart, and Winston, 1960); and V. O. Key, *The Responsible Electorate* (Cambridge: Belknap Press of Harvard University Press, 1966).

25. Even the experts in government have the good sense to specialize, Schattschneider wrote. Observers of the Congress have long known that the most respected members often speak out only on a narrow range of topics. In recent years, Senator Sam Nunn (D-Georgia) was often followed on military policy, but little else. Senator Daniel Patrick Moynihan (D-New York) is widely held in high regard in the field of welfare policy, as is Senator Richard Lugar (R-Indiana) on foreign affairs.

26. Mathematicians have provided formal proof that when decision-makers must choose from among three or more options by comparing two at a time, the results can be arbitrary and chaotic. This topic is dealt with in detail in Chapter 5.

27. It is difficult or impossible to tell how, when, or whether a decision-making process has been manipulated.

28. The following discussion comparing divine will and popular will in politics was inspired by William Riker, *Liberalism against Populism* (San Francisco: W. H. Freeman, 1982), 239.

29. It is important to note that the evangelical Protestant denominations, the largest of which are Southern Baptists, are by far the fastest growing of all denominations or religions in the United States. They are also the ones that tend toward conservative activism in public affairs. See James L. Guth, *Bully Pulpit* (Lawrence: University of Kansas Press, 1997); Robert Booth Fowler, Allen D. Hertzke, and Laura R. Olson, *Religion and Politics in America* (New York: Westview Press, 1999); James L. Guth, "Politics in a New Key," *Western Political Quarterly* 43 (1990): 153–179; and James L. Guth and John C. Green, *The Bible and the Ballot Box* (Boulder: Westview Press, 1991).

30. Representative institutions are only "elitist" in the sense that a select group of people is charged with making decisions. But this is a promiscuous use of the term; after all, all organizations and polities of any size depend on select groups to make decisions. The term "elitist" is appropriate in the context of situations where those who make policy decisions are not directly accountable to the people. I argue in this book that representative democracy has some elitist qualities, but policy-making by plebiscite may actually be more elitist.

31. In populism's most virulent form, election results are construed to invest in the elected leader the unchallenged authority to speak for the people on policy.

32. In Chapter 6 we will look in great detail at what it might take to ensure that representative institutions meet these criteria: representativeness and account-ability.

Chapter 2: The Heritage of
Populism in the United States

1. Michael Kazin, *The Populist Persuasion* (Ithaca, N.Y.: Cornell University Press, 1995), 1.

2. Alexander Hamilton, James Madison, and John Jay, *The Federalist Papers* (New York: Random House, 1937), Paper No. 10.

3. In their view, there was a natural tension between order and liberty. Too much freedom would lead to disorder, which would in turn make liberty not worth having. By the same token, too much order would tend to encroach on the most valuable liberties, including free speech. See James McGregor Burns, *The Vineyard of Liberty* (New York: Alfred A. Knopf, 1982), for a detailed discussion of the so-called liberty/order tension.

4. The Founders regarded regular and frequent elections to be both crucial and extremely difficult to achieve. Their logic went like this: regular and frequent elections are necessary to keep elected officials from infringing on the people's liber-ties, but politicians in power would be very tempted to postpone or suspend elec-tions they felt they might lose; the separation of powers was the means by which no one elected official or branch would amass enough unopposed power to be able to suspend elections.

5. See Jackson Main Turner, *The Anti-Federalists* (Chapel Hill: University of North Carolina Press, 1961); John D. Lewis, *The Anti-Federalists Versus the Federalists* (San Francisco: Chandler, 1967); and Christopher M. Duncan, *The Anti-Federalists and Early American Thought* (DeKalb: Northern Illinois University Press, 1995).

6. Many of the most important aspects of the Constitution were the result of compromises to make the document viable for ratification. These included the de-cision to have a bicameral legislature (to give each state, regardless of size, an equal voice in the Senate, and to represent the population equally in the House of Representatives) and the notorious three-fifths compromise, which counted slaves as three fifths of a person for the purposes of calculating representation in the House, among many others.

7. See Thomas Cronin, *Direct Democracy* (Cambridge: Harvard University Press, 1989), 25.

8. See Richard Brookhiser, *Alexander Hamilton, American* (New York: Free Press, 1999).

9. See James S. Young, *The Washington Community, 1800–1828* (New York: Harcourt Brace and World, 1966).

10. See James Ceaser, *Presidential Selection* (Princeton: Princeton University Press, 1979), for a discussion of the changes in the party system at that time. Martin van Buren, in particular, articulated the rationale for parties made up of political professionals and organized from the grass roots on up. Party leaders in

a competitive party system would be motivated to meet the needs of the rank and file in their efforts to win elections.

11. See Kazin, *The Populist Persuasion,* and Michael Nelson and Sidney M. Milkis, *The American Presidency: Origins and Development, 1776–1998* (Washington, D.C.: Congressional Quarterly, 1999).

12. The first national bank, part of Alexander Hamilton's economic planning, had been chartered by the federal government in 1791 after a long political battle. Its charter had expired in 1811. Ultimately the second Bank of the United States was chartered in 1817.

13. Ironically, Democrats like Jackson, although especially suspicious of an overbearing central government, were willing to exert strong, unilateral executive leadership seemingly in the Federalist tradition. Jackson's rationale was that strong executive leadership was needed temporarily in order to correct an imbalance between federal and state authority that had developed along Hamiltonian/Federalist lines. This sort of rationale has become something of an American tradition; in more recent times, both Richard Nixon and Ronald Reagan similarly used it to justify strong executive action to return authority to the states.

14. Decentralized party organizations that were closed to ordinary citizens and were tightly controlled by political professionals remained the norm in the United States until the 1970s.

15. See Lawrence Goodwyn, *The Populist Moment* (New York: Oxford University Press, 1978); Steven Hahn, *The Roots of Southern Populism* (New York: Oxford University Press, 1983); Michael E. McGerr, *The Decline of Popular Politics* (New York: Oxford University Press, 1986); and Robert McMath, *American Populism* (New York: Hill and Wang, 1993).

16. Thanks in part to a lavishly financed campaign, the Republican William McKinley was able to convince enough of the working class that government policy that was good for business was also good for working folks to win the election in a landslide. In all, the populist Bryan received the Democratic nomination three times, and lost badly each time.

17. One of the ironies of the era was that the Progressives—a largely middle-class group whose brain trust and leadership were constituted in part of members of the eastern elite—took over the movement for reform from agrarian populists with whom they had little or nothing in common. In fact, there were real antagonisms between the "benighted" farm folks and the Henry Cabot Lodges and Henry Adamses and other Progressive thinkers and leaders.

The historian Richard Hofstadter contends in *The Age of Reform* (New York: Alfred A. Knopf, 1955) that both the farmers being overrun by railroad trusts and the bankers and the old money elite were suffering from status anxiety in the late 1800s. The newly rich industrialists were taking incredible power in the society at the expense of both. Many in the younger generation of the well-educated middle class and the old-money elite saw the need for social and political reform and understood the grievances of the dispossessed among farmers and workers. They, too, were suffering a loss of power and prestige at the hands of what they regarded as rapacious monopolists.

18. See William Deverell and Tom Sitton, *California Progressivism Revisited* (Berkeley: University of California Press, 1994); Martin Sklar, "Periodization and Historiography: Studying American Political Development in the Progressive Era, 1890s–1916," *Studies in American Political Development* 5 (Fall 1991): 173–213; Martin Sklar, *The United States as a Developing Country* (Cambridge: Cambridge University Press, 1991); and Richard McCormick, *The Party Period and Public Policy* (New York: Oxford University Press, 1986).

19. Hofstadter, *Age of Reform*, 5.

20. From Benjamin Parke DeWitt, *The Progressive Movement* (New York: Macmillan, 1915), quoted in Arthur Mann, ed., *The Progressive Era* (New York: Holt, Rinehart, and Winston, 1963), 2.

21. See Charles A. Beard, *The Economic Interpretation of the Constitution* (New York: Macmillan, 1914).

22. See Hofstadter, *Age of Reform*.

23. The impulse to use government to rid people of their darker impulses remains in full force today; witness the efforts of mainstream reformers to raise taxes on tobacco products and litigate against the tobacco companies to the brink of extinction. Some of the more zealous reformers are lobbying the Food and Drug Administration to outlaw tobacco.

24. John D. Hicks, "Populist Origins," in Mann, *The Progressive Era*, 19.

25. See Herbert Croly, *The Promise of American Life* (New York: Macmillan, 1910).

26. Wilson, *Congressional Government* (New York: Houghton Mifflin, 1887), wrote about the need for parliamentary government; as president he worked to enforce party discipline within the Democratic caucus on Capitol Hill. In the first years of his presidency he had a great deal of success in pushing through his program.

27. The twentieth-century political philosopher Isaiah Berlin provided a useful way to think about these conflicting ideas about the role of government in a democracy. His concepts of "negative liberty" and "positive liberty" correspond well to the clash between constitutionalism and populism. With negative liberty, freedom is thought of as the absence of any infringement on the individual from outside forces. With positive liberty, freedom may take the form of a people acting corporately to reach their aspirations. We will return to this topic in Chapter 6.

28. Franklin Roosevelt's New Deal was in part redistributionist, but in the main it was characterized by massive federal efforts to give people a sense of economic security in hard times; the reforms of the sixties and seventies tended toward social reform, including civil rights, environmentalism, and consumer advocacy.

29. This development is dealt with in greater detail in the next chapter.

30. See Dan T. Carter, *The Politics of Rage* (New York: Simon and Schuster, 1995), and Stephan Lesher, *George Wallace, American Populist* (Reading, Mass.: Addison-Wesley, 1993).

31. See Stanley B. Greenberg, *Middle Class Dreams* (New Haven: Yale University Press, 1996), and Thomas B. Edsall and Mary D. Edsall, *Chain Reaction* (New York: Norton, 1991) for excellent treatments of the success Republicans had in exploiting divisions in the Democratic coalition on hot-button racial issues.

32. Democrats retained control of at least the House and usually both the Senate and the House despite their failures at the presidential level. There are a good many reasons for this, including the fact that Republicans tended to field weak candidates, at least in House races. See Gary Jacobson, *The Politics of Congressional Elections* (New York: HarperCollins, 1992). But perhaps the number one reason is the fact that southern Democrats could run in their districts as moderates and conservatives and win easily. In fact, throughout the 1970s (with the exception of the 1976 election), '80s, and early '90s the South was both the most Republican region in presidential politics and the most Democratic in House politics.

33. Ironically, it was Jefferson who as president was maneuvered by Chief Justice John Marshall into supporting a ruling establishing the concept of judicial review in the *Marbury v. Madison* (1803) decision.

34. Roosevelt's infamous court-packing scheme in 1937 was an effort to get the Supreme Court better to reflect the popular will. While the scheme failed, the Court did ultimately end up changing direction, some would say in response to public opinion, and permitting many of the more controversial parts of the New Deal to become law.

35. Ventura has since left the Reform party, largely because of the increasing influence within the party of radicals of the right and left. In 1999, the life-long right-wing Republican Pat Buchanan joined the Reform party, and for a time he received the support of Lenora Fulani, the onetime Freedom party presidential candidate who has been at the vanguard of a therapeutic-Marxist movement for a couple of decades. Fulani believed she and Buchanan could find common ground. To her the party represented an effort by a disparate group of people to be heard in a political system she and others believe shuts them out.

36. See Bob Woodward, *The Agenda* (New York: Simon and Schuster, 1994).

37. Clinton pledged to "end welfare as we know it" during the 1992 campaign. Early in his first term he resisted Republican attempts to end Aid to Families with Dependent Children, the main welfare program, as a federal entitlement. Ultimately, in 1996, he signed landmark legislation to do just what he had said, end welfare as it had been known. He was able adroitly to claim as much credit for the achievement as the GOP because of his campaign pledge. In addition, he pushed through a crime bill that aimed to put 100,000 new police officers on the streets, and he has managed to make gun control an anticrime position. These accomplishments are among the most important in his terms, as he has successfully shed the pro-welfare, criminal-coddling image that hampered the Democrats for some thirty years.

38. See David Broder, "Whose Government Is This?," *Washington Post*, July 13, 1999, A17.

39. See Stephen C. Craig, "The Angry Voter: Politics and Popular Discontent in the 1990s," in Stephen C. Craig, ed., *Broken Contract* (Boulder: Westview Press, 1996), 46–49.

40. Eighteen state legislatures now have term limits. All of these terms limits were instituted in the 1990s. In addition, nine more governors are term-limited now than were a decade ago, bringing the total to thirty-eight.

41. See the *Washington Post*, February 21, 1999, B5.

42. John Geer, *From Tea Leaves to Opinion Polls* (New York: Columbia University Press, 1996).

43. Quoted in Geer, *From Tea Leaves to Opinion* Polls, 130. In my experience working on Capitol Hill, on any really tough vote, members can be expected to hold a conference call involving pollsters as well as policy and political staff.

44. Joe Klein, "Talk Politics," *New York*, February 27, 1989, 28.

45. Eleanor Clift, "The Tea Bag Revolution," *Newsweek*, February 6, 1989, 18.

46. Carroll J. Doherty, "Rank and File Draw a Line Against Aid for Mexico," *Congressional Quarterly Weekly Report*, January 21, 1995, 215.

47. Doherty, "Rank and File...," 215.

48. John Greenwald, "Don't Panic: Here Comes Bailout Bill," *Time*, February 13, 1995, 34.

49. Greenwald, "Don't Panic," 34.

50. Carroll J. Doherty, "Collapse of Mexican Loan Plan Exposes Leaders' Limitations," *Congressional Quarterly Weekly Report*, February 4, 1995, 372.

51. William Schneider, "The Populist Takeover of Congress," *National Journal*, February 11, 1995, 394.

52. Schneider, "The Populist Takeover of Congress," 394.

53. Thomas Friedman, "The Critics Were Wrong," *New York Times*, February 25, 1996, A21.

54. Nancy Gibbs, "Thumbs Down," *Time*, February 1, 1993, 28.

55. Quoted in Benjamin I. Page and Jason T. Tannenbaum, "Populistic Deliberation and Talk Radio," *Journal of Communication* 46, no. 2 (1996): 42.

56. Gibbs, "Thumbs Down," 28.

57. Jill Smolowe, "How It Happened," *Time*, February 1, 1993, 34.

58. Page and Tannenbaum, "Populistic Deliberation and Talk Radio," 51–52.

59. In *McCullough v. Maryland* (1819) the Supreme Court established the doctrine of "dual federalism." The doctrine was based on the interstate commerce clause in Article I of the Constitution, which was in this case was interpreted as permitting federal regulation only on commerce between or among states. In 1937 the Court switched gears with its ruling in *National Labor Relations Board v. Jones and Laughlin Steel Corporation*. With that decision, the Court permitted regulations on businesses that conducted commerce with entities outside their state. Nearly all businesses engage in some such activity.

60. See especially James L. Sundquist's seminal work, *The Decline and Resurgence of Congress* (Washington, D.C.: Brookings, 1981), for a discussion of the resurgence of Congress in the 1970s as a response to presidential abuse of power in foreign affairs (especially by Lyndon Johnson and Richard Nixon) and in the domestic and electoral arena (Nixon). In the seventies Congress "rearmed," as it were, by giving itself more resources to compete with the president on budget policy, economic policy, and foreign, defense, and intelligence policy, in particular.

61. In the last fifty years, only Johnson and, to a lesser extent, Reagan enjoyed a free ride to pass whatever they wanted when first elected. In Johnson's case, the legislative onslaught went on for more than a year; in Reagan's case, the honey-

moon was much shorter. Newt Gingrich tried to claim a mandate to vote into law within one hundred days his ten-point program, the "Contract with America," which had helped to bring the Republicans into power in the House in 1994 for the first time in forty years. His mandate was shorter-lived still. Significant mandates in American politics are extremely rare and always short.

Chapter 3: Direct Democracy: Past, Present, and Future

1. Sullivan spread the word about initiatives and referenda in the 1890s. See Thomas Cronin, *Direct Democracy* (Cambridge: Harvard University Press, 1989), 48–49.

2. Cronin, *Direct Democracy*.

3. See Chapter 2 for a discussion of the reforms of the party system that were central parts of the Progressives' agenda.

4. See Woodrow Wilson, *Congressional Government* (Boston: Houghton Mifflin), 1885.

5. The Republican party had almost no presence in the South from the late 1800s until the 1960s. The Democratic party held control of the region as long as the national party stayed mum on civil rights issues. In the 1960s, when Lyndon Johnson and other Democrats on the national stage took the lead in the fight for civil rights for African Americans, the party lost the support of many southern whites, opening up opportunities for Republicans in the region.

6. See Howard Reiter, *Selecting the President* (Philadelphia: University of Pennsylvania Press, 1985), for an excellent discussion of the gradual decades-long decline in the power and control of party leaders over delegates at the national conventions of both parties. The unit rule, which used to enforce state party unanimity at the conventions, became much rarer by midcentury, and as early as the 1930s candidates for president began to woo delegates directly without going through party leaders.

7. The 1968 Democratic Convention in Chicago was a nightmare for the party in a lot of ways. For one thing, the divisions within the party on Vietnam led to violence in the streets of Chicago, some of it nationally televised, and even some tussles on the convention floor. The party appeared to be in shambles, and in many ways it was. As a result, in the aftermath of the convention there was a need to patch things up with all factions of the party—including the rebellious ones.

8. Between 1968 and 1976 the number of states holding primaries doubled, from eighteen to thirty-six. But those numbers actually understate the importance of the change, because before the reforms in 1969 and 1970, many primaries were only "beauty contests" with no direct impact on the selection of delegates to the convention.

9. The case that pitted the Illinois Democrats against the national party was *Cousins v. Wigoda (1975)*. See David E. Price, *Bringing Back the Parties* (Washington, D.C.: Congressional Quarterly, 1984), 139–142.

10. The best treatment of this subject is probably in Byron E. Shafer, *Quiet Revolution* (New York: Russell Sage Foundation, 1983).

11. In fact Democrats ran into exactly this sort of problem during the period from about 1968 into the 1990s. The party's liberal wing was in the majority, but by nominating liberals for president, in presidential elections Democrats regularly lost a large chunk of their more moderate or conservative voters to the Republicans.

12. There are about as many self-described independents as there are those who identify with one of the parties. In the 1950s the vast majority of voters expressed a clear preference for one party over the other. In more recent years, voters are as likely to be neutral toward the two major parties as to express a clear preference.

13. See Alan Ehrenhalt, *The United States of Ambition* (New York: Times Books, 1991).

14. Parties have proved to be surprisingly malleable in some issue positions to suit the convenience of their candidates. A recent example: Vice President Al Gore and other Democrats now trumpet their support of the use of faith-based organizations to deliver social services, a position that just ten years ago was held by only the more conservative members of the Republican party.

15. Contrary to some conventional wisdom, Richard Nixon presided over a period of tremendous expansion of the federal government. Nixon rhetorically attacked such expansion, while his administration supported the creation of the Environmental Protection Agency, the use of federal guidelines for affirmative action, and a considerable increase in regulations relating to consumer protection, as well as many, many other programs.

16. See Jonathan Rauch, *Demosclerosis* (New York: Times Books, 1995), Chapter 3.

17. See especially Alan Rosenthal, *The Decline of Representative Democracy* (Washington, D.C.: Congressional Quarterly), 1998.

18. See John Geer, *From Tea Leaves to Opinion Polls* (New York: Columbia University Press, 1996).

19. For a good overview of the changes in campaign finance laws, see Herbert E. Alexander, *Financing Politics* (Washington, D.C.: Congressional Quarterly, 1992).

20. The same sort of thing was happening at the state level. Nearly everywhere around the country, legislators were becoming more and more responsive to citizens and organized interests. Well-organized interest groups find the legislative process remarkably permeable if one employs good tactics and appeals to the electoral interests of the members through their constituents. See Rosenthal, *The Decline of Representative Democracy*.

21. In the 1999 appropriations process it was business as usual as there were "dozens of windfalls for business salted into annual appropriations bills that have been enacted, or await final congressional approval," according to Dan Morgan and Juliet Eilperin, "Spending Bills' Small Print Can Be Fine for Business," *Washington Post*, 22 October 22 1999, A1. These reporters detail a $15 million item for research on "supersonic aircraft noise mitigation" slipped into the Senate bill to benefit Gulfstream aircraft; special provisions for bankrupt cellular phone companies, including one in the House Majority Leader's district; rules on health labeling for cigar companies; wording in the Environmental Protection Agency appropriation identical to that supported by a lobbyist for the Chemical

Manufacturers Association and the American Petroleum Institute, and myriad other small projects for the districts or states of well-placed members.

22. These three programs alone account for over 40 percent of federal spending, including spending to cover interest on the national debt. By some time in the first couple of decades of the twenty-first century these programs will account for nearly two thirds of federal spending.

23. Most people blamed the GOP for the standoff. Though it is hard to be certain who was to blame, it is the case that some prominent Republican members were enthusiastic about the prospect of forcing a showdown with the Clinton Administration over the scope of government spending.

24. Grossman, *The Electronic Republic*, 145.

25. Democracy 21 press release, 10 May 1999. Wertheimer is president of this organization, which focuses on "using the communications revolution to strengthen democracy."

26. See David Magleby, "Direct Legislation in the American States," in David Butler and Austin Ranney, editors, *Referendums Around the World* (Washington, D.C., 1994), 237–242.

27. Magleby wrote before the recent uses of initiatives on affirmative action in California and other states and communities.

28. Term-limits proposals vary. The most popular proposal for the U.S. House of Representatives would limit members to three two-year terms. Similar term limits apply to state legislators in some states.

29. George Will makes this case in *Restoration* (New York: Free Press, 1992).

30. See Cronin, *Direct Democracy*.

31. The tax revolt in California and other states is described in Daniel A. Smith, *Tax Crusaders and the Politics of Direct Democracy* (New York: Routledge, 1998).

32. The scientific measurement of public opinion is based on the selection of a random sample of citizens. It can be shown mathematically that the views of a random sample of several hundred people are very likely—95 percent likely—to approximate the views of the entire population.

33. See Benjamin I. Page and Robert Y. Shapiro, *The Rational Public* (Chicago: University of Chicago Press, 1992), for a discussion of the evidence that citizens' responses to poll questions sometimes vary randomly.

34. Good sources on these and other difficult issues regarding polling are Robert S. Erikson and Kent L. Tedin, *American Public Opinion* (Boston: Allyn and Bacon, 1995); and Herbert B. Asher, *Polling and the Public* (Washington, D.C.: Congressional Quarterly, 1999).

35. For more on these and other similar efforts, see F. Christopher Arterton, Jeffrey B. Abramson, and Gary R. Orren, *The Electronic Commonwealth* (New York: Basic Books, 1988); and F. Christopher Arterton, *Teledemocracy* (Newbury Park, Calif.: Sage Publications, 1987).

36. See Theodore L. Becker and Richard A. Couto, eds., *Teaching Democracy by Being Democratic* (Westport: Praeger, 1996).

37. The prominent pollster and political analyst Dick Morris has written a book focusing on the web site, [vote.com], and *The National Review* and other publications have published commentary about it.

38. See Kevin A. Hill and John E. Hughes, *Cyberpolitics* (Lanham: Rowman and Littlefield, 1998).

39. See Tracy Westen, "2004: A Digital Election Scenario," in Anthony Corrado and Charles M. Firestone, *Elections in Cyberspace* (Washington, D.C.: Aspen Institute, 1996), 59–61.

40. The Democracy Network is more ambitious in some ways than the better-known Project Vote Smart. Project Vote Smart provides voters across the nation with a great source of information on issues and politicians running for office, but it does not bring candidates into an interactive format as the Democracy Network does.

41. Arterton, *Teledemocracy*, 118–122.

42. See Arterton, *Teledemocracy*; and Arterton, Abramson, and Orren, *The Electronic Commonwealth*.

43. See Hill and Hughes, *Cyberpolitics*.

44. See James S. Fishkin, *Democracy and Deliberation* (New Haven: Yale University Press, 1991); and James S. Fishkin, *The Voice of the People* (New Haven: Yale University Press, 1995).

45. Unfortunately the participants only numbered about 450 in the end.

46. Similar experiments have been conducted in Great Britain. The Granada Television Studio in Manchester, England, has done something similar to what Fishkin did on several occasions in the last twenty-five years. The so-called "Granada 500" is five hundred people chosen as a representative sample of the population (though not necessarily randomly selected). The participants read about major issues—crime, for example—and are asked whether they would be willing to take the opportunity to quiz officials on the issue and be a part of discussions involving experts. Many of these discussions have been on national television.

47. See Robert A. Dahl, *Democracy and Its Critics* (New Haven: Yale University Press, 1989).

48. See Fishkin, *Democracy and Deliberation*.

49. Critics of this idea point to the value of the civic ritual of going to a public place to vote. If voters are required to weigh in on multiple complicated ballot measures, this advantage of the traditional way of voting may have to be balanced against the advantages of voting by mail or electronically. Already, Oregonians can vote by mail.

50. See Grossman, *The Electronic Republic*, 153.

51. In the next chapter I will discuss the vigorous debate among academics and activists on the suitability of the mass public for making informed judgments in a plebiscite.

52. See Arterton, *Teledemocracy*, and Arterton, Abramson, and Orren, *The Electronic Commonwealth*.

53. See Michael Schudson, *The Good Citizen* (New York: Martin Kessler Books, 1998).

54. See Arterton, *Teledemocracy*, and Arterton, Abramson, and Orren, *The Electronic Commonwealth*.

55. Over 60 percent of Americans old enough to vote do not participate in off-year elections. Usually just a little over half participate in presidential elections.

56. Article IV, Section 4 (the so-called "Guarantee Clause") states, "The United States shall guarantee to every State in this Union a Republican Form of Government." There will be a great deal more discussion on this and related controversies in Chapter 4.

57. Proposition 13, passed by Californians in 1978, froze or strictly limited increases in property taxes for many Californians.

58. A Field poll conducted in California in August of 1999 indicated that most people in the state supported the use of referenda and initiatives for the "big questions," but thought it best to rely on representatives for legal and technical matters.

Chapter 4: Direct Democracy
Versus Representative Democracy

1. See Benjamin Barber, *Strong Democracy* (Berkeley: University of California Press, 1984); and Barber, *A Passion for Democracy* (Princeton: Princeton University Press, 1998).

2. See Theodore L. Becker and Richard A. Couto, eds., *Teaching Democracy by Being Democratic* (Westport, Conn.: Praeger, 1996); and Theodore L. Becker, "Elements of a Transformational and Teledemocratic Political Communications System," from the Web site of the Initiative and Referendum Institute in Washington, D.C., at [www.iandrinstitute.org].

3. Barber, *Strong Democracy*, 24.

4. Barber, *A Passion for Democracy*, 120.

5. Barber, *A Passion for Democracy*, 121.

6. Barber, *A Passion for Democracy*, 128.

7. Barber seems to say that a tradition of a more participatory citizenship has been lost in the United States and needs to be reinvigorated.

8. Barber, *Strong Democracy*, 4.

9. Barber, *Strong Democracy*, 151.

10. Barber, *Strong Democracy*, 132.

11. Barber, *Strong Democracy*, 160.

12. Barber envisions these institutions as having initially only a deliberative role. Eventually, as citizens become accustomed to the new responsibilities, the assemblies would draft laws.

13. Barber, *Strong Democracy*, 256. A Civic Communications Cooperative would be set up to oversee civic education and electronic town meetings and to guarantee access to information for all citizens.

14. Barber, *A Passion for Democracy*, 240–241.

15. See Chapter 3 for detailed descriptions of these two proposals.

16. James S. Fishkin, *Democracy and Deliberation* (New Haven: Yale University Press, 1991), 67. Most observers on both sides of the debate acknowledge this.

17. Robert A. Dahl, *Democracy and Its Critics* (New Haven: Yale University Press, 1989), 311.

18. See Benjamin I. Page and Robert Y. Shapiro, *The Rational Public* (Chicago: University of Chicago Press, 1992).

19. Not only that, they acknowledge that the information available to people may often be skewed and/or inaccurate.

20. Page and Shapiro emphasize that it is the people *when taken as a whole* that are rational. This is in part, they say, a result of irrational views' canceling each other out, as I have said. However it is a rather curious usage of the term "rational" to suggest that aggregations of frequently irrational judgments can be "rational." Although they do contend that there is some deliberating going on among ordinary people and that people on the whole have good judgment, the gist of their argument is not that the people are rational in the sense that most people would use the term: using their good judgment to consider carefully opposing, well thought out options on complex policy questions. Rather they define rational as an artifact of haphazard, unstructured discussion and statistical probability. It would probably be more accurate for them to have concluded that people have good instincts, rather than that they are rational. It follows, then, they say, that because of their good instincts people should be the ones to decide among options that have been put in front of them by experts who know the issues in more detail.

21. See Daniel Lazare, *The Frozen Republic* (New York: Harcourt Brace, 1996).

22. See the discussion of Woodrow Wilson's views on the party system in Chapter 3.

23. See James L. Sundquist, *Constitutional Reform and Effective Government* (Washington, D.C.: Brookings, 1992).

24. This quote is from an electronic mail correspondence with Eric O'Keefe on June 29, 1999.

25. At this writing, U.S. Term Limits is actively targeting for the 2000 election cycle members of Congress who are reneging on earlier pledges to self-limit their terms. Most of them are Republicans. The organization promises to spend millions of dollars on television ads and other media to identify to the public those who have not kept their word.

26. Various efforts along these lines are being pursued in Colorado, Oregon, California, and other states. Usually they involve increasing the number of signatures required for certain types of ballot measures and/or regulating the collection of signatures.

27. Kevin Phillips, *Arrogant Capital* (Boston: Little Brown, 1995), xii.

28. Phillips, *Arrogant Capital*, 113.

29. Phillips, *Arrogant Capital*, 116.

30. Phillips, *Arrogant Capital*, 175.

31. Benjamin Barber freely acknowledges that the population would need to be retrained in order to participate in policy-making in a meaningful way. He does, however, seem to suggest that a meaningful participatory tradition only needs to be reinvigorated.

32. Michael Schudson, *The Good Citizen* (New York: Martin Kessler Books, 1998).

33. See especially David Magleby, *Direct Legislation* (Baltimore: Johns Hopkins University Press, 1984), Chapters 7 and 10.

34. See Lynn Baker, "Direct Democracy and Discrimination: A Public Choice Perspective," *Chicago-Kent Law Review* 67 (1991): 707.

35. See Arthur Lupia, "Shortcuts Versus Encyclopedias: Information and Voting Behavior in California Insurance Reform Elections," *American Political Science Review* 88 (1994): 63–76.

36. See Susan A. Banducci, "Searching for Ideological Consistency in Direct Legislation Voting," in Shaun Bowler, Todd Donovan, and Caroline J. Tolbert, eds., *Citizens as Legislators* (Columbus: Ohio State University Press, 1998). To anticipate an argument developed in Chapter 5, the level of ideological consistency demonstrated by voters in a plebiscite may often be irrelevant to the quality of the outcome of that plebiscite. This is the single most glaring oversight on the part of almost all observers, academic and otherwise, in the consideration of the wisdom of having voters decide individual policy matters. *The fact is that fully rational and ideologically consistent voters can easily produce irrational results when the final result is tabulated.*

37. The most recent work on the subject is David Broder's *Democracy Derailed* (New York: Harcourt Brace, 2000).

38. See Charles Mahtesian, "Grassroots Charade," *Governing* (November 1998): 38–42.

39. Successful initiatives to restrict racial preferences and limit government services to illegal immigrants were also political footballs for Wilson.

40. Mahtesian, "Grassroots Charade," 40.

41. See Daniel A. Smith, *Tax Crusaders and the Politics of Direct Democracy* (New York: Routledge, 1998).

42. Perhaps that is the reason that voter alienation has not receded with the increase of participatory and direct forms of democracy in recent years. The lack of accountability when decisions on major public policy questions are made in the uproar of public initiative campaigns may lead to more frustration with the political system. There is also evidence of "voter dropoff" in plebiscites. Fewer people vote in these than in candidate elections; some suggest this is due to confusion about the measures, which may be exacerbated by the conduct of the campaigns.

43. See Elisabeth R. Gerber, *The Populist Paradox* (Princeton: Princeton University Press, 1999); and Elisabeth R. Gerber, "Legislative Response to the Threat of Popular Initiatives," *American Journal of Political Science* 40 (1996): 99–128.

44. It is important also to note that the distinction between political professionals and grassroots movements is often blurry in initiative politics. Truly grassroots groups sometimes begin the process of putting an initiative on the ballot, but then require the services of the pros to carry that aim out.

45. See Magleby, "Direct Legislation in the American States," in David Butler and Austin Ranney, eds., *Referendums Around the World* (Washington, D.C.: American Enterprise Institute, 1994); and Susan A. Banducci, "Direct Legislation: When Is It Used and When Does It Pass?," in Bowler, Donovan, and Tolbert, *Citizens as Legislators.*

46. See Magleby, *Direct Legislation*, Chapter 10.

47. The source for these examples is M. Dane Waters, president of the Initiative and Referendum Institute in Washington, D.C.

48. There is also a variety of limitations on the types of legislation that may be voted on in the states. Only the courts in California have explicitly established that the initiative process is a right of a sovereign people and not a privilege granted by the state.

49. For excellent overviews of the controversies surrounding the single-subject rule, see James Gordon and David Magleby, "Pre-election Judicial Review of Initiatives and Referendums," *Notre Dame Law Review* 64 (1989): 298; and Daniel H. Lowenstein, "California Initiatives and the Single-Subject Rule," *UCLA Law Review* 30 (1983): 936.

50. See Julian Eule, "Judicial Review of Direct Democracy," *Yale Law Review* 99 (1990): 1504.

51. See especially Robin Charlow, "Judicial Review, Equal Protection, and the Problem with Plebiscites," *Cornell Law Review* 79 (1994): 527.

52. See Eule, "Judicial Review of Direct Democracy"; and Hans A. Linde, "Who is Responsible for Republican Government?" *University of Colorado Law Review* 65 (1994): 709.

53. Derrick Bell, in "The Referendum: Democracy's Barrier to Racial Equality," *Washington Law Review* 54 (1978): 1–29, makes a strong case for how plebiscites can have a negative impact on African Americans, in particular, as well as other groups. Hans A. Linde, in "When Initiative Lawmaking Is Not Republican Government: The Campaign Against Homosexuality," *Oregon Law Review* 72 (1993): 20–39, and John F. Niblock, in "Anti-Gay Initiatives: A Call for Heightened Judicial Scrutiny," *UCLA Law Review* 41 (1993–4): 153, make a similar case regarding plebiscites and homosexuals.

54. D. P. Haider-Markel, "The Politics of Gay and Lesbian Rights," *Journal of Politics* 58 (1996): 332–349, develops this argument well.

55. Elisabeth R. Gerber and Simon Hug, "Minority Rights and Direct Legislation," unpublished manuscript, show that antiminority sentiment will only be exacerbated by plebiscites when the voting majority holds strongly antiminority views on the issue in question. They argue that on many issues dealing with minority rights, such as hate crimes, the majority is not antiminority, and in those cases the initiative serves to protect rather than undermine minority rights.

56. See Peter Schrag, *Paradise Lost* (New York: New Press, 1998).

57. See Todd Donovan and Shaun Bowler, "Responsive or Responsible Government," in Bowler, Donovan, and Tolbert, eds., *Citizens as Legislators*, for figures on the tendency of voters to turn down measures that might threaten minority rights.

58. During the period of massive resistance in the South in the 1950s and into the '60s, it was common practice for politicians to play on racial prejudices and there were often electoral rewards. The most famous case of racial politics was that of George Wallace, who lost a gubernatorial primary as a moderate in the mid-fifties before taking a rigidly pro-segregation position, which proved successful.

59. See Baker, "Direct Democracy and Discrimination: A Public Choice Perspective."

60. She shows that majorities in a legislature can be produced by narrow victories at the ballot box. If the majority party were to win most of its seats by slim margins and the minority party were to win its seats by much larger margins, it would easily be possible that more voters support minority party candidates even though a legislative majority is not achieved. That majority party would then be in a position to pass unpopular legislation, perhaps including legislation that would threaten a minority group's rights.

61. See William H. Riker, "Comment on Baker, 'Direct Democracy and Discrimination: A Public Choice Perspective,' " *Chicago-Kent Law Review* 67 (1991): 791.

62. Julian Eule, "Representative Government: The People's Choice," *Chicago-Kent Law Review* 67 (1991): 777.

63. In most initiative and referendum states judges must stand for reelection. See Julian Eule, "Crocodiles in the Bathtub: State Courts, Voter Initiatives, and the Threat of Electoral Reprisal," *University of Colorado Law Review* 65 (1994): 733. Obviously, the electoral pressures on judges at the state level make the potential of plebiscites to threaten vulnerable minorities' rights a more serious consideration still.

64. See Rosenthal, *The Decline of Representative Democracy.*

65. The median voter is the voter whose position on a given policy issue is right in the middle—half of the voters are to her right and half are to her left.

66. See John G. Matsusaka, "Fiscal Effects of the Voter Initiative: Evidence from the Last Thirty Years," *Journal of Political Economy* 103 (1995): 587–623.

67. Frequently polls indicate opposition to particular taxes enacted by legislatures.

68. States are prevented from engaging in deficit spending, but may finance capital projects. Tight budgets in direct democracy states, which may be due in part to tax and spending limitations, sometimes result in increased pressure from interest groups and the public for more spending. This may in turn lead to increases in debt limits and the use of accounting gimmicks in order to satisfy these demands.

69. See Gary C. Jacobson, *The Electoral Origins of Divided Government* (Boulder: Westview Press, 1990), for a description of poll results that indicate deep ambivalence about spending priorities on the part of the American public. Also, Edward L. Lascher, M. Hagen, and S. Rochlin, in "Gun Behind the Door: Ballot Initiatives, State Policies, and Public Opinion," *Journal of Politics* 58 (1996): 760–775, make the case that initiatives in some states have worked to thwart the public's desire for some types of social spending.

70. See Diane Dwyer, M. O'Gorman, J. Stonecash, and R. Young, "Disorganized Politics and the Have Nots: Politics and Taxes in New York and California," *Polity* 27 (1994): 25–47; and Donovan and Bowler, "Responsive or Responsible Government?"

71. Schrag, *Paradise Lost.*

72. George F. Will, "Faustian Deal in California," *Washington Post*, 24 May 1998, C7.

73. See Baker, "Direct Democracy and Discrimination: A Public Choice Perspective," and Cronin, *Direct Democracy*, for an exposition of these and other suggestions for remedying some of the more serious problems with institutions of direct democracy.

74. There are some notable examples of members of Congress choosing the public interest over electoral considerations. In 1993, Congresswoman Marjorie Margolies-Mezvinsky (D-Pennsylvania) cast a vote on the Clinton economic package; she argued that the measure was good for the country, yet clearly the vote led directly to her defeat in 1994. Senator Albert Gore (D-Tennessee) lost his seat in 1970 as a result of his controversial stand against the Vietnam War, a position he tried hard but was unable to sell back home.

75. See Hanna F. Pitkin, *Representation* (New York: Atherton Press, 1969), for one of the best developments of this argument.

76. See Bernard Crick, *In Defense of Politics* (Chicago: University of Chicago Press, 1992).

77. See John Hibbing and Elizabeth Theiss-Morse, *Congress as Public Enemy* (New York: Cambridge University Press, 1995).

78. Rosenthal, *The Decline of Representative Democracy*, 340.

79. Baker, "Direct Democracy and Discrimination: A Public Choice Perspective," 776. Her reference to "Platonic Guardians" seems to mean appointed judges.

Chapter 5: Dispelling the Populist Myth

1. Probably the best effort was made by William Riker in *Liberalism Against Populism* (San Francisco: W. H. Freeman, 1982), and *The Art of Political Manipulation* (New Haven: Yale University Press, 1986). But even these books are pitched at a level that requires some training in the esoteric lingo of public choice.

2. The canonical works in the early days of public-choice research include Kenneth Arrow's *Social Choice and Individual Values* (New Haven: Yale University Press, 1963); Duncan Black's *The Theory of Committees and Elections* (Cambridge: Cambridge University Press, 1963); and Anthony Downs's *An Economic Theory of Democracy* (New York: Harper, 1957). Excellent treatments and summaries of some of the key findings described in this chapter can be found in William Riker and Peter Ordeshook, *Introduction to Positive Political Theory* (Englewood Cliffs, N.J.: Prentice Hall, 1973); Peter Ordeshook, *A Political Theory Primer* (New York: Routledge, 1992); and Kenneth Shepsle and Peter Ordeshook, *Political Equilibrium* (Boston: Kluwer-Nijhoff, 1982).

3. See Brian Barry and Russell Hardin, eds., *Rational Man and Irrational Society?* (Beverly Hills: Sage Publications), 1982.

4. It needs to be noted that, in a free society, there are always in principle more than two choices in any policy decision that anyone cares about. Both direct and representative political institutions either permit voters or legislators to choose

from among multiple alternatives, or they are arranged to narrow choices down to two in order to produce a clear majority winner.

5. *New York Times*, 22 September 1998, D9.

6. Interestingly, winners in recent British elections have secured parliamentary majorities *without* popular vote majorities. Even the "landslide" Labour victory of 1997 was achieved with fewer than half of the votes. In effect, in Britain a plurality of less than 50 percent frequently gains the authority to ram legislation through nearly without impediment by managing to elect a legislative majority. This state of affairs is due to the existence of a third party, the Liberal Democrats, that regularly secures substantial support even though either the Conservative or Labour party have gained the majority and thus the right to form the government.

7. The Senate was designed to protect the interests of the states by providing equal representation to each state: two senators, regardless of population. Originally states did not even permit the direct election of senators. Senators were usually chosen by the state legislature. This was changed by constitutional amendment in 1913, which provided for the direct election of U.S. senators.

Thus, a group of senators representing only a small portion of the population can have a disproportionate influence on legislation. Informal rules, such as the use of holds on legislation and the filibuster, further enable a minority to thwart the majority will. At the extreme, the filibuster enables a group of senators representing only about 11 percent of the nation's population—two senators from each of the nation's twenty-one least populous states—to prevent any movement on legislation. In fact, given rules governing the distribution to the states of federal funds for some programs, this extreme situation is not all that rare. Essentially, these senators can prevent changes in legislation that would call for distribution of funds by a formula based solely on population.

8. See John Haskell, *Fundamentally Flawed* (Lanham, Md.: Rowman and Littlefield, 1996), Chapter 1, for a more detailed description of the concept of "plebiscitary legitimacy."

9. We should keep in mind that even with the strong two-party tradition in the United States, frequently more than two candidates have received a substantial number of votes in the race for president. *The winner has failed to get a majority of the vote four times in the last ten presidential elections.* Even in a system that does its best to engineer a clear either/or choice, there are always other options—often, other options popular enough to deny the winner majority support.

10. See Jules Witcover, *Marathon* (New York: Viking Press, 1977).

11. Of these three, only Johnson came into office with both chambers of Congress controlled by his party. Although Reagan was reelected in 1984 with a split Congress, it could be said that the House, while Democratic, had a working conservative majority on some issues. Nixon came in with a strongly Democratic Congress in 1972 despite his large margin of victory over the Democratic nominee, George McGovern.

12. Public choice scholars have developed the idea of coalitions of minorities in formal mathematical terms. The first to develop formal theories on the subject were William Riker, in *A Theory of Political Coalitions* (New Haven: Yale University Press, 1963), and Anthony Downs, in *An Economic Theory of Democracy*.

13. This example is drawn from William Riker, *Liberalism Against Populism* (San Francisco: W. H. Freeman, 1982).

14. Wallace received about 14 percent of the popular vote and carried five states as an independent candidate. His independence enabled him to express in a purer form than Nixon was able to the smoldering discontent over social unrest that many felt.

15. To this day Democrats are still more trusted on Social Security and Medicare and gain a great deal of electoral mileage from charging that the Republicans in Congress are a threat to these programs. Of course, some Republican politicians, most notably the former House Speaker, Newt Gingrich, and House Majority Leader Dick Armey, have fed the fears of some voters by off-hand comments about Medicare "withering on the vine."

16. George McGovern, Nixon's 1972 opponent, was depicted as the AAA candidate—acid, amnesty, and abortion—because of his support for decriminalizing some illegal drugs, amnesty for draft evaders, and abortion rights.

17. See Thomas Edsall and Mary Byrne Edsall's *Chain Reaction* (New York: Norton, 1991).

18. The larger point here is that at some stage in the decision-making process for filling almost any public office or for deciding any public policy question anyone cares about there will be more than two options. The question is: How does the political system narrow down those options? Is that done openly using electoral procedures? Or do party leaders determine the options as in the old days? In investigating whether the will of the people is done we must assume that the process is open. If it is not, the question is moot; there is no expectation from the start that the will of the people will be done.

19. In addition to the fact that it is simpler to consider political decision-making scenarios with three options instead of four or more, it is also important to note that the same principles apply when there are more options. In fact, the problems that crop up in trying to identify the true will of the voters when there are three options are more likely to arise when there are more choices.

20. Academics call the most preferred choice the Condorcet winner, after a seventeenth-century mathematician who first discovered the paradox of voting.

21. When the field of candidates or choices reaches five, there may be at least an even chance that there is no candidate who can beat all others in one-to-one matchups. One way that some scholars suggest to determine which is the strongest option or candidate when no candidate can beat all the others is to determine which choice would win the most of these one-to-one pairings. This is similar to what is done in some European soccer tournaments, when all the teams play all the other teams in what is called a round-robin arrangement. The winner is the team that wins the most games, even if it does lose to one or more of the others.

The important thing to remember is that even if one option wins more matchups than any other, if it does not win them all then that means it cannot be said to be clearly the people's favorite, since another option can beat it. See especially Samuel Merrill III, *Making Multicandidate Elections More Democratic* (Princeton: Princeton University Press, 1988).

22. Taking off where I left off in the last footnote, there are many other ways to select a winning candidate or policy option than just choosing the top finisher (Rule I here, the plurality winner rule) or the run-off (Rule II here). Steven Brams has long advocated approval voting, which permits people to choose as many options on a list that they approve of (see Steven Brams and Peter Fishburn, *Approval Voting* [Boston: Birkhauser, 1983]). So if one likes two of the three policy options, one can vote for both of them. The winning option would be the one to receive the most total votes.

Approval voting has been shown to be considerably better at identifying the most preferred candidate or the one who would win a round-robin tournament (see note 21) than the plurality winner method, and in most circumstances about as good as the run-off. There are other methods of voting, most of which require people to list all the options or candidates in order of preference. Some of these outperform the run-off and all outperform the plurality winner method in identifying the most preferred candidate. It should be noted that all methods of voting are imperfect, either because they are subject to manipulation by strategic voters or because they do not always identify the most preferred candidate, or both. In the end, uncertainty always wins the day because we can never be sure whether the outcome has been manipulated or whether the group even has a clear preference, and all voting methods are flawed—though some are clearly superior to others.

23. Samuel Merrill's *Making Multicandidate Elections More Democratic* (Princeton: Princeton University Press, 1988) compares the performance of many different voting methods, using computer simulations that take into account a variety of possible voter preference orderings.

24. See in particular the following articles by Steven Brams, Marc Kilgour, and William Zwicker: "The Paradox of Multiple Elections," *Social Choice and Welfare* 15, no. 2 (1998): 211–236; and "Voting in Referenda: The Separability Problem and Possible Solutions," *Electoral Studies* 16, no. 3 (1997): 359–377. Also, for related insights on similar voting problems, see Hannu Nurmi, *Voting Paradoxes and How to Deal with Them* (Berlin: Springer-Verlag, 1999); and Dean Lace and Emerson Niou, "A Problem with Referendums," *Journal of Theoretical Politics* 12, no. 1 (2000): 5–31.

25. The way this often works is that opponents of a measure that has qualified for ballot access will come up with a countermeasure that has the kill clause written into it.

26. Brams, Kilgour, and Zwicker have suggested that voters be permitted to vote for *combinations* of measures. That is, Kevin would support the combination of measures that he feels is best, which would be YNN. They go further to suggest that Kevin and the others be permitted, under approval voting rules, to vote for all combinations they approve of. In that case, Kevin might also cast a vote for NNY, as might Chris. The idea would be that both men were interested in supporting one or the other of the more moderate environmental regulations, and they both disapproved of B. We could assume that Nisha would approve of all combinations that included a regulation—YYY, YNN, YNY, NYN, and NNY, disapproving only of NNN.

The combination that ended up winning with normal voting rules, YNY, would have received at most one approval vote, from Nisha. Kevin and Chris would have voted for both YNN and NNY, and only those options. The likely outcome would have been unanimous support for the two moderate combinations, with the unpopular combination that won using normal rules garnering only Nisha's support. (We could imagine that a coin flip would determine which of the two combinations that tied for first would become policy.) This outcome with approval voting is superior to the outcome using the traditional method of determining outcomes. It identifies two combinations favored by all the voters, whereas the traditional method awards victory to an unpopular combination.

Brams has long championed the use of approval voting for primary elections, and more recently for initiative and referendum campaigns. As mentioned earlier, approval voting is superior in identifying the most preferred option to the method usually used today (plurality winner, or "first past the post," as the British refer to it). Of course it is not perfect, as every electoral method is subject either to manipulation by strategic voters or to identifying other than the most preferred option or to both. Despite its imperfections, there is no doubt and no debate that approval voting is superior to the traditional method.

Its use would, however, present voters with more complexity. Furthermore, the debate about which plebiscite measures should be voted on in combination would surely become heated and controversial. How do we determine which measures would be considered together? Aren't voters taxed enough just to keep up with the details of single measures without having to consider the ramifications of combinations of measures?

Still, if initiatives and referenda are to be used, there is no doubt that allowing voters to consider combinations is better than the method currently used, just as Brams and others say. Realistically, however, the complexity of implementing it and the problems that would crop up in determining which measures to consider together will probably render such a reform impossible to enact.

27. Brams, Kilgour, and Zwicker bring up another interesting related point in "The Paradox of Multiple Elections." It may be that voters, in considering their options in Senate, House, and presidential races, might vote differently for a given office if they knew who would win the White House or control the House. The evidence indicated that, in 1980, the most popular combination of outcomes was for a Republican sweep of both Houses of Congress as well as the White House. The second most popular combination was a Democratic sweep. The third most popular was a Democratically controlled Congress with a Republican president. The eventual outcome—GOP control of the Senate and the presidency with the House going Democratic—was preferred by still fewer voters.

28. See Shaun Bowler, Todd Donovan, and Caroline Tolbert, eds., *Citizens as Legislators* (Columbus: Ohio State University Press, 1998), 147.

Chapter 6: Curing the Mischief of Plebiscite

1. The Initiative and Referendum Institute in Washington, D.C., has accumulated data from many surveys that indicate this. (Their web site is [www.iandrinstitute.org].) David Broder in *Democracy Derailed* (New York: Harcourt, 2000), Chapter 5, gives a good summary of some of these polls.

2. For some examples, see Clark Forsythe, "First Steps," *National Review,* 20 December 1999, 42–45.

3. One of the most common criticisms of the public choice analysis of decision-making is that it assumes individuals' preferences to be set in stone. Public choice scholars are said to take a snapshot of people's views, drawing conclusions on that basis, when in fact people's views are fluid and flexible. This criticism has a great deal of merit—people's views on issues are fluid and they are open to compromise and the "middle ground." The point I am making here is that representative institutions better reflect those very qualities of people's thinking on complex issues. These are flexible institutions that are in a position to respond if changing circumstances dictate.

It is direct democratic institutions that view preferences as static. (This is why they can be assessed using the analytical tools of public choice, just as I did in Chapter 5.) The result of a plebiscite is said to represent the people's inviolable will. The discoveries in public choice are valuable precisely because they undermine this unsophisticated understanding of people's preferences.

4. David Mayhew, *Divided We Govern* (New Haven: Yale University Press, 1991).

5. See Isaiah Berlin, *Four Essays on Liberty* (New York: Oxford University Press, 1969).

6. Ron Unz, "California and the End of White America," *Commentary,* November 1999.

7. See, for example, Carol Swain, *Black Faces, Black Interests* (Cambridge: Harvard University Press, 1993).

8. Californians rejected a modest version of this proposal that appeared on the ballot in March 2000. The California proposal did not have any teeth. Even if "none of the above" won, the top vote getter would still be put in office. The voters would just be "sending a message."

Bibliography

Aldrich, John H., and Richard G. Niemi. "The Sixth American Party System." In *Broken Contract*, ed. Stephen C. Craig. Boulder: Westview Press, 1995.

Alexander, Herbert. *Financing Politics*. Washington, D.C.: Congressional Quarterly, 1992.

Arrow, Kenneth. *Social Choice and Individual Values*. New Haven: Yale University Press, 1963.

Arterton, F. Christopher. *Teledemocracy*. Newbury Park, Calif.: Sage Publications, 1987.

Arterton, F. Christopher, Jeffrey B. Abramson, and Gary R. Orren. *The Electronic Commonwealth*. New York: Basic Books, 1988.

Asher, Herbert. *Polling and the Public*. Washington, D.C.: Congressional Quarterly, 1999.

Baker, Lynn. "Direct Democracy and Discrimination: A Public Choice Perspective." *Chicago-Kent Law Review* 67 (1991): 707.

Banducci, Susan. "Direct Legislation: When Is It Used and When Does It Pass?" In *Citizens as Legislators,* ed. Shaun Bowler, Todd Donovan, and Caroline Tolbert. Columbus: Ohio State University Press, 1998.

———. "Searching for Ideological Consistency in Direct Legislation Voting." In *Citizens as Legislators*, ed. Shaun Bowler, Todd Donovan, and Caroline J. Tolbert. Columbus: Ohio State University Press, 1998.

Barber, Benjamin. *Passion for Democracy*. Princeton: Princeton University Press, 1998.

———. *Strong Democracy*. Berkeley: University of California Press, 1984.

Barry, Brian, and Russell Hardin, eds. *Rational Man and Irrational Society?* Beverly Hills: Sage, 1982.

Beard, Charles. *The Economic Interpretation of the Constitution*. New York: Macmillan, 1914.

Becker, Theodore, and Richard A. Couto, eds. *Teaching Democracy by Being Democratic*. Westport, Conn.: Praeger, 1996.

Bell, Derrick. "The Referendum: Democracy's Barrier to Racial Equality." *Washington Law Review* 54 (1978): 1–29.

Berlin, Isaiah. *Four Essays on Liberty*. New York: Oxford University Press, 1969.

Black, Duncan. *The Theory of Committees and Elections*. Cambridge: Cambridge University Press, 1963.

Bowler, Shaun, Todd Donovan, and Caroline Tolbert, eds. *Citizens as Legislators*. Columbus: Ohio State University Press, 1998.

Brams, Steven, and Peter Fishburn. *Approval Voting*. Boston: Birkhauser, 1983.

Brams, Steven, Marc Kilgour, and William Zwicker. "The Paradox of Multiple Elections." *Social Choice and Welfare* 15 (1998): 211–236.

———. "Voting in Referenda: The Separability Problem and Possible Solutions." *Electoral Studies* 16 (1997): 359–377.

Broder, David. *Democracy Derailed.* New York: Harcourt, 2000.

———. "Whose Government Is This?" *Washington Post*, 13 July 1999, A17.

Brookhiser, Richard. *Alexander Hamilton, American.* New York: Free Press, 1999.

Burns, James McGregor. *The Vineyard of Liberty.* New York: Knopf, 1982.

Carter, Dan. *The Politics of Rage.* New York: Simon and Schuster, 1995.

Ceaser, James. *Presidential Selection.* Princeton: Princeton University Press, 1979.

Charlow, Robin. "Judicial Review, Equal Protection, and the Problem with Plebiscites." *Cornell Law Review* 79 (1994): 527.

Clift, Eleanor. "The Tea Bag Revolution." *Newsweek*, 6 February 1989: 18.

Craig, Stephen. "The Angry Voter: Politics and Popular Discontent in the 1990s." In *Broken Contract*, ed. Stephen Craig. Boulder: Westview Press, 1996.

Crick, Bernard. *In Defense of Politics.* Chicago: University of Chicago Press, 1992.

Croly, Herbert. *The Promise of American Life.* New York: Macmillan, 1910.

Cronin, Thomas. *Direct Democracy.* Cambridge: Harvard University Press, 1989.

Dahl, Robert. *Democracy and Its Critics.* New Haven: Yale University Press, 1989.

Deverell, William, and Tom Sitton. *California Progressivism Revisited.* Berkeley: University of California Press, 1994.

Dionne, E. J. *Why Americans Hate Politics.* New York: Simon and Schuster, 1992.

Doherty, Carroll. "Collapse of Mexican Loan Plan Exposes Leaders' Limitations." *Congressional Quarterly Weekly Report*, 4 February 1995.

———. "Rank and File Draw a Line Against Aid for Mexico." *Congressional Quarterly Weekly Report*, 21 January 1995.

Downs, Anthony. *An Economic Theory of Democracy.* New York: Harper, 1957.

Duncan, Christopher. *The Anti-Federalists and Early American Thought.* DeKalb: Northern Illinois University Press, 1995.

Dwyer, Diana, M. O'Gorman, J. Stonecash, and R. Young. "Disorganized Politics and the Have Nots: Politics and Taxes in New York and California." *Polity* 27 (1994): 25–47.

Edsall, Thomas, and Mary D. Edsall. *Chain Reaction.* New York: Norton, 1991.

Ehrenhalt, Alan. *The United States of Ambition.* New York: Times Books, 1991.

Erikson, Robert, and Kent L. Tedin. *American Public Opinion.* Boston: Allyn and Bacon, 1995.

Eule, Julian. "Crocodiles in the Bathtub: State Courts, Voter Initiatives, and the Threat of Electoral Reprisal." *University of Colorado Law Review* 65 (1994): 733.

———. "Judicial Review of Direct Democracy." *Yale Law Journal* 99 (1990): 1504.

———. "Representative Government: The People's Choice." *Chicago-Kent Law Review* 67 (1991): 777.

Fishkin, James. *Democracy and Deliberation.* New Haven: Yale University Press, 1991.

———. *Voice of the People.* New Haven: Yale University Press, 1995.

Fowler, Robert Booth, Allen D. Hertzke, and Laura R. Olson. *Religion and Politics in America.* New York: Westview, 1999.

Friedman, Thomas. "The Critics Were Wrong." *New York Times*, 5 September 1996, A21.

Geer, John. *From Tea Leaves to Opinion Polls*. New York: Columbia University Press, 1996.

Gerber, Elisabeth. "Legislative Response to the Threat of Popular Initiatives." *American Journal of Political Science* 40 (1996): 99–128.

———. *The Populist Paradox*. Princeton: Princeton University Press, 1999.

Gerber, Elisabeth, and Simon Hug. "Minority Rights and Direct Legislation." Unpublished manuscript.

Gibbs, Nancy. "Thumbs Down." *Time*, 1 February 1993: 28.

Goodwyn, Lawrence. *The Populist Moment*. New York: Oxford University Press, 1978.

Gordon, James, and David Magleby. "Pre-election Judicial Review of Initiatives and Referendums." *Notre Dame Law Review* 64 (1989): 298.

Greenberg, Stanley. *Middle Class Dreams*. New Haven: Yale University Press, 1996.

Greenwald, John. "Don't Panic: Here Comes Bailout Bill." *Time*, 13 February 1995: 34.

Grofman, Bernard, and Chandler Davidson, eds. *Controversies in Minority Voting*. Washington, D.C.: Brookings, 1992.

———. *Quiet Revolution in the South*. Princeton: Princeton University Press, 1994.

Grossman, Lawrence. *The Electronic Republic*. New York: Viking, 1995.

Grunwald, Michael, et al. "At Home, Lawmakers See Debt-Cutting's Deep Appeal." *Washington Post*. 7 September 1999, A1.

Guth, James. *Bully Pulpit*. Lawrence: University of Kansas Press, 1997.

———. "Politics in a New Key." *Western Political Quarterly* 43 (1990): 153–179.

Guth, James, and John C. Green. *The Bible and the Ballot Box*. Boulder: Westview, 1991.

Hahn, Steven. *The Roots of Southern Populism*. New York: Oxford University Press, 1983.

Haider-Markel, D. P. "The Politics of Gay and Lesbian Rights." *Journal of Politics* 58 (1996): 332–349.

Haskell, John. *Fundamentally Flawed*. Lanham, Md.: Rowman and Littlefield, 1996.

Hibbing, John R., and Elizabeth Theiss-Morse. *Congress as Public Enemy*. New York: Cambridge University Press, 1995.

Hicks, John. "Populist Origins," In *The Progressive Era*, ed. Arthur Mann. New York: Holt, Rinehart, and Winston, 1963.

Hill, Kevin, and John E. Hughes. *Cyberpolitics*. Lanham, Md.: Rowman and Littlefield, 1998.

Hofstadter, Richard. *The Age of Reform*. New York: Alfred A. Knopf, 1955.

Howe, Neil, and Phillip Longman. "The Next New Deal." *Atlantic*, April 1992, 88–90.

Husted, Thomas, and Lawrence Kenney. "The Effect of the Expansion of the Franchise on the Size of Government." *Journal of Political Economy* 105 (1997): 54–82.

Initiative and Referendum Institute. Web page: [www.iandrinstitute.org].

Jacobson, Gary. *The Electoral Origins of Divided Government*. Boulder: Westview, 1990.

———. *The Politics of Congressional Elections*. New York: HarperCollins, 1992.

Kazin, Michael. *The Populist Persuasion*. Ithaca, N.Y.: Cornell University Press, 1995.

Key, V. O. *The Responsible Electorate*. Cambridge: Belknap Press, 1966.

King, Anthony. *Running Scared*. New York: Martin Kessler Books, 1997.

Klein, Joe. "Talk Politics." *New York*. 27 February 1989: 28.

Lacy, Dean, and Emerson Niou. "A Problem with Referendums." *Journal of Theoretical Politics* 12 (2000): 5–31.

Lascher, Edward, M. Hagen, and S. Rochlin. "Gun Behind the Door: Ballot Initiatives, State Policies, and Public Opinion." *Journal of Politics* 58 (1996): 760–775.

Lazare, Daniel. *The Frozen Republic*. New York: Harcourt Brace, 1996.

Lesher, Stephan. *George Wallace, American Populist*. Reading, Mass.: Addison-Wesley, 1993.

Lewis, John. *The Anti-Federalists Versus the Federalists*. San Francisco: Chandler, 1967.

Linde, Hans. "When Initiative Lawmaking Is Not Republican Government: The Campaign Against Homosexuality." *Oregon Law Review* 72 (1993): 20.

———. "Who Is Responsible for Republican Government?" *University of Colorado Law Review* 65 (1994): 709.

Lowenstein, Daniel. "California Initiatives and the Single-Subject Rule." *UCLA Law Review* 30 (1983): 936.

Lupia, Arthur. "Shortcuts Versus Encyclopedias: Information and Voting Behavior in California Insurance Reform Elections." *American Political Science Review* 88 (1994): 63–76.

Madison, James, Alexander Hamilton, and John Jay. *The Federalist Papers*. New York: Random House, 1937.

Magleby, David. *Direct Legislation*. Baltimore: Johns Hopkins University Press, 1984.

———. "Direct Legislation in the American States." In David Butler and Austin Ranney, eds., *Referendums Around the World*. Washington, D.C.: AEI Press, 1994.

———. "Let the Voters Decide? An Assessment of the Initiative and Referendum Process." *University of Colorado Law Review* 66 (1995): 13–46.

Mahtesian, Charles. "Grassroots Charade." *Governing* (November 1998): 38–42.

Mann, Arthur, ed. *The Progressive Era*. New York: Holt, Rinehart, and Winston, 1963.

Matsusaka, John. "Fiscal Effects of the Voter Initiative: Evidence from the Last Thirty Years." *Journal of Political Economy* 103 (1995): 587–623.

Mayhew, David. *Congress: The Electoral Connection*. New Haven: Yale University Press, 1974.

———. *Divided We Govern*. New Haven: Yale University Press, 1991.

McCormick, Richard. *The Party Period and Public Policy*. New York: Oxford University Press, 1986.

McGerr, Michael. *The Decline of Popular Politics*. New York: Oxford University Press, 1986.

McMath, Michael. *American Populism*. New York: Hill and Wang, 1993.

Merrill, Samuel. *Making Multicandidate Elections More Democratic*. Princeton: Princeton University Press, 1988.

Morgan, Dan, and Juliet Eilperin. "Spending Bills' Small Print Can Be Fine for Business." *Washington Post*, 22 October 1999, A1.

Nelson, Michael, and Sidney M. Milkis. *The American Presidency: Origins and Development, 1776–1998*. Washington, D.C.: Congressional Quarterly, 1999.

New York Times. 22 September 1998, D9.

Niblock, John. "Anti-Gay Initiatives: A Call for Heightened Judicial Scrutiny." *UCLA Law Review* 41 (1993–4): 153.

Nurmi, Hannu. *Voting Paradoxes and How to Deal with Them*. Berlin: Springer-Verlag, 1999.

Ordeshook, Peter. *A Political Theory Primer*. New York: Routledge, 1992.

Page, Benjamin, and Jason Tannenbaum. "Populistic Deliberation and Talk Radio." *Journal of Communication* 46 (1996).

Page, Benjamin, and Robert Y. Shapiro. *The Rational Public*. Chicago: University of Chicago Press, 1992.

Phillips, Kevin. *Arrogant Capital*. Boston: Little Brown, 1995.

Pitkin, Hanna. *Representation*. New York: Atherton Press, 1969.

Price, David. *Bringing Back the Parties*. Washington, D.C.: Congressional Quarterly, 1984.

Rauch, Jonathan. *Demosclerosis*. New York: Times Books, 1995.

Reiter, Howard. *Selecting the President*. Philadelphia: University of Pennsylvania Press, 1985.

Riker, William. *A Theory of Political Coalitions*. New Haven: Yale University Press, 1963.

———. *Liberalism against Populism*. San Francisco: W.H. Freeman, 1982.

———. *The Art of Political Manipulation*. New Haven: Yale University Press, 1986.

———. "Comment on Baker, 'Direct Democracy and Discrimination: A Public Choice Perspective.'" *Chicago-Kent Law Review* 67 (1991): 791.

Riker, William, and Peter Ordeshook. *Introduction to Positive Political Theory*. Englewood Cliffs: Prentice Hall, 1973.

Rosenthal, Alan. *The Decline of Representative Democracy*. Washington, D.C.: Congressional Quarterly, 1998.

Schattschneider, E. E. *The Semisovereign People*. New York: Holt, Rinehart, and Winston, 1960.

Schneider, William. "The Populist Takeover of Congress." *National Journal*, 11 February 1995: 394.

Schrag, Peter. *Paradise Lost*. New York: New Press, 1998.

Schudson, Michael. *The Good Citizen*. New York: Martin Kessler Books, 1998.

Shafer, Byron. *Quiet Revolution*. New York: Russell Sage Foundation, 1983.

Shepsle, Kenneth, and Peter Ordeshook. *Political Equilibrium*. Boston: Kluwer-Nijhoff, 1982.

Sklar, Martin. "Periodization and Historiography: Studying American Political Development in the Progressive Era, 1890s–1916." *Studies in American Political Development* 5 (Fall 1991): 173–213.

———. *The United States as a Developing Country*. Cambridge: Cambridge University Press, 1991.

Smith, Daniel. *Tax Crusaders and the Politics of Direct Democracy*. New York: Routledge, 1998.

Smolowe, Jill. "How It Happened." *Time*, 1 February 1993: 34.

Stark, Steven. "Too Representative Government." *Atlantic*, May 1995, 92–106.

Sundquist, James. *Constitutional Reform and Effective Government*. Washington, D.C.: Brookings, 1992.

———. *The Decline and Resurgence of Congress*. Washington, D.C.: Brookings Institution, 1981.

Swain, Carol. *Black Faces, Black Interests*. Cambridge: Harvard University Press, 1993.

Turner, Jackson Main. *The Anti-Federalists*. Chapel Hill: University of North Carolina Press, 1961.

Unz, Ron. "California and the End of White America." *Commentary*, November 1999.

Washington Post. 21 February 1999, B5.

Wertheimer, Fred. Democracy 21, press release, 10 May 1999.

Westen, Tracy. "2004: A Digital Election Scenario." In *Elections in Cyberspace*, ed. Anthony Corrado and Charles M. Firestone. Washington, D.C.: Aspen Institute, 1996.

Will, George. "Faustian Deal in California." *Washington Post*, 24 May 1998, C7.

———. *Restoration*. New York: Free Press, 1992.

Wilson, Woodrow. *Congressional Government*. New York: Houghton Mifflin, 1887.

Witcover, Jules. *Marathon*. New York: Viking Press, 1977.

Woodward, Bob. *The Agenda*. New York: Simon and Schuster, 1994.

Young, James. *The Washington Community, 1800–1828*. New York: Harcourt Brace and World, 1966.

Index